THE POLICY PROCESS IN A PETRO-STATE

The Policy Process in a Petro-State

An analysis of PDVSA's (Petróleos de Venezuela SA's) internationalisation strategy

CESAR E. BAENA
Professor
Instituto de Estudios Superiores de Administración (IESA)
Caracas, Venezuela

Ashgate

Aldershot • Brookfield USA • Singapore • Sydney

Published by
Ashgate Publishing Ltd
Gower House
Croft Road
Aldershot
Hants GU11 3HR
England

Ashgate Publishing Company
Old Post Road
Brookfield
Vermont 05036
USA

HD
9574
.V44
P423
1999

Ashgate website: http://www.ashgate.com

British Library Cataloguing in Publication Data
Baena, César E.
  The policy process in a petro-state : a decision-making analysis
  of PDVSA's internationalisation policy. - (The political
  economy of Latin America)
  1. International business enterprises - Venezuela
  2. Petroleum industry and trade - Venezuela 3. Venezuela -
  Economic policy
  I. Title
  338.8'8987

Library of Congress Catalog Card Number: 99-73393

ISBN 0 7546 1070 5

Printed and bound by Athenaeum Press, Ltd.,
Gateshead, Tyne & Wear.

Contents

List of Tables

Preface

A journey into the unknown is the best way to describe the writing of a book, especially when that book is the result of research undertaken as work for a PhD thesis. Often, the destination seemed to be a far away point; arriving there was anything but in a straight line. Many feelings sprang up during this time, ranging from the darkest to the brightest. This journey was not only mental, but also physical. Many situations were encountered along the way; many people as well. I express my most sincere gratitude to those who helped me reach my destination in one way or another.

I am thankful to my thesis supervisor at the London School of Economics and Political Science (LSE), George Philip, who was able to zero in on the main arguments within sargassoes of information. I am also most grateful to the thesis examiners, Peter Odell and Francisco Panizza, for incisive and pertinent observations. My most sincere gratitude to all those who agreed to be interviewed; their insightful and anecdotal conversations revealed the fascinating world of the oil industry, until then largely unknown to me. My highest appreciation to María Concha Gómez, who encouraged me even during the most turbulent paths of the journey. And also to my mother.

This work could have never been carried out without the financial and institutional help of The British Council, Fundación Gran Mariscal de Ayacucho, and CONICIT, which made my stays in London and at the LSE possible. One journey leads to another. And the time has come to undertake others that had been postponed during the accomplishment of the one that now has reached its destination.

List of Abbreviations

AD	Acción Democrática. Social Democratic party
AGROPET	Agrupación de Orientación Democrática
BCV	Central Bank of Venezuela
b/d	Barrels per day
CEN	Comité Ejecutivo Nacional. AD's highest decision-making assembly
COPEI	Comité para la Organización Política y la Elección Independiente. Social Christian party
CVP	Corporación Venezolana de Petróleo
DCMN	Developing-country multinational
DCSOE	Developing-country state-owned enterprise
DFI	Direct Foreign Investment
ISI	Import-substitution industrialisation
MAS	Movimiento al Socialismo
MEM	Ministry of Energy and Mines
MEP	Movimiento Electoral del Pueblo
MN	Multinational
OAPEC	Organisation of Arab Petroleum Exporting Countries
OECD	Organisation for Economic Cooperation and Development
OPEC	Organisation of Petroleum Exporting Countries
PDVSA	Petróleos de Venezuela, S. A.
SOE	State-owned enterprise
VIF	Venezuelan Investment Fund

Chapter 1
Introduction

1 Introduction

The mere mention of multinationals from developing countries (DCMNs) generates disbelief and outright scepticism. Multinationals (MNs) are believed by many solely to originate in industrialised countries. However, the internationalisation of companies from developing countries has become a significant phenomenon on the world economic scene, providing an interesting subject for the analysis of important policy-making issues (Khan, 1987; Riemens, 1989; Kumar, 1981; Wells, 1983; Agmon, ed., 1977). Although works on the activities of MNs from industrialised countries are abundant, multinationals from developing countries (DCMNs) have attracted little attention in the specialised literature. Most available works on the subject look at the foreign operations of DCMNs in lesser-developed countries (Khan, 1987; Wells, 1983), indirectly looking at cases where companies from developing countries have made inroads in OECD areas. With the exception of a few isolated studies (Kumar, 1981; Riemens, 1989; Díaz-Alejandro, 1977), little attention has been paid to the foreign operations of state-owned enterprises (SOEs) from developing countries. Furthermore, such works tend to exclude the study of cases from oil exporting countries, considering them atypical, due to their capital-intensive features, in contrast to more commonly labour-intensive enterprises from developing countries.

By analysing the internationalisation policy of *Petróleos de Venezuela* (PDVSA), a major state-owned oil industry from a developing country, this study attempts to fill the gaps and enlarge the limits of the existing literature on DCMNs. This study argues that the analysis of the policy-making process set in motion to adopt and implement the internationalisation of Venezuela's state-owned oil industry in OECD areas offers a fertile ground for gaining insight into the balance between politics and corporate strategy in a developing country.

Loosely defined, a MN is any enterprise that possesses direct foreign investments (DFIs) -in the form of asset ownership, production or/and service facilities- in one or more countries other than its home one (Kumar, 1981: xv; Wells, 1983: 9[1]). The rise of MNs has been commonly identified with the highest state of global capitalism, where free trade becomes an essential feature. However, it is the very absence of free trade that provides the basic rationale for MNs. Indeed, local market imperfections and trade restrictions both in the industrialised world as in the developing one have fostered the establishment and growth of MNs (Riemens, 1989: 3).

Wells (1983) was among the first to coin the term 'new multinationals' for companies from developing countries with DFIs. The recent appearance of MNs from developing areas –although still amounting to a small fraction when compared to the international activities of MNs from OECD countries– has called for a reassessment of the most common theoretical models used to explain the nature, operations and impact of traditional MNs. Among such theories the most commonly found in the academic literature are international trade, efficient markets, imperialism, product-cycle and cycle-related models, internalisation, and eclectic theory[2]. It is beyond this study's scope to dwell on the different paradigms of such models. It is sufficient to say that in the absence of any solid theoretical foundation to explain DCMNs, most existing works tend to rely on the theories used to explain traditional MNs, providing, as a result, partial explanations for phenomena stemming from developing contexts. Government policy-making processes are different in a developing context, and need to be given particular attention as determinant factors in the internationalisation efforts of a large firm, even more so in the case of a SOE operating in a key economic sector.

Most available works often attempt to study the existence of DCMNs by assessing how similar or dissimilar they are in their motivations and behaviour from the more typical MNs from industrialised countries. Some authors, Riemens (1989: ii) and Kumar (1981) for instance, argue that there is no fundamental difference between DCMNs and industrialised country MNs: the main difference is one of nature and not of motives. Wells (1983: 3), on the contrary, argues that the foreign investment from DCMNs behaves quite differently from that of traditional MNs from industrialised countries, largely due to their competitive advantages resulting from their experience in developing country contexts. Among the competitive advantages commonly attributed to DCMNs in their operations in developing contexts are their capacity to adapt their technological know-how to a smaller scale ('descaling'), their usually smaller size, their labour-intensive operations, trade mark exposure and lower pricing. Nevertheless, the capacity of companies from industrialised countries to adapt to the specifics of the home environment has rendered these features less distinctively advantageous of companies from developing countries (Lall, 1983; Riemens, 1989). Moreover, such alleged competitive features only prove really competitive when applied in a developing country context, and not in a more industrialised economy. For capital intensive, large size, high-risk companies such as oil industries needing state-of-the-art technology and operating in both industrialised and developing country contexts (Mikdashi, 1986) those features do not represent any secure advantage in comparison to companies from industrialised countries.

Another useful way of assessing the behaviour of DCMNs is looking at the factors and motivations that prompted their expansion. Often, companies decide to expand abroad in order to preserve export markets and penetrate new ones, to exploit raw materials, to minimise market risks, to assert competitive advantages, to bypass quota restrictions, to search for lower costs, to strengthen contact with kin groups, and to diversify operations. This study will assess to what extent these motivations apply to PDVSA in its efforts to become a vertically integrated MN.

A preferred form of DFI by DCMNs is the joint venture. DFIs can be undertaken in the form of exports, licensing, totally or partly owned subsidiaries, and minority or majority equity joint ventures. Mainly due to their low set-up costs, joint ventures are a preferred option for companies seeking to expand internationally, especially for those of developing countries (Wells, 1983: 3). Joint ventures provide an option between licensing and wholly owned subsidiaries. In many cases, joint ventures are the only form allowed by the host country, whose legislation may require the foreign company to join a local one in order to operate. Usually, the local partner will contribute toward asset formation, technological expertise, risk sharing, and access to markets; it will also provide the foreign company with useful knowledge about the local market, the country's legislation and domestic politics. Often, non-economic factors contribute to the adoption of a joint venture as a form of investment (Riemens, 1989: 13). When the joint venture involves a SOE, non-economic factors take an even greater significance, due to the strategic importance in which the joint venture will operate and to the complex political arrangements that shape policy-making in that sector.

PDVSA's internationalisation policy

The high degree of vertical integration achieved by PDVSA has placed it among the most important world oil companies. PDVSA is one of the world's largest refiners. In 1997, PDVSA had a total installed refining capacity of 3.77 million b/d, that is 1.28 million b/d in Venezuela and 2.49 million b/d abroad (including *Refinería Isla* in neighbouring Curaçao). In 1995, it ranked third as the world's largest refiner, preceded by Royal Dutch Shell (4.2 million b/d) and Exxon (3.9 million b/d)[3] . Among OPEC members, PDVSA possesses by far the largest DFIs in the form of refinery assets. After the oil industry was nationalised in 1975, decision-makers of the newly created oil SOE set out to create channels for the distribution of crude oil, independent from those until then offered by the vertically-integrated oil MNs operating in the country. The policy of creating PDVSA's independent downstream outlets through the acquisition of refinery assets in order to enlarge market share and create independent means of reaching the final consumer was termed 'internationalisation'. As formulated by PDVSA, the internationalisation policy took the form of the acquisition of refinery assets abroad through the creation of joint-venture associations, usually with 50% equity ownership. Besides enabling PDVSA to expand market share and gain access to technical know-how, the internationalisation policy allowed industry policy-makers to maximise their freedom to decide over corporate strategies and to create an international network of operations, farther away from the government's unexpected fiscal demands and from Congress' meddling.

The antecedents to the internationalisation policy can be traced to the transition to nationalisation, when the first policy steps were taken by government decision-makers for the creation of distribution channels for the soon-to-be nationalised oil industry. Even before concessions were written off by the end of 1974, executives from the state CVP (*Corporación Venezolana de Petróleo*) had begun negotiating some of the terms that led to the establishment of working agreements between the oil MNs and the nationalised oil industry. The need to reproduce the vertically integrated branches of the foreign companies continued to be a major concern for oil policy-makers following nationalisation. The nationalisation of the oil industry in Venezuela would have been only partially complete had the nationalised oil industry kept relying on the distribution outlets belonging to the oil MNs.

Conflict-ridden nationalisation actions such as the ones that took place in Mexico (1938) and Iran (1951) had hampered future collaboration between the nationalised oil industry and the expelled oil MNs. On the contrary, in Venezuela the virtual absence of conflict during the nationalisation process allowed the nationalised oil industry to develop a successful and convenient working relationship with the foreign concessionaires, whose technical know-how and distribution channels were badly needed by the nascent oil SOE.

Many observers of the oil industry and especially the decision-makers who conceived it often say that PDVSA's internationalisation policy was a success story. With low initial set-up costs, the benefits of creating a refinery network abroad were appealing: the industry could expand market share and gain access to key consumer markets. By establishing a network of DFIs in the form of refinery assets, the industry could diversify its financial sources and its freedom to operate, beyond the dynamics of domestic public policy-making and government fiscal demands.

As a result of government's excessive dependence on revenues from the oil sector, the political leadership in Venezuela is particularly sensitive to oil policy issues. Oil is the government's main source of revenues for creating public goods, both material and political. Any attempts by the oil industry to limit government controls over its actions are likely to generate conflict with the executive and Congress. Traditionally, PDVSA's policy-makers have increasingly sought to assert their policy-making freedom from the executive and the legislature.

Initially, PDVSA's efforts to become a vertically integrated oil MN met the opposition of Congress. The decision-making process that shaped the policy's adoption, formulation, and implementation phase was neither a straightforward nor an easy one. During the first phase of policy implementation, industry policy-makers struggled to minimise the adverse reaction of political actors in Congress. It was the first time since nationalisation that Congress and the industry confronted each other in such a vehement way over a policy choice. Congress felt threatened by the freedom of action exerted by the industry's policy-makers who were asserting their role as main actors in the process of oil policy-making. With the implementation of the policy, some of the industry's decision-making powers would be transferred outside the country's boundaries. By establishing joint-venture associations, the industry was bound to negotiate many policy issues with a foreign partner, a formula that inevitably met the opposition of the most nationalistic members of Congress.

PDVSA's internationalisation strategy soon became entangled in the highly politicised process of public policy-making. Opponents of the government's performance used the industry's policy as an instrument to advance in the political game. In turn, industry policy-makers partly underestimated the political implications of the implementation of PDVSA's first internationalisation contract with Germany's Veba Oel in 1983. However, the contract was a pioneering one, the first of its kind signed by the nationalised oil company. Not only did the contract entail a joint-venture association with a foreign partner, but it also implied the international operation of the state oil company. During the first phase of policy implementation, besides Congress attacks, industry policy-makers also had to grapple with unexpected cash demands from the treasury and with a low barrel price which sharply affected the company's finances.

During the impasse that resulted from the signing of the contract with Veba Oel, the controversial Article 5 of the Nationalisation Law, determining PDVSA's freedom to associate with foreign oil companies, was put to the test for the first time. Created as part of the Nationalisation Law of 1975, this Article was devised to regulate the industry's association with foreign companies. The Article reflects two distinctive and often irreconcilable ideological stances. That of those who wanted to preserve the industry's freedom to associate with foreign capital for its operations and those who thought that this was unnecessary. In any case, Congress legitimacy was considered a prerequisite for association with foreign capital. At the root of the ideological debate around Article 5 lay the tension that has characterised most of the issues concerning PDVSA's international expansion: the persistence of opposite sets of values in oil policy-making. This study builds upon this assumption and, by looking at the process of policy-making behind PDVSA's efforts to expand its operations abroad, shows the balance between politics and corporate strategy in practice.

During the negotiations leading to the establishment of the joint-venture agreement with Veba Oel, PDVSA and the Ministry of Energy had consulted the *Procurador General de la República* (Republic's Solicitor General) on the matter of whether the contract needed legislative approval prior to its implementation. Based on an interpretation of Article 5, the Solicitor General's opinion was that gaining Congress legitimacy was not necessary. However, most Congress representatives thought otherwise. Bypassing Congress triggered a major decision-making conflict among the actors involved in oil policy. Congressional debates evolved around themes such as the executive's autonomy to dispose of the natural resource, the oil industry's accountability to the legislature, the unchecked freedom of its policy-makers, and the industry's association with foreign partners.

The main political obstacle to policy implementation was finally removed when an arrangement at the highest political level was achieved, after the main opposition party (AD) won the 1983 national elections and secured a majority representation in Congress. Further criticism of government policy had thus lost justification. Despite early attacks from the opposition in Congress during the first phase of policy implementation, PDVSA's decision-makers succeeded in the medium term in implementing the internationalisation policy, accomplishing the objectives laid down from the outset.

Despite Congress' decision not to veto the implementation of the contract with Veba Oel, no other joint-venture associations for the purchase of refinery assets abroad were signed during the three years following the policy-making impasse between PDVSA and Congress. Some of the negotiations that had been under way for the establishment of other internationalisation contracts were postponed. The impact of the policy-making impasse created as a result of the contract with Veba Oel had been felt both by the industry and by its potential partners, who showed apprehension and reluctance in partnering with a company that had negotiated and implemented a major contract without due Congress approval.

In 1986, the political obstacle was finally overcome and a second, more aggressive phase of policy implementation took place as PDVSA established further joint-venture contracts abroad. This new phase in the internationalisation policy stemmed from the pressing need to enlarge market share as a way to minimise the dramatic effects of the 1986 price fall in the oil barrel. Contracts to establish joint-venture associations in refinery complexes were then signed with Swedish Axel Johnson, Southland Petroleum Corporation, and Union Pacific Corporation. The leasing of the Curaçao refinery in the Caribbean was also achieved during this phase.

The beginning of a third phase of policy implementation can be identified in 1989, when PDVSA became Citgo's sole owner after acquiring 50% shares from its partner Southland Petroleum. During the Pérez (1989-93) and Caldera (1994-99) administrations, decision-makers' concerns shifted towards the implementation of the policy named *Apertura*, consisting of associations with foreign companies to carry out upstream activities in the country. However, attempts to continue expansion of the network of refineries abroad were not abandoned. Especially during the Caldera administration, a new *élan* was given to the policy of internationalisation.

The study

Venezuela offers a unique case and thus a fertile ground for the study of oil policy-making processes. This is mainly due to three factors. First, the dominant role played by the oil sector in the economy, a situation which finds no parallel in any other Latin American country. Second, the special status of PDVSA as having both a tradition as private company and the evident international character of its operations. The need to assert corporate strategies in order to be competitive in the international oil market, and at the same time be able to satisfy the demands of an excessively dependent government, reflects the dual private-SOE character of the company. Third, unlike the rest of OPEC's members, Venezuela's political system functions as a democracy, where political parties are strong and Congress, as representative of people's pluralist choices, plays a decisive role in public policy-making. In general, the existence of democratic bargaining as the core of public policy-making processes sets Venezuela apart from its counterparts in OPEC, where democratic institutions are either weak or non-existent.

It was stated earlier how little attention has been paid in the academic literature to the study of the significant phenomenon of MNs from developing countries with DFIs in OECD areas. In Venezuela, the absence of public policy-making studies is even more glaring. With the exception of a handful of works dealing with selected government policy decisions (Clark, 1968; Bond, 1975; Martz and Myers, eds, 1986; Arroyo, 1983; Gil, 1978; Torres and Salcedo, 1988; Naím, 1993), policy studies about government policy-making processes in Venezuela have occupied limited space in the political science literature. Some studies have concentrated on the analysis of specific economic policy decisions (Hausmann, 1985; Rodríguez, 1987; Palma, 1989; Toro Hardy, 1992) and others on the performance of SOEs, only partially discussing government policy-making issues (Kelly, ed., 1985). A salient neglect is found in the specific area of government-SOE interaction in Venezuela. This study attempts to cover some aspects of this unexplored field.

Due to its great importance for the Venezuelan economy, the oil industry has attracted particular attention from social scientists (Tugwell, 1974; Vallenilla, 1975; Philip, 1982; Coronel, 1983; Villalba, 1985; Randall, 1987; Mommer, 1990; Boué, 1993; Giordani, 1995). One study (Johnson, 1987) looked at the oil industry from the perspective of the managers' adaptability to the new post-nationalisation context; although not analysed from a policy-making view, PDVSA's internationalised strategy is given indirect treatment and the Veba Oel case is explained in an appendix. Two undergraduate theses (Barrios, 1989; Lorenzo, 1992) deal specifically with the industry's internationalisation policy. Barrios assesses the alleged economic benefits of the policy. In turn, Lorenzo looks at the policy from a media perspective. Neither study addresses policy-making issues. None of the studies mentioned above thoroughly explores the dynamics inherent in the policy-making process, nor the arm's length interaction between the industry and the executive; the central issue of the industry's accountability to the legislature remains equally unexamined. By analysing PDVSA's internationalisation policy, this study attempts to fill these gaps in the existing literature on oil policy-making processes in Venezuela.

This book aims to gain insight into a process whose complexity has never been unravelled and whose implications for further oil policy-making processes in Venezuela and other developing countries need to be adequately assessed. By analysing the complexities and the dynamics of the policy-making process that featured PDVSA's internationalisation, this study deepens the understanding of government policy-making processes in

Venezuela, thus contributing to the literature, on one side, on public policy and public administration and, on the other, on DCMNs.

By focusing on the political constraints imposed by government and Congress on PDVSA's internationalisation strategy, this book explores the difficulties encountered by a major SOE from a developing country in its efforts to grow beyond national borders. Also, the study stresses the impact of democratic bargaining on the process of oil policy-making in Venezuela. The tension between politics and corporate strategy are highlighted as the core of the policy-making process. Specifically, this study examines the intricate policy-making process that shaped the origins and the development of PDVSA's internationalisation policy, emphasising the events that shaped each one of the three distinguishable phases of the policy-making process: adoption, formulation, and implementation. The study also looks at the relationship between the oil industry and the other two key decision-making bodies involved in the oil policy-making process: the Energy Ministry and Congress. In exploring the ways in which each one of them sought to influence policy outcome, the study attempts to gain insight into the main factors that prompted the tensions among the policy actors involved.

Striking a balance between pursuing corporate policies and meeting government demands is a hard dilemma for a SOE. The adoption and implementation of the internationalisation policy by Venezuela's most important SOE polarised key issues inherent in the process of oil policy-making and in the distribution of power among Congress, the Ministry and the SOE. Issues such as the right of PDVSA to associate with foreign companies and the behaviour of its policy-makers were at the centre of the discussion surrounding PDVSA's internationalisation strategy.

There exists an underlying contradiction between the company's goal to become a vertically integrated MN and its role as the country's most important SOE. The dynamics inherent in the need to strike a balance between these two imperatives lies at the core of oil policy-making issues in Venezuela. This study attempts to explore how PDVSA's policy-makers reconciled these two apparently contradictory objectives. Seeking to solve this conundrum, this study is guided by a concern to solve the following puzzle: **How did PDVSA reconcile its efforts to become an oil MN with its role as the country's most important SOE?**

At the core of the controversy that followed the implementation of the industry's internationalisation policy, the need to strike a balance between those two key objectives posed interesting political and public policy-making questions for both the oil industry and the government. Some such questions will be explored throughout this book: (i) How successful was the oil industry in minimising the impact of executive and Congress demands? (ii) How did policy-makers reconcile accountability to Congress while asserting their policy-making freedom? (iii) To what extent did this policy experience shift the distribution of power among the oil industry, the executive, and Congress in the process of oil policy-making? (iv) Were the main sources of conflict among policy-making actors resolved? (v) Is the SOE more independent from political and government demands as a result of its international expansion?

Three environments, or pressure-generating centres, constantly exert influence over the oil industry: the oil market, the domestic political context and the government's financial situation. By seeking to determine what was the industry's response to their pervasive influence over policy formulation and implementation, this study aims to ascertain the extent to which these variables influenced the decision-making process that brought about the industry's internationalisation policy. As the variables shifted over time, so did the industry's responses to them. This non-static and dependent interaction between the major environments identified and the oil industry will be assessed in this study within the framework provided by the internationalisation policy.

Five main arguments lay at the core of this study. First, the internacionalisation policy not only enabled PDVSA to enlarge market share and minimise market uncertainties, but it also provided a platform to enhance its freedom of action away from goverment interference and Congress meddling.

Second, oil policy outcomes largely reflected PDVSA's policy choices. The decision-making power within the process of oil policy-making has been shifting from the executive and Congress to the SOE. Since nationalisation, PDVSA has been consolidating its position as the most important policy actor in oil policy-making processes. The Ministry is weak and tends to follow the industry's choices. Despite its veto power over policy decisions, Congress frequently chooses to grant legitimacy to PDVSA's policy choices. The decision-making pattern characteristic of most public policy-making processes was reversed by two factors: a) the unrivalled significance of the company for the country's economy and b) the constant tendency to assert its corporate freedom by minimising executive and Congress controls. Thus, the equation Congress-Ministry-SOE makes virtually no sense in this case. A pattern SOE-Ministry-Congress represents better the behaviour of oil policy-making processes in Venezuela.

Third, industry policy-makers implemented the *fait-accompli* approach in order to secure policy implementation and solve the dilemma imposed by the exercise of executive and Congress controls over corporate decision-making. By going ahead with policy implementation prior to obtaining

Congress legitimacy, this approach allowed the industry to pursue policy choices. Once the legislature knew about the implementation of the policy, it proved to be less inclined to exercise its veto powers, since reversing the policy was more costly than allowing it to continue. In the long run, the policy was not only continued but also expanded.

Fourth, policy implementation was affected by the way it was previously implemented. In a process that had several distinctive implementation phases, each phase had an impact on the way future policies were to be implemented. It is argued here that it was not the content of the policy that changed, but the way it was implemented. Policy content did not vary: objectives remained basically the same throughout the implementation phases. What varied was the way in which policy-makers, seeking to pursue policy implementation, sought to minimise the negative impact of external variables on the policy-making process.

Fifth, necessary political legitimacy for policy implementation was finally granted, not because of a consensus on oil policy, but because of an arrangement achieved at the highest political level. A partial legitimacy followed the absence of a decision over the industry's policy choice. Thus, political opposition to the industry's views regarding many of the issues inherent in the industry's internationalisation policy remains latent. A reconciliation of stands between the political leadership and the industry's policy-makers over oil policy issues has yet to be reached.

Oil policy-making in a democracy: the tension between corporate strategies and political bargaining

The analysis of the Veba Oel case and the controversy it generated in Congress, causing an impasse within the state's policy-making process, highlighted the latent tension between the SOE and the legislature. These two sets of policy actors regard the administration of oil from opposite ideological platforms. For policy-makers of the oil industry, oil is a commodity subject to the fluctuations of the international market, a domain quite separate from the domestic logic of politics. For the political leadership, the oil industry is a strategic one as it is the main source enabling government to create public goods, both political and material.

Tension among policy actors constitutes an inherent part of the process of public policy-making. At the core of democratic practice, the SOE, the executive and Congress clash over decisions leading to public policy adoption and implementation. Such a struggle represents the diversity of views and values found within the state, reflecting the very pluralism of society. Policy outcomes mirror such diversity. The difficult relationship between governments and SOEs reflects the constantly changing mixture of long-term and short-term objectives. This dichotomy between the long-term corporate goals pursued by the SOE and the short-term objectives sought by the executive and Congress epitomises one of the main dilemmas of democratic practice. Often, Congress may regard a policy issued from within the state's structure -from a SOE, for instance- as a threat to the interests of the people that it represents. In turn, in the case of a powerful SOE such as PDVSA, policy-makers may argue that what is best for the industry is also good for the people, as successful corporate strategies have often been translated into higher revenues for the government and have fostered economic growth. Many successful policies that at the outset did not enjoy Congress' acquiescence were finally implemented, resulting in higher fiscal contributions for the treasury. In such a context, PDVSA may dispute with Congress the role of deciding what is best for the country.

PDVSA's policy to expand its international operations exacerbated the latent tension existing between the SOE and Congress. During its first phase of policy implementation, the short-term gains of the internationalisation strategy were not clearly apprehended by Congress. The short-term benefits of the deal –i.e. increasing petroleum exports to Germany– were not convincing enough to justify the logic of the internationalisation policy as a whole. Had the first internationalisation contract been translated into immediate and more substantial contributions to the treasury, opposition to the policy in Congress would plausibly have been less harsh.

Tension over policy-making issues occurs not only outside the SOE –i.e. in Congress– but also within it. Kelly (1985) argued that there are usually two types of SOE policy-makers: 'engineers' and 'commissars'. The most distinctive difference between the two is whether they concentrate their main interests within the SOE, 'engineers', or outside it, 'commissars'. The former group behaves as traditional profit-maximisers for the industry; promotion and professional recognition become significant values within the context of the SOE. The latter, on the contrary, place their interests outside the firm, mainly in the political sphere; for them, the SOE serves as an instrument to maximise personal and political gains. The behaviour of a typical SOE is usually the result of a constant tension between 'engineers' and 'commissars'. Modified, this distinction partially fits this study. As it is generally considered, the oil sector is made of the industry and the Ministry, with oil policy outcomes resulting from the interaction between the two. For analytical purposes, if 'engineers' were placed neatly within the industry and 'commissars' in the Ministry, then oil policy outcomes would be the result of the tension and constant interaction between these two sets of policy actors. Thus modified, and provided that politics remain outside the industry, this scheme could fit PDVSA's case.

As both a MN and a SOE, PDVSA behaves and responds differently to the variables acting upon most typical SOEs. After a general discussion about Latin American MNs and about the nature of SOEs, the subsequent sections explore the specifics of PDVSA's dual role, as the country's most important SOE and as an internationally integrated oil MN with important DFIs. One of the industry's main challenges is precisely how to strike a balance between the two aspects of this duality.

Latin American Multinationals

Latin American MNs were among the first to spring from the developing world. The growth in the international expansion of companies from Latin America has accompanied the different industrialisation processes unevenly experienced throughout the region at different times (White, 1981). For decades, efforts to promote an industrialisation based on an import-substitution strategy did little to foster the international expansion of Latin American companies. On the contrary, such a strategy, based on the implementation of protectionist policies aimed to strengthen domestic markets, resulted in the establishment in the region of numerous MNs, seeking to circumvent existing import restrictions[4]. By the late 1960s, the ISI (import-substitution industrialisation) policy started to face serious challenges, being gradually replaced by policies aimed at encouraging exports. This new export-oriented strategy paved the way both ideologically and financially for the international expansion of several Latin American companies.

Earlier industrialisation processes in Argentina fostered the foreign operations of three private companies –Bunge y Born, Siam Di Tella, Alpargatas– with operations in Brazil and other neighbouring countries as early as the turn the century (Katz and Kosacoff, 1983; White, 1981). In Brazil, many companies sought to internationalise their operations largely as a response to the abandonment of the ISI policy. Unlike Argentina where the bulk of firms with foreign operations were privately owned, the participation of Brazilian SOEs in the international expansion trend has been significant (Villela, 1983). In the light of limited oil findings in the national territory (Philip 1982: 368-400), PETROBRAS' subsidiaries –INTERBRAS and BRASPETRO– have pursued an important international expansion policy aimed at trading and exploration activities. SIDERBRAS and, to a lesser extent, Vale do Rio Doce, operating in iron and steel respectively, have also attempted international ventures, although in the case of the latter significant results have not been achieved (Kelly, 1982: 121). Mexico is the other large Latin American country whose companies operating in the manufacturing, oil, paper, and engineering sectors have pursued international expansion. The state-oil company, PEMEX, has exported its refining technology to other countries in the region, and has purchased refinery stakes in the US and Europe. Other Latin American countries whose companies, both private and state-owned, have attempted internationalisation strategies in the past two decades include Chile, Colombia, and Venezuela.

PDVSA is by far Venezuela's most important MN, in terms of both size and magnitude of operations. PDVSA possesses significant DFIs through its totally or partially owned refineries in Europe, the US and the Caribbean. Abroad, PDVSA's presence is felt through direct sales, co-operation programmes, technological assistance, or/and DFIs in the form of assets in refineries and storage facilities. Several Venezuelan private companies –notably, Organización Diego Cisneros, SUDAMTEX, MAVESA, POLAR, INELECTRA, SIVENSA; ASERCA and several banks– have established DFIs across Latin America and the US. However, the bulk of their DFIs remains insignificant compared to PDVSA's.

Considerations over government-SOE relations

The analysis of the decision-making process that shaped PDVSA's internationalisation policy reveals many of the issues that affect the interaction between SOEs and governments. Therefore, a brief discussion about the levels of analysis commonly found in the literature on SOEs is next introduced in this chapter. Set apart from the rest of SOEs in Venezuela, PDVSA is a different state company, both because it resulted from the amalgamation of a set of private companies and because of its unequalled position as administrator of the government's most important source of income.

Covering the analysis of the rationales for analysing their creation, performance and management, the specialised literature on SOEs is vast. In varying degrees, SOEs play a major role in industrialised and developing countries alike. Studies focusing on developing countries highlight the importance of SOEs as an essential part of the planned development process of such countries (Ramanadham, 1984: 209). Despite their often poor financial performance and the current debate over the desirability of their privatisation and/or divestiture, SOEs continue to exercise an important role in the economies of many developing countries.

One of the problems most commonly alluded to by the literature on SOEs is their need to fulfil numerous and often contradictory objectives (Jones, 1982: 4). Usually, SOEs are created as policy instruments intended to be economically efficient and at the same time be able to respond to the government's financial and political needs. SOEs are confronted with the need to fulfil multiple objectives, rarely ranked according to priorities. These objectives are: profitability, provision of cheap services and cross-subsidies, minimisation of market imperfections, generation of foreign exchange, creation of employment, national and/or regional development, and to keep foreigners out of activities considered of strategic importance or national interest (Aharoni, 1984).

Since the 1950s, Latin American governments have created SOEs not only in the more traditional areas of public services and natural resources, but also in manufacturing, banking, and commerce. Many of them sprang up within the import substitution strategy that spread throughout most of the region during the 1950s and 1960s. Other SOEs emerged, as did PDVSA, as part of a wave of nationalisations, especially in the petroleum and mining sectors during the 1970s (Vernon, 1983). The substantial size of the public sector in many Latin American countries largely resulted from the rise in foreign borrowing that swept throughout the region during most of the 1970s. In 1974, just before the Venezuelan government nationalised the petroleum industry, SOEs contributed 5% of GDP. Almost ten years later, when PDVSA signed its first internationalisation contract in 1983, SOEs were contributing 29% of GDP, of which 22% came from the oil sector (Kelly, 1984). More recently, as new loans became scarcer following the debt crisis of the 1980s, many Latin American governments set out to reappraise the role of SOEs (Larrain and Selowsky, 1991). In the absence of a particularly strong private sector, many SOEs have been used in Venezuela to foster and diversify economic activity away from the oil sector. As in most Latin American countries, in Venezuela widespread consensus over the need to rationalise the government's scope of involvement in the economy has recently provided an ideological platform for the reassessment of the functions of SOEs (Galal, 1991).

Oil policy-making in Venezuela: the interaction between a powerful SOE and an overdependent government

The analysis of PDVSA's internationalisation policy suggests that the general considerations concerning most SOEs and their relationship with the executive and Congress do not quite explain the specifics of the Venezuelan case. As already stated, PDVSA was created as a large state holding as a result of a smooth nationalisation process. One of the most immediate objectives with its creation was to boost the operations of the decaying national oil industry. The key significance of the oil sector for the country's economy and for government performance soon placed the nationalised oil industry at the centre of most economic decisions. Oil policy-making occupies a pivotal place in the government agenda. The legal structure conceived for PDVSA upon its creation reflected the need to make the industry increasingly productive while keeping it under close government control. Combining corporate policies with meeting government demands has been a constant dilemma for the industry's policy-makers.

Government dependence on oil revenues has characterised the country's democratic period which began in 1958. Nowhere in Latin America, not even in Mexico where oil ranks undisputed above the rest of economic sectors, is a government as dependent on one sector as is Venezuela's on its oil sector. The preponderant role occupied by the oil resource in the economy of Venezuela places the oil industry way above the rest of SOEs in significance. In 1995, the contribution of oil exports to the government's total fiscal revenues reached over 60%. For the same year, the share of oil in the country's export bill exceeded 80% and payments to the treasury amounted to 8.8% of GDP[5].

PDVSA's structure combines both the legal status of a SOE and the embodiments of a large private holding company. Such an arrangement was the result of the combination of two often-contradictory sets of elements. First, the need to keep the company subordinate to the state through executive and legislative controls. As with most SOEs, the Minister, in this case the Energy Minister, leads the company's annual assemblies. Most policy directions need the Minister's ratification. Certain key policy decisions -especially those regarding association with foreign capital- require the approval of Congress for their implementation. However, in practice, such a structure of power separation does not take place neatly. Largely as a result of the company's pivotal role in public policy-making processes, Congress and executive controls over it tend to be weak and often rhetorical. The preponderance of the oil sector for the country's economy and politics creates its own policy-making dynamics, away from the straightforward legal path stipulated for the industry's functioning and its relationship with the government. A close look at oil policy-making issues shows that most decisions emanate from the industry. Having developed efficient ways of minimising adverse reactions from Congress and from a rather weak Ministry, industry policy-makers shape and decide most oil policy decisions. As stated previously, the usual policy-making pattern Congress-Ministry-SOE makes virtually no sense in the case of Venezuela. Policy decisions describe their own pattern with PDVSA as generator of most decisions and strongly influencing each of the other bodies involved in the policy process: the Ministry and Congress.

Second, there exists the need to maintain the private features necessary for the company's sound commercial performance. An important element that ranks PDVSA as an unusual type of SOE is its tradition as a private and foreign-owned company prior to nationalisation in 1975. The possession of the tradition and the organisational culture of a private company is a distinctive trait that singles the oil industry out from the rest of domestically born SOEs in Venezuela. Meritocracy and low degrees of politicisation are among the main features of this legacy. Despite a few isolated cases, in PDVSA the goals to keep politics out and to respect work merits have been erected into respected principles. Besides its dual status as a SOE with a strong private company ethos, another important element which differentiates PDVSA from the other SOEs is having the freedom to decide upon its own budget. The budgetary exercise is one of the government processes that has the most decisive and immediate effect on SOEs. Contrary to the rest of SOEs, PDVSA is exempted from the uncertainties of government budget allocations, being able to decide upon its own operational budget. However, PDVSA's budgetary independence is not in practice totally devoid of conflict. Often, government financial pressures can result in the modification or postponement of an investment plan considered excessively costly by the executive and/or by Congress. The government can force the company to transfer significant sums to the treasury, as occurred in 1982 when a significant part of PDVSA's reserves deposited abroad were transferred to the Central Bank. When a devaluation of the local currency was decreed soon after, the industry lost a considerable amount of its international reserves.

Deciding over the best corporate policy choice, that at the same time will produce more cash for the treasury, constitutes a dilemma for industry policy-makers. The need to establish a balance between both these objectives encourages SOE policy-makers to adopt and implement policies which will enable them more freedom of action and which at the same time will diminish executive and Congress control mechanisms. The internationalisation policy provided the industry with the possibility of meeting both these objectives. The industry's attempts to become an oil MN minimised executive and Congress controls over it. Aharoni (1984) noted that in those SOEs involved in the sale of raw materials in international markets, Congress and executive efforts to direct those enterprises as if they were state monopolies often turn out to be futile. This was true of the policy case studied here: despite Congress attempts to thwart policy implementation, PDVSA's policy-makers succeeded in continuing with their policy choice.

Legislative and executive controls over the SOE: an undefined agenda

In Venezuela Congress is a key actor in oil policy-making. The issue of accountability to the legislative body is a delicate one. It became the major source of conflict during the first implementation phase of PDVSA's internationalisation policy. A cause-effect relationship emerges from the exercise of legislative control over the SOE. The spaces that escape the exercise of control are used by the SOE to increase administrative and financial autonomy. In turn, the more a SOE is autonomous, the more the legislature sees its control functions threatened. As Aharoni (1986: 249) asserted:

> The diminished status of the legislature is evident when the question of its relationship with SOEs and its control over them is analysed. The problem of accountability to Parliament is even more difficult than accountability to government.

Parliamentary control over the executive and over the SOE tends to be weak in countries where the public sector is usually large and where the decision-making process is characterised by the complex bargaining dynamics of democratic practice. As mentioned earlier, Venezuela has both a large public sector and a political system characterised by democratic bargaining, where the role of Congress and of political parties in government policy decisions is significant. With the exception of cases where policy outcomes clearly reflect the actions of a reduced group of actors such as the country's President (Torres and Salcedo, 1988), in Venezuela government policy-making processes share more characteristics with similar practices in democratic states than with those in authoritarian or quasi-authoritarian regimes, where Congress and political parties are either non-existent or whose impact on government policy processes is negligible.

The issue of political legitimacy is a complex one whose implications can be felt in both government policy-making processes and in the political system itself. Congress usually grants political legitimacy for SOE policy choices. In cases where the legislature fails to do so, the President of the country can grant legitimacy over a given policy. In PDVSA's internationalisation policy, the President's decision finally enabled its continuation. Nevertheless, such outcomes might suggest a partial legitimacy. This, despite the high political standing of the figure of the President: legislative opposition to the industry's policy choice remains latent and are likely to reappear at a later phase of the policy implementation process.

Largely as a result of the existence of undefined and constantly shifting agendas for both the SOE and the government, the interaction between them is usually difficult and complex. Mainly through the Ministry, the government is charged with the role of controlling agent. In turn, the SOE is faced with the need to maximise its freedom to implement corporate policies. The classic dilemma, for both the government and the SOE, is how to manage the tension between executive control and industry autonomy (Vernon 1985). SOE policy-makers face what Aharoni (1984:12) calls the 'crucial question'; that is:

How to preserve the advantages of independent operation while at the same time ensure accountability to bodies that represent the state, tax payers and the political process.

The imposition of accountability standards by the executive or the legislature entails the exercise of a form of control over the SOE. As governments possess several decision-making centres, each with different objectives and programmes (Allison, 1971), control of the SOE is often diffuse and imprecise. Usually, there are no fixed rules for the exercise of control. Forms and procedures often vary according to the specificity of the policy case and/or the SOE in question, and seldom do they respond to defined guidelines. In the case of PDVSA, mainly due to its sheer dominance in the country's economy, government control mechanisms over it are difficult to exercise. Many policies originate in the industry and are then ratified by a rather weak Ministry. The high degree of technicalities involved in the policies implemented often prevents Congress representatives from clearly determining their viability and overall benefits. Often, Congress sanctions a policy choice according to the short-term, non-corporate objectives assigned to most SOEs. Political interests and the dynamics of government policy-making play an important role here: corporate decisions are caught up in the process of democratic bargaining.

Accountability to the legislature is an important element for any SOE, one that confers legitimacy to performance and policy choices. For Congress, as embodiment of the people, accountability provides a way of keeping track with the SOE's performance and policy plans. As Aharoni (1986: 249) pointed out:

Accountability means a responsibility or liability to reveal, explain and justify what one does, to account for one's action, to report on the actions and the results arising from the exercise of authority. Since managers of SOEs have the authority to exercise discretion over the use of public funds and to exercise economic power associated with diverse social consequences, they must be accountable for their decisions to the representatives of the public.

The search for an effective interaction between the government and the SOE is usually fruitless; its results are usually unsatisfactory for both the government and the SOE (Vernon, 1984, 1985). Increasing executive or legislative control may result in less SOE autonomy. In turn, SOE policy-makers may experience opposition from the executive or Congress for their policy choice. Often, they develop alternative strategies for minimising the impact of such opposition on policy outcomes. One way of doing this is by implementing policies before obtaining full executive or Congress approval. Perhaps at first implemented in an unconscious manner, and despite the risk of Congress vetoing the policy, the *fait-accompli* approach enabled PDVSA's policy-makers to continue with policy implementation.

The question as to who and how should effectively represent the government in its dealings with the SOEs is never devoid of ambiguity. Although such a figure is usually the Minister, often the country's President intervenes to impose a decision or to act as referee over Ministry-industry policy impasses. Whatever formal mechanisms the government uses to control its SOE, there are also less tangible factors that influence their usually arm's length interaction. The strength of the personality of the President of the country is one. Equally important are the personalities of the SOE's president and the Minister in charge. Furthermore, as in the case of PDVSA, the strength and importance of the SOE plays a significant role in this interaction. As political bargaining constitutes an intrinsic part of public policy-making, the nature of the political coalition in Congress too has a definite impact on the way the legislature seeks to control the SOE and its policies as embodiments of government policy guidelines.

When a SOE interacts with the government, it is usually the case of a large firm interacting with a large bureaucracy (March and Simon, 1958). As mentioned, in the case of oil policy-making in Venezuela, the Ministry is weaker than the oil industry. When executive officials and industry managers interact around the regulation of SOEs, it is usually the latter who possess the skills and knowledge to set policies more suitable for the industry. Ministries often lack the necessary financial and professional means to take the best technical decisions. Factors such as the technical expertise of SOE policy-makers, the importance of the resources they produce for the country and their degree of organisation undermine the Ministry's decision-making powers. Due to the importance they gain within government policy-making processes, Vernon argued that SOE managers can become a political force in their own right (Vernon, 1985, 1985). The ascension of PDVSA policy-makers as the most important actors within the oil policy-making process since nationalisation has often made them a key group to be reckoned with by both government policy-makers and the political élite.

Policy-making as a subject of analysis

There is not one best conceptual definition to explain what a policy entails. Several authors have ventured different definitions to grasp the complexities and scope of a concept that encompasses too many decisions and factors during an imprecise time span. Highlighting the difficulties in describing the term, Heclo wrote that policy may be regarded as 'a course of action or inaction rather than specific decisions or actions' (1972: 85). In turn, Easton explained policy as a 'web of decisions' (1953: 130), and Jenkins as 'a set of interrelated decisions concerning the selection of goals and the means of achieving them within a specified situation' (1978: 15). Wildavsky argued that the term policy 'is used to refer to a process of decision-making' (1979: 387), and also to the product of that process.

Policy is rarely the result of only one decision. Frequently, it involves groups of decisions which more often than not can be considered as a mere orientation, an ill-defined set of values evolving over time, fading to surge again at a later phase of the policy-making process, as Ham and Hill (1993: 11-12) put it:

> Policy will often continue to evolve within what is conventionally described as the implementation phase rather than the policy-making phase of the policy process.

Public policy analysis is used to describe the study of government decision-making processes (Dye, 1976; Jenkins, 1978; Wildavsky, 1979; Hogwood and Gunn, 1984; Ham and Hill, 1993). Often, policy analysis is considered as a normative discipline (Dye, 1976: 108), conceived 'to better policy-making' (Dror, 1971: ix), and 'to aid interaction between people' (Wildavsky, 1979: 17; cited by Ham and Hill: 5-6).

Several models can be used to analyse the policy-making process subject of this case study. Policy-making is basically a multidisciplinary discipline, which relies on the combination of different conceptual paradigms (Dye 1992: 17, 21; Wildavsky, 1979: 3). Among the several theoretical models that could offer relevant insights into the analysis of the policy-making case subject of this study are: rational actor (Dror, 1968; Dye, 1992; Dunleavy and O'Leary, 1987: 172, 282; Simon: 1957; March and Simon, 1958: 169-171; Ham and Hill, 1993: 84); organisational (Allison, 1969: 699; Dye, 1993: 22; Selznick, 1957: 5; Ham and Hill: 125), bureaucratic-politics (Allison, 1971; Halperin, 1974), and policy-as-a-process models (Dye, 1992: 23-26; Jones, 1978; Pressman and Wildavsky, 1973; Naím, 1983: 1). This book is not the most adequate place for restating already abounding discussions on these theoretical models. Suffice it to mention that such models provide partial explanations that could be applied to the study of most policy-making cases. In an attempt to bring out the specific features of PDVSA's internationalisation policy and to shun over-generalisation, this research analyses this policy case using the levels of analysis commonly found in works dedicated to DCMNs and SOEs, earlier discussed in this chapter.

In its concern with identifying a structure in the course of the policy-making process studied, this research claims to be partly inspired by the policy-as-a-process model. This analytical approach provides a useful pattern for identifying the different phases found in the policy-making process. PDVSA's internationalisation policy reflected well the phases suggested by this model.

Policy-making: a process evolving through distinctive phases

The separation of the process of government decision-making in a series of distinctive activities passing through more or less distinguishable phases has often been regarded as the main focus of the analysis of policy-making processes (Jones, 1978). Although not in an orderly manner, policy processes usually evolve through several identifiable phases. First, problem identification, when decision-makers recognise the need to change existing policies in order to redress a situation or accomplish a goal. Second, policy formulation, where an agenda is usually set for public discussion and concrete programmes are proposed to solve the problem. Third, policy legitimisation implies seeking support for policy choice in the executive, Congress or with the President. Fourth, policy implementation, calling for the organisation of a bureaucracy, agency or set of individuals charged with the task of carrying out the policy adopted. Fifth, policy evaluation, where results of the implementation of the policy are assessed and reported to top decision-makers or government; the impact of policy implementation on the organisation, society and on the subsequent development of the policy itself is evaluated (Dye, 1992: 23-26).

Although policy processes seldom reflect a neat development as prescribed in the policy-as-a-process approach, an effort will be made in this study to identify these constantly interacting phases without, nevertheless, neglecting to understand the substance and content of the policy choice itself and its impact on subsequent implementation phases.

As the case provided by the analysis of PDVSA's internationalisation policy demonstrates, the way the policy process was carried out –i.e., during its first phase, implemented before having obtained legitimacy from Congress– had an impact on the subsequent phases of policy implementation. Policy formulation and implementation are linked concepts; both phases are constantly interacting and influencing each other (Pressman and Wildavsky, 1973; Naím, 1983: 1). Often, a policy outcome can reflect more the way that it was implemented than the way the policy was formulated. Too rigid a separation between the phases through which policy processes evolve is analytically misleading, since it does not take into account the highly dynamic interdependence among all its phases. A differentiation between policy adoption and implementation is only justifiable in order to discern more clearly the policy's course, in an attempt to identify the variables and actors exerting influence upon it. Although it attempts to distinguish each policy phase, this study stresses the close interaction between policy formulation and policy implementation. Furthermore, this analytical approach not only helps to bridge the gap between political science and administration studies, but it also reveals more adequately the constant influence of politics on all the phases of the process of public policy-making.

Instruments and procedures of the study

Most material on PDVSA's internationalisation policy is scattered between internal industry material and unpublished documents, as well as in limited publications intended for outside the industry. The most valuable information on the internationalisation strategy dwells in the minds of the policy-makers that conceived it. Over sixty interviews were conducted throughout this study. Largely, subjects were policy-makers in PDVSA and in the Energy Ministry. Among the former group, most managers from PDVSA's Strategic Planning Unit were interviewed, as well as other decision-makers in the affiliated companies who had been involved in the different stages of the internationalisation policy. Retired PDVSA presidents and vice-presidents were also interviewed, as well as several oil market analysts. Unfortunately, access to the acts of PDVSA's assemblies was denied, its content having been classified as confidential by the industry.

When the *in situ* research for this work was carried out during the autumn of 1993, Venezuela was in the midst of political turmoil. The country was preparing for the first general elections after the two *coups d'état* attempts of 1992, and after the impeachment and subsequent ousting of President Carlos Andrés Pérez. The efforts to interview politicians who had been involved in Congress debates during the Veba Oel controversy in 1983 proved fruitless. Most of them were still active in politics, and were unable or unwilling to be interviewed.

Congress archives, the primary source for the analysis of key congressional debates, turned out to be poorly kept, not being adequately indexed by computers. Press reports on congressional debates and on speeches by politicians are here used to counterbalance the inaccessibility to certainly more adequate Congress sources. By and large, the media in Venezuela keeps a fairly good up-to-date coverage of oil related issues. Subject to the necessary degree of scepticism and comparative scrutiny, media reports on many of the issues involved in this study proved to be a valuable source of material.

Book structure

This book consists of eight chapters. The following two chapters are devoted to the nationalisation process and to the formative years of the nationalised industry respectively. In Chapter II it is argued that in the nationalisation programme the political leadership and executive officials played an active role in bringing about the transition to a nationalised oil industry. Such a process was characterised by the absence of conflict with the oil MNs. Already during the consensual process that led to nationalisation, the first contacts with the oil MN were taking place in order to secure for the nationalised oil industry the necessary distribution channels and latest technical know-how. Chapter III looks at the first policy objectives of the nationalised oil company. The internationalisation policy was the natural outgrowth of the accomplishment of those initial corporate objectives. Chapter IV examines the first phase of policy implementation, identifying the antecedents to the establishment of the first internationalisation joint-venture contract in 1983. The chapter explores the policy-making process set in motion in order to establish PDVSA's first joint venture abroad. By focusing on the policy-making impasse created between Congress and the oil sector –the oil industry and Energy Ministry– as a result of PDVSA's effort to become an oil MN, Chapter V explores the impact of politics over corporate strategy. The tensions found at the core of oil policy-making processes were brought to the surface during this controversy among policy-making actors. Chapter VI deals with the second phase of policy implementation, after the main political obstacle to the internationalisation of the industry was removed. Existing joint ventures were expanded and new ones were established during this phase, consolidating PDVSA's position as oil MN. The chapter explores how corporate strategy succeeded over politics in the process of policy-making. Chapter VII focuses on the third phase of policy implementation, when the internationalisation policy was further pursued. The chapter also engages in an evaluation of the different policy options -notably the establishment of netback deals- other than the purchase of refinery assets as a way to enlarge market share. The experience of other oil exporting countries is assessed. In the Conclusion, Chapter VIII, the main findings of the study are analysed based on the arguments stressed in the Introduction and throughout the whole work. The tensions inherent in oil policy-making processes are examined as a reflection of the constant interaction between corporate strategy and politics, and of PDVSA's dual role as oil MN and as the country's most important SOE.

Notes

1   Often, stricter definitions have been applied to determine whether a company qualifies as a MN. According to the Multinational Enterprise Project undertaken by the Harvard Business School, in order for a company to qualify as MN, it had to have manufacturing subsidiaries in six or more foreign countries. Due to their unusually small size, only a handful of developing country MNs were included in such a study (Wells: 1983, 9).
2   Riemens (1989) offers a good and succinct account of such theoretical models.
3   *Annual Reports*. PDVSA, 1995 and 1997; *PDVSA. CONTACT*. Newsletter. No 46. August-September 1995.
4   Writing about Brazil, Villela (1983: 243) points out that the establishment of MNs was not only the result of the import-substitution policy, but also an important part of it. The entrance of MNs in the country was in fact encouraged, as a way to foster the growth of certain sectors of the economy. In a major effort to bring about an all-out industrialisation, the import-substitution strategy was accompanied by the creation of numerous SOEs and the increase in government incentives to protect local firms.
5   *Annual Report*. PDVSA, 1995.

Chapter 2
The nationalisation policy:
A combination of political
and strategic motives

2 The nationalisation policy: A combination of political and strategic motives

Introduction

The decision to nationalise the oil industry was basically a political one which took place in a context of growing state capitalism in Venezuela. From the perspective of the political leadership, to exert unhindered controls over the oil industry meant controlling the state, rendered ever more powerful thanks to uninhibited access to the oil wealth. By having access to an enormous source of wealth, governments would be able to fulfil most of their objectives while avoiding unwanted confrontation with key sectors of society. Nationalisation of the oil industry was a milestone in the democratic, conflict-avoidance design of the Venezuelan political élite. Furthermore, nationalisation of the oil sector enabled the socialisation of a large part of the economy: an essential component for the democratisation programme of the political élite. Following nationalisation of the oil industry and the 1974 oil windfall, the public sector grew impressively during the second half of the 1970s. Because of its unrivalled importance for government performance, oil policy-making occupies a unique place among government public policy-making processes in Venezuela.

The consensual and negotiated way in which the nationalisation of the Venezuelan oil industry took place had a decisive influence on the development of the policies the industry was to pursue thereafter. Despite the nationalist outbursts of some radical politicians of the far left who, voicing their discontent at a half-way nationalisation, opposed any form of indemnity for the assets to be expropriated from the oil MNs, by 1974 most politicians did not advocate a radical action. The negative legacies of previous conflict-ridden nationalisation actions in other oil producing countries discouraged Venezuelan politicians from adopting drastic measures.

Too much would have been at stake had the Pérez administration (1974-79) nationalised the oil industry in a radical way. The consensual form taken by the nationalisation process allowed for the continuation of the working relationship between the oil MNs and the nationalised oil industry. The newly

31

created oil industry needed to maintain ties with the foreign concessionaires if it was to secure the sale of crude oil and access to much needed technology. The oil industry was able to establish a series of tightly knit technical and marketing agreements with the foreign oil concessionaires. Contracts with the oil MNs had been negotiated even before the nationalisation action came into being. 'Rather than a jump into a void'[1], nationalisation was the result of a carefully planned strategy to minimise damage and maintain the international links of the nationalised oil industry.

Instead of confrontation, bargaining with the oil concessionaires was the policy-making approach adopted by the government. The need to secure the treasury a constant and ever growing flow of income was another reason for the adoption of a smooth passage to nationalisation. Depending on the oil industry for almost two-thirds of its income, government policy-makers made sure that the nationalisation process did not interrupt or reduce the industry's sale of crude. As the Minister of Energy, Valentín Hernández Acosta, pointed out:

> It is much better for the country not to have [nationalised] heroically because that would not have allowed the oil industry to continue bringing in the income which the country requires for its development[2].

This chapter examines the factors and the context that contributed to the formulation and implementation of the nationalisation policy in Venezuela. The well-rooted nationalist aspiration of the political élite to control the oil industry since the end of the dictatorship in 1958 paved the way towards nationalisation of the industry in 1975. A past of common mistrust and uncomfortable cohabitation between governments and oil MNs had increasingly fed the nationalist feelings of the political élite. In this chapter it is argued that the nationalisation policy was largely devised by the political élite, and that the role played in this process by managers of the oil industry was of limited significance. Among the main elements that fostered the adoption of nationalisation were the need to reverse the long-term trend of disinvestment in the oil industry –both as a result of the 1958 'no-more-concessions' policy and of increasingly severe taxation schemes– and a favourable oil market situation after the First Oil Shock of 1974.

The background to nationalisation

When nationalisation came into being in 1975 the convergence of economic, political and technical factors was favourable to a change in the status quo. Although nationalisation was the result of a historical process of bargaining between the foreign concessionaires and successive Venezuelan governments since the end of the Gómez dictatorship in 1936[3], the international context during the mid-1970s favoured the implementation of a consensual nationalisation policy. In the early 1970s the major oil MNs had in general seen their bargaining power eroded in the international oil market. The balance of power was increasingly leaning in favour of the oil exporting nations to the detriment of the MN companies, in a manner that resembled a zero-sum distribution. The importance of the oil MNs in the stake of the world markets had, by and large, diminished by the mid-1970s, as the data in Table 2.1 show.

Table 2.1 Crude oil production by ownership, 1950-1979 (in percentage) *

	1950	1957	1966	1970	1979
Seven majors**	98.2	89.0	78.2	68.9	23.9
Other companies	1.8	11.0	21.8	22.7	7.4
Producing country oil companies	(a)	(a)	(a)	8.4	68.7
Total	100.0	100.0	100.0	100.0	100.0

(*) Excluding crude oil produced in the US and the ex-communist bloc.

(**) The Seven Majors: Standard Oil of New Jersey, Gulf Oil Corporation (Gulf), Texaco, Standard Oil of California (SOCAL), Mobil Oil Corporation (Mobil), Royal-Dutch Shell (Shell), British Petroleum Corporation Ltd. (BP). Often added to this group is Compagnie Française des Pétroles, later to become Total.

(a) Negligible.

Sources: Vernon, R. The Hungry Giants: The United Nations and Japan in the Quest for Oil and Ores, Cambridge, Mass., 1983, adapted from Brian Levy, 'World Oil Marketing in Transition', International Organization 36, No.1 (Winter 1982, p. 117); Shell Briefing Service, The Changing World Oil Supply, June, 1980, p. 7; Annual Reports from leading oil companies, from 1970 to 1979; Zuhayr Mikdashi. The Community of Oil Exporting Countries. A study of Governmental Co-operation. George Allen & Unwin Ltd. London, 1972, pp. 35-36.

Most oil producing countries had nationalised their oil industries totally or partially by the time Venezuela did so. Argentina, Chile, Uruguay, Bolivia and Mexico nationalised their oil industries during the 1930s. In 1975, around the same time as Venezuela, Kuwait and Saudi Arabia decreed the reversion of all their oil concessions[4]. Venezuela's late action proved beneficial, allowing it to gain insight from the negative effects of previous nationalisation experiences. Following the nationalist ideals of the Revolution and after an uncomfortable history of mutual mistrust between Mexican governments and the oil MNs, Mexico nationalised its oil industry in 1938, expropriating a large part of their assets. Affected by ever-growing politicisation and labour disputes, one of the main objectives of the oil state company Petróleos Mexicanos (PEMEX) after nationalisation was the fulfillment of the domestic market through production of cheap oil. The result was a chronic capital shortage and a significant loss of international market share[5]. Mexico provided an example that had to be avoided. When Venezuelan policy-makers considered nationalisation of the oil industry, fear of 'Pemexisation' of the new oil industry was an important variable to be taken into consideration. In Venezuela, prior to the implementation of the nationalisation policy, governments opted for divesting and regulating the terms for the tenure of oil concessions, while imposing severe fiscal schemes on the oil companies[6].

In the mid-1970s Venezuelan oil policy-makers found a favourable context that in the short-term enabled them to press for convenient agreements with the oil MNs. Obvious advantages resulted from this *entente*. The Venezuelan government was able to establish co-operation agreements with the foreign oil companies for technical assistance and managed to secure access to marketing facilities enabling the nationalised oil company to commercialise its crude. The foreign companies, in turn, received indemnity from the expropriation of wells whose concession was due to expire in 1984.

Driving the foreigners out in a gentleman-like way –i.e. asking them to leave and still keep in touch– aided the scheme envisaged by the government and the political leadership, as the outcome would not bring about major disruptions to the oil business. In that sense, political parties and government policy-makers at the time of the Pérez administration behaved as income-maximisers whose analyses of the oil situation were tainted by strong nationalist feelings, as demonstrated by the debates held in Congress to approve the nationalisation bill[7]. However, this set of actors managed to minimise the counter effects of their nationalist discourse by avoiding radical actions. The favourable combination between context and historical factors, both at the domestic and international levels, rendered unnecessary the implementation of too radical an action.

If badly implemented, the nationalisation policy could have produced dangerous consequences for the country's economy. The expropriated companies could have retaliated and decided on a sudden pull-out, leaving the nationalised oil industry cut off from its communicating branches with the oil markets. However, during the first half of the 1970s the bargaining power of the major oil companies had badly deteriorated. As a result of the 1958 no-more-concessions policy and of a series of disputes with successive administrations over taxation and investment conditions, the oil concessionaires had lost many battles in Venezuela and were forced to pay ever-increasing taxes for their operations[8]. Since 1958 the concessionaires had been engaging in a major disinvestment policy in Venezuela. They had been reducing the scope of their activities in the country due to declining world prices and local tax increases, while at the same time increasingly shifting their upstream operations to other areas such as the Middle East, where production costs and taxes were lower than in Venezuela[9]. The foreign companies' response to unfavourable domestic conditions was disinvestment in the oil industry, causing a decline in Venezuelan crude in the world markets. The oil companies could hardly afford to invest in projects that would only provide returns close to or beyond 1984, when all concessions were to be returned to the state. According to a 1983 analysis, only 10% of the potential areas for discovering new oil were exploited by the foreign companies, which were concentrating on the extraction of crude from wells already being exploited[10]. The foreign concessionaires had ceased investment in activities other than the ones considered indispensable for operating and keeping installations. Also, they continuously reduced personnel[11]. By the time nationalisation took place, oil production in Venezuela had indeed declined since its unrivalled 1973 peak level of approximately 3.3 million b/d. In 1976, production had gone down to a level of 2.3 million b/d[12], a significant slump of one million over a three-year period. For the year 1975 production averaged 2.34 million b/d, which meant a reduction of 630,000 b/d in comparison to the previous year. The exorbitant oil revenues resulting from the First Oil Shock had in fact stimulated the reduction of Venezuela's crude in the international markets. As of 1976, the government received about $8,860 million for its fuel exports, for a considerably inferior amount of exports in relation to the year 1973, when the treasury only registered $4,433 million for a peak production of over three million b/d[13].

The political background to the nationalisation policy

During the electoral year 1973, most candidates adopted a moderate stance with regard to oil nationalisation. Petroleum matters did not occupy a conspicuous place in the electoral debate. Lorenzo Fernández, candidate of the Social Christian party COPEI, stressed the need to accelerate the nationalisation process, while AD's Carlos Andrés Pérez pointed out that it was unlikely that the country could wait until most concessions were due to be handed back to the state in 1984. At the time, only the parties of the left advocated outright expropriation of foreign oil assets[14].

In his farewell speech to Congress in February 1974, President Caldera (1969-74) exhorted his successor, AD's Carlos Andrés Pérez, to nationalise the oil industry. The call was a radical shift from Caldera's earlier policy of accommodation towards the foreign concessionaires which he had pursued up until 1970. President Caldera, whose administration nationalised the gas industry in 1970, had grown gradually disillusioned with the companies' lack of co-operation with his government's policy of increasing upstream activities in the country.

Most efforts to minimise the disinvestment tendency that the oil MNs had maintained in Venezuela since the early 1960s had given little results. In 1969, net investment in the oil sector had averaged $365.7 million; in 1972 that amount had been reduced to an alarming $232 million[15]. Cessation of further investment in oil activities had been the companies' response to increasing domestic taxes on oil production, to the no-more-concessions policy, and, during the Caldera administration, to the terms of the service contracts[16]. A long-time manager of the oil industry commented that,

The basic error was to announce the no-more concessions policy ten years prior to nationalisation. As a result, the companies stopped investing[17].

Moreover, the oil MNs deemed that the state oil company, the CVP (*Corporación Venezolana del Petróleo*), created in 1960 to take over part of the national market for the sale of oil products[18], was allotted excessive control over their operations. Subsequently, when the CVP sought their co-operation to develop its own distribution channels to commercialise Venezuelan oil products, the oil MNs reacted in a non-committal way. The oil concessionaires were weary of ever-increasing taxes and unexpected cash demands by the government. A former PDVSA director pointed out that,

Before nationalisation, the Ministry of Finance used to call the treasurers of the foreign companies to ask them for advances on tax payments[19].

The lack of co-operation from the oil concessionaires in finding outlets for oil was important in changing the attitude of government policy-makers, who increasingly regarded nationalisation as the only means to reverse the deterioration of the local oil industry. COPEI, after having failed to achieve a satisfactory accommodation during the last years of Caldera's administration, ended up adopting a more nationalistic stance towards the oil MNs than traditionally nationalistic AD. In this context, and allegedly as a reaction against the opposition received by his party's proposal concerning oil policy decisions, Caldera's administration nationalised the gas industry in 1970[20].

President Caldera's experience had demonstrated that, despite the ever-demanding taxation schemes that the successive Venezuelan governments had been able to impose on the foreign companies, the presence of the MNs in the national soil had for a long time fed the nationalist feelings of the political leadership. A history of mistrust and uncomfortable cohabitation between Venezuelan governments and foreign oil companies rendered a possible accommodation unlikely.

Besides the need to increase investments as a rationale for adopting a quick nationalisation policy, there remained the fact that the oil MNs were reminiscent of the unequal north-south economic world order commonly challenged at the time. No matter how much bargaining power was taken away from them by the host government, the MNs responded to decision-making centres outside the national boundaries, thus creating mistrust and exacerbating nationalist feelings among local politicians. In Venezuela, the foreign companies became increasingly alienated, thus losing any useful support among the political élite.

The Pérez administration (1974-79) and nationalisation

AD's Carlos Andrés Pérez won the December 1973 elections by a comfortable margin, with 48.6% of the vote. The Social Christian party COPEI had come next with 36.8% followed by the parties from the left, MAS (*Movimiento al Socialismo*) and MEP (*Movimiento Electoral del Pueblo*) with percentages not exceeding five percent each. AD was able to secure a majority representation in Congress, in a proportion of 44.3% in relation to 30.3% for COPEI[21]. The results of this election were important because, while putting an end to a past of political fragmentation, they reiterated the standard of two party polarisation that characterised Venezuelan politics until 1993. After 1958, Venezuelan voters had usually chosen between AD and COPEI, increasingly reducing the importance of the parties from the left. The polarisation AD-COPEI eased the implementation of the tacit accords contained in the *Pacto de Punto Fijo* (Punto Fijo Pact)[22] signed by COPEI, AD and URD (*Unión Republicana Democrática*) in 1958 during the transition period from dictatorship to democracy. Advocating democratic bargaining and minimising confrontation, the Pact set out the basis for political behaviour in the new democratic regime. By alienating the left, the parties from the political centre agreed on a set of rules for the construction of what Karl called a 'pacted democracy'[23] . They agreed on the minimum consensus over economic policy and preservation of democracy by fighting communism and keeping the military at arm's length. By signing the *Pacto Institucional* (Institutional Pact) in 1970 AD and COPEI ratified the tacit system of minimum consensus earlier introduced by the Punto Fijo Pact. In the light of the increasing two-party polarisation, AD and COPEI were able to strengthen the terms of the 'pacted democracy' installed since 1958, from where stemmed a political system characterised by tacit consensus on key issues at the highest party decision-making echelons. Control of the oil industry would strengthen this tendency. With nationalisation, the high level decision-making centres of AD and COPEI became a political oligarchy in themselves. Thanks to the control over the oil sector, the governments installed by AD and COPEI were able to maintain a tight clientelist network and, consequently, rely on a strong popular support. Access to oil revenues provided the two dominating parties with a comfortable basis for appeasing conflict, and for adopting a policy-making approach based on the avoidande of conflict.

In his first post-election speech, the newly elected president, Carlos Andrés Pérez, was more precise about his position regarding the nationalisation issue. He highlighted the need to implement the policy in the short term.

> The private companies are maintaining their exploratory activities at minimum levels, and we run the risk that our industry will rapidly deteriorate. It would be wise to proceed in the immediate future to a nationalisation which would secure our sovereignty in the industry and which would set out new formulas for the participation of foreign companies in those spheres in which we need their technical resources[24] .

In order to gain experience in the problems of nationalisation and minimise the apprehensions of the oil companies, the Pérez administration nationalised the iron-ore industry in the first place. The nationalisation of this industry was an exercise that provided the government with useful experience for the much more significant nationalisation of the petroleum industry. With the smooth nationalisation of the iron-ore industry, the Pérez administration showed the international community –both oil companies and foreign governments– that the country was able to implement consensual nationalisation policies.

The implementation of the nationalisation policy was eased by the bonanza created by the First Major Oil Shock, as huge oil revenues made possible the indemnity of the foreign companies for the anticipated end to their concessions. Furthermore, based on the high inflow of cash as a result of the oil windfall, it was not difficult for the AD administration to implement an expansive economic policy, characterised by multiple subsidies and huge infrastructure projects[25]. Under such a scheme, nationalisation of the oil industry was a crucial element for the accomplishment of the government's short-term political and economic programmes. Nationalisation of the most important sector of the economy secured the government sufficient funds to redistribute wealth and adopt a policy-making approach based on the avoidance of conflict. In this context, and through a complex system of taxation over the oil industry, the government became the undisputed administrator of the oil rent[26].

The international context

Venezuela nationalised its oil industry at a time when OPEC member states were in the position of unchallenged managers of the world's most important natural resource. Or at least they thought so, encouraged by their much more powerful position resulting from the First Major Oil Shock of 1973-74. This major oil crisis, which caused the barrel price to reach excessively high levels, was triggered by events in the Middle East, in a conflict known as the Fourth Arab-Israeli war[27]. As a retaliatory measure against US support of Israel during the conflict, the OAPEC member states[28] decided to reduce oil supply to the western countries and to impose a total embargo on the US[29]. As the data in Table 2.2 show, within a short period following the beginning of the conflict in the Middle East the price of the barrel rocketed, to the distress of the OECD economies and to the benefit of OPEC governments.

Table 2.2 Posted prices of OPEC members: selected dates and countries ($ per barrel)

	Venezuela	Saudi Arabia	Iran	Libya
January, 1973	3.36	2.59	2.55	3.77
November, 1973	7.80	5.12	5.34	8.92
January, 1974	14.25	11.56	11.87	15.78

Note: The average API level for Venezuelan crude is here 35°; for the rest of crudes API level is 34°.
Sources: Petroleum Economist. Tables; *Petroleum Intelligence Weekly.* Tables.

The shock in the world oil markets had effects reflecting the enormous importance that oil was gaining in the development of the post-WWII period. Economic growth had been accompanied by ever increasing oil demand. The supply-demand relation was dangerously tight; any disruption in the former part of the equation could result in a world economic downturn. The OPEC producers, controlling the largest part of the oil market, knew this too well. They had become the key actors of a new economic order. The OECD countries feared the decisions of OPEC and the Third World looked up to its members as the challengers of the unfair economic north-south division. In the 1970s there was a transcendental shift of world power from the oil consuming countries to the producer ones, a change so deep that has been called a 'world oil revolution'[30].

The immediate impact of the First Oil Shock on the industrialised world was economic recession. The new hikes in the price of the barrel suddenly brought deep economic dislocations. Inflation introduced its nasty and continually haunting presence into the economies. Unemployment rates soared. Western Europe, the US, and Japan found themselves drastically experiencing negative signs in their balance of payments' accounts. GDP in the US decreased 6% between 1973 and 1975; unemployment had reached 9% as of 1975. For the first time in the post-WWII period, Japan's GDP decreased. In turn, the purchasing power of the oil producing countries grew in a zero-sum game proportion in relation to that of the importing countries. This redistribution of the oil rent in favour of the OPEC members became known as the 'OPEC-tax', launching a dramatic recession in the industrialised world[31].

The impact of the oil windfall on Venezuela's economy

When the decision to nationalise the oil industry was adopted, the Venezuelan government was enjoying the bonanza resulting from the First Oil Shock. The barrel price was still high and OECD dependence on oil had not been significantly curbed. The oil market situation facilitated the adoption of the nationalisation policy in 1974, as the treasury relied on sufficient wealth to pay for the expropriated assets of the oil MNs. By the mid-1970s, Venezuela, like most OPEC nations, was receiving exceptionally high-income volumes for its crude sales, despite a reduction in production levels, as Table 2.3 shows.

Table 2.3 Oil production in Venezuela, 1970-1974

	Output (Million b/d)	Income (Million $)	Export Price ($ per barrel)
1970	3,760	2,357	2.0
1972	3,450	3,092	2.64
1973	3,462	3,959	3.09 Jan., 1st
1974	2,976	10,308	14.26 Jan., 1st

Sources: Petroleum Economist, February 1992; *International Financial Statistics*, IMF. Vol. XLV, No. 4, April 1992.

As a result of the sudden hike in oil prices, government income jumped from $4,418 million in 1973 to more than $14,418 million in the year 1974[32]. According to Mommer, in 1974 the state achieved the highest ever level of rent rate over the natural resource: 134%[33]. In order to prevent the over-heating and the inflationary effects of the sudden injection of petrodollars into the economy, in 1974 the Pérez administration created the Venezuelan Investment Fund (VIF). Between 1974 and 1977 the VIF received a total of around $5,300 million[34]. Despite the measures implemented to minimise the negative effects of the oil windfall, a policy of great spending, subsidies and non-restricted foreign borrowing was the result of the oil economic boom. In this context, fiscal spending seemed to be limitless[35].

The policy-making process leading to nationalisation

Several factors fostered the adoption of the nationalisation policy in 1974. First, there was the urgent need to capitalise the oil industry. Second, the favourable financial situation of the government as a result of the oil windfall. Third, the long and cumulative process of friction between the oil concessionaires and Venezuelan politicians. Upon realisation of the favourable oil market context for a smooth passage to nationalisation, the Pérez administration set out to obtain political support for nationalisation. The policy-making process leading to nationalisation was characterised by bargaining and interaction among the actors involved: Congress, executive, pressure groups, and oil managers. Political actors and executive officials were the most significant policy-making groups in this process.

Nationalisation counted on a high degree of political support, and the problems that arose in the policy-making process were due to technical and programmatic issues, rather than to political ones. There was little public debate over the policy; politicians, executive officials and managers of the oil industry had usually dealt with oil policy issues.

As opposed to previous nationalisation actions where the oil MNs and their governments exerted pressure to influence policy events, in Venezuela the oil companies hardly sought to modify the course of the process. As a result of unfavourable tax conditions and more attractive opportunities elsewhere, the oil MNs had limited interest in continuing operations in the country and did not oppose being expropriated as long as they received an indemnity. Despite the sporadic talks between government and oil companies over technical matters, the oil MNs played a somewhat passive, although vigilant role in the whole process. Seeking to benefit from the nationalisation outcome, both government and oil MNs decided to avoid conflict situations[36]. By agreeing to establish technical and co-operation agreements with the nationalised oil industry, the oil MNs showed their approval of the way the process was being carried out.

As of 1973 all political parties advocated nationalisation. Differences of opinion did appear regarding the characteristics the process was to take and the terms of the Nationalisation Law. Nationalisation of the oil industry became the nationalist card played by the Pérez administration; COPEI and the parties from the left followed suit. Not even traditionally conservative oil policy-makers such as Pérez Alfonzo, the most influential oil figure in Venezuela at the time, opposed the convenience of immediate action[37].

The political parties, notably AD with its majority representation in Congress, took the lead over the nationalisation issue. COPEI, in the best consensual spirit of the Punto Fijo Pact, did not object to the AD-led policy move. Public debate over nationalisation was in fact moderate. A former PDVSA policy-maker pointed out that,

> The action was the nationalist flag of AD and the parties from the left. Nobody could have opposed to it; besides, there were no reasons to have done so. There was the international context, the seventies...[38].

At an early stage, negotiations took place in the political parties at the highest echelons, which in Venezuela are often crucial decision-making centres[39]. Once consensus was reached by AD and COPEI, other sectors of society were brought in to broaden the consensual basis in support of the nationalisation action. They were integrated into the *Comisión*

Presidencial para la Reversión de la Industria Petrolera (Presidential Commission for the Reversion of the Petroleum Industry) appointed on May 16, 1974. Resulting from a whole year's work, the Commission's document, the *Magna Carta* of nationalisation, established a diagnosis of the situation of the oil industry, and suggested immediate implementation of the nationalisation policy[40].

The Commission was composed of members from the executive, the political parties, several sectors of society and the armed forces. AD's representation was the most visible. The Commission was assisted by a *Comité de Coordinación* (Coordination Committee) which represented different sectors of society, such as professional guilds, universities, unions, entrepreneurs, and so on, many of which had close ties with AD. The lawyers who assisted the Commission, Florencio Contreras and Carlos D'Empaire, had participated as legal advisors in the nationalisation of the iron-ore industry that took place in April 1974, at the beginning of the Pérez administration.

As nationalisation was to be implemented in the immediate future, in 1975 President Pérez appointed observers from the Ministry of Energy and Mines to the boards of directors of the major oil companies. The purpose was to observe the transition process and oversee the management of the oil business in preparation for the upcoming period. The role of the Ministry of Energy was of great significance here. The process of preparing Venezuelan nationals for the challenge of nationalisation began at an early stage of the transition process. When nationalisation was implemented many Venezuelan employees of the foreign oil companies found themselves suddenly promoted to very high posts in the nationalised oil industry[41].

Besides the groups of government officials and political parties which, grouped in the Commission, influenced the development of the policy formulation process leading to nationalisation, there was a number of Venezuelan managers working in the foreign concessionaires who formed a pressure group called *Agrupación de Orientación Petrolera* (Oil Orientation Group). This group was known as AGROPET and became the representative body of the oil industry workers. Feeling somewhat alienated from the process underway, where the political actors in Congress and executive officials played the leading roles, oil managers sought to influence the outcome of the nationalisation policy. As the government's nationalisation plans approached, several oil managers became increasingly apprehensive about the outcome of the action, wondering about the degree of efficiency of a process largely commanded by the political élite and government.

AGROPET soon went from a handful of members to over one hundred oil workers who intended to find governmental response to the opinions of the oil sector. Its representatives delivered speeches and wrote in the press about the need to keep the tradition of meritocracy for the nationalised oil industry and of the advantages of maintaining the private company ethic that prevailed under the foreign companies. Although not summoned to be a part of it, AGROPET submitted to the Commission its views on the nationalisation policy. Summarised, the group's recommendations were a) to establish a holding company with a board of eight to nine full-time members with considerable experience in the oil industry, b) to create three to four integrated companies after a process of administrative rationalisation, c) to establish a sharp separation between the oil industry and the political establishment; the oil minister should not be present at the industry's board meetings, d) to create an institute for research and development, e) to begin the exploration of the heavy-oil Orinoco region[42]. With some modifications, many of AGROPET's concerns were reflected in the Nationalisation Law.

As a result of the political character of the discussions, public opinion felt somewhat overwhelmed and paid little attention, as most people did not clearly understand what was at stake with nationalisation. An opinion survey carried out during September and October 1974 among several key sectors of society and especially among blue and white-collar employees of the oil industry, including the state's CVP, showed the mistrust of the interviewees towards the state handling of the oil industry[43]. The oil managers highlighted 'the incapacity of the state to administer its enterprises in an objective, efficient and profitable manner'[44]. The oil managers, as inheritors of the private enterprise of the oil MNs, mistrusted the political élite and had clear apprehensions concerning government handling of the oil industry. Constant political interference in the management of the nationalised industry was a major concern among the oil workers, who considered the public sector as,

> An archaic structure controlled by mediocre, selfish and corrupted interests of the lowest kind such a structure, which permits dishonesty, subsidises mistakes and where cronyism is rampant, cannot guarantee the normal functioning of the oil industry and, much less, its profitability[45].

The role of oil managers in the policy-making process was, as mentioned above, less significant than that of the executive and the political leadership. Many oil managers advocated alternatives to the nationalisation option. A form of association with the foreign oil companies could have been possible, without having to implement the more radical action of nationalising the assets of the fourteen companies operating in the country. The following are comments by PDVSA's policy-makers on nationalisation:

The country could have negotiated a sort of profit-sharing agreement with the MNs[46]. Nationalisation was a means for politicians to gain access to power[47]; it was a way to gain full access to the natural resource[48].

Although some managers of the oil industry considered that nationalisation was not the only policy option available to reverse the decline of the industry, most of them did not openly oppose the action. The oil managers followed the policy process and, through AGROPET, sought to influence its outcome, without overtly opposing it. Politicians were well aware of the opinions of many oil managers regarding the government's decision to nationalise and did not consider them as allies in carrying out the policy. Oil managers alienated themselves from a policy process that, in turn, alienated them. Had it been up to them, it was perhaps unlikely that they would have opted for nationalisation. The oil managers' allegiance to the MNs was strong and long-dated. Most of them did not clearly understand the motivations of the political élite, their nationalist arguments, and their intention of turning the oil industry into a SOE. They feared politicisation of the oil industry's management and constant interference in their corporate decisions. However, opposition to nationalisation by the oil managers would have meant open criticism to the goverment's policy and that would have had negative consequences on their future careers in the nationalised industry.

Most oil managers were concerned with the short-term implications of the nationalisation policy over the continuation of the industry's activities. The apprehensions of the oil industry employees are included in the following comments by a PDVSA policy-maker:

> Nationalisation meant cutting the chain between upstream and downstream operations. Such was the preoccupation of the oil managers. When we nationalised, we were left in the hands of two or three large companies to commercialise our oil. We were very vulnerable[49].

In spite of these concerns and of the highly political character of the action, not all oil managers failed to recognise the positive implications of the nationalisation action. Despite their passive criticisms of the government's decision to nationalise, most oil managers believed in the capacity of Venezuelan nationals to face the challenges ahead and had faith in the preservation of the meritocratic system that prevailed under the oil MNs[50]. The following comments reflect well the current feeling of most oil managers regarding the decision of the political forces to nationalise the oil industry in 1975:

Nationalisation was done in an impeccable form...The oil technocrats would not have nationalised the industry. The politicians did it, and that was a good thing[51].

Not one of the people who worked for the concessionaires and now is in the high command of PDVSA disagrees with nationalisation. At the time, some Venezuelans protested the move, and went even as far as to propose a coup as a solution to stop the nationalisation move...The Venezuelan employees were loyal; they had faith in the system of meritocracy[52].

In turn, many politicians held the view that the Venezuelan employees of the oil industry served foreign interests and cared little for their country. This view largely stemmed from the times of the military regime of Marcos Pérez Jiménez (1948-58), when the MNs, indifferent to the nature of the regime, had continued operating in the country, while most of the democratic political forces were either in prison or in exile. The opposite views of these two sets of policy-makers –on one side, executive officials and political actors, and on the other, industry managers– has been at the centre of many controversies over oil policy-making in Venezuela since nationalisation.

In the last stage of the policy formulation process of the nationalisation policy, Congress, which evaluated the terms of the document drawn up by the Commission, heard in audience spokesmen from different sectors of society[53]. They were willing to voice their opinions on the nationalisation action, as well as on related subjects such as energy policy, the oil fleet, the economy, the decision-making process itself and so on. It is difficult to determine to what extent their considerations were reflected in the final draft of the Nationalisation Law. Nevertheless, the fact that numerous organisations and oil-related personalities were heard in Congress imbued the policy formulation process with a certain degree of democratic legitimacy. However, even though the opinion of several sectors were taken into consideration in drawing up the final nationalisation document, its outcome reflected more the visions of political actors and executive officials over the handling of the oil resource than of any other group involved in the process of oil policy-making.

Important issues such as the decision-making process between the Ministry and the oil industry, the terms in which the industry was to be accountable to Congress, and the demands of government agencies such as the Central Bank and the VIF were left largely undefined. These unresolved issues lay at the root of the many oil policy-making conflicts that ensued after nationalisation. The neglect of such significant policy-making issues at the time of nationalisation demonstrated that policy-makers of the Pérez administration did not really look ahead in order to grasp the overall long-term implications of the action for the oil industry and for the oil policy-making process in particular. At the time of nationalisation, the debate was mainly conducted on the basis that the key issue, as the following chapter will demonstrate, was the need to recover a declining industry and to secure international links to channel crude volumes. However, nationalisation was to bring about a significant change in the way in which not only oil policy-making but also government policy-making was to be conducted.

The Commission's draft reviewed by Congress was finally submitted to the executive in the Council of Ministers' meeting on March 11, 1975. At the same time there were two other projects of Nationalisation Law, one presented by MEP and another by COPEI. These alternative projects were considered only marginally in Congress. In fact, the final outcome of the Nationalisation Law mirrored closely the text produced by the Commission, where AD's representation was the most conspicuous. Although the policy-making process for the adoption of nationalisation was characterised by bargaining and participation among the parties involved, the results reflected more the idea that government policy-makers had of the action.

The executive formally sanctioned the Nationalisation Law on August 29, 1975[54]. All concessions, most of which were due to end by 1984, were to be written off on December 31, 1975. The total compensation bills for the assets expropriated to the oil companies amounted to $2,085 million, of which $231.61 million were paid cash and $1,853.5 million in government bonds[55].

Article 5 of the Nationalisation Law

In Congress discussions had evolved around the most controversial articles. For the purposes of this research, special attention will be allotted to Article 5, which set out the guidelines for future associations between the nationalised industry and the private sector including the foreign companies. Using the experience of similar clauses included in the laws of countries that had nationalised their oil industries, government policy-makers left the door open for associations with the private sector, national or foreign. Highly controversial, the following clause determined the association of the newly created oil industry with private sector partners:

> In special cases, and whenever it concerns the public interest, the executive or its entities could sign association agreements with private entities, with a participation that would enable the state control over it and up to a limited

length of time. For the signing of such association agreements, previous
Congress authorisation will be required, in joint session by both Chambers,
according to the conditions determined, and after having been informed by
the executive of the pertinent circumstances[56].

By setting the legal basis for future association agreements with
foreign oil companies, the inclusion of Article 5 also intended to foster the
confidence of the international oil community and the private sector. By
including Congress legitimacy as a requisite for association with private
capital, Article 5 appeased the most fervent politicians who were concerned
with a return to the system overthrown with nationalisation.

The private sector, represented by FEDECAMARAS, did not consider
it necessary for the oil industry to seek approval from the legislature in
order to establish agreements with the private sector. The private sector
deplored the fact that Article 5 gave Congress the power to interfere in
the freedom of association of the nationalised oil industry. Article 5 limited
the freedom of PDVSA's policy-makers to associate with private and
foreign capital.

Most political factions of the left were not satisfied with the wording
of the article either, since they did not consider it necessary for the oil
industry to associate with the private sector in order to carry out any of its
activities. Alarmed at the possible implications of this article, the *Juventud
Revolucionaria Copeyana* (COPEI's Revolutionary Youth) decided to
create a united front to 'fight those who pretended to use the petroleum
business to favour private enterprise groups'[57]. The radical left was, not
surprisingly, even more opposed to Article 5, considering that it implied
relinquishing the country's sovereignty to private capital interests. The
Communist Party identified in Article 5 the intrigues of the foreign and
domestic private capital that at the last moment had convinced government
policy-makers to secure a space for their participation in the nationalised
oil industry. Even AD's Pérez Alfonzo opposed the Article, not seeing the
need to envisage further association with foreign companies.

Not all political leaders opposed the co-operation between the private
sector and the nationalised oil industry. Despite its leftist credo, MAS
considered that private capital was to have an important role in the activities
of the nationalised oil industry and it did not oppose the Article. AD's
Gonzalo Barrios, important figure in the high-level decision-making centre
of the party, believed that a space should be left open for the possibility of
establishing mixed ventures with the private sector, both domestic and
foreign, in case this should prove convenient for the nationalised industry
in the future. Barrios, who in fact was not totally in favour of establishing

such associations, provided the middle ground in which opposing sides found accommodation. His position reflected AD's high decision-making centre, and became the seal that ended the discussions around the Article's content[58]. The nationalised oil industry was in need of the oil concessionaires' expertise to carry out essential activities, and ruling out association with foreign capital was considered inconvenient. As will be seen in Chapter III, soon after nationalisation, several agreements for technical co-operation and commercialisation were signed between the newly created oil industry and the ex-concessionaires.

When the first major association with a foreign company, the German Veba Oel, took place in 1983, Article 5 was for the first time put to the test. Following the advice of the *Procurador General de la República* (Republic's Solicitor General), PDVSA implemented the joint-venture association without seeking Congress approval. When the legislature learned of the contract's implementation, a major controversy originated. As will be examined in Chapter IV, the different and opposing views that caused much controversy during the elaboration of Article 5 of the Nationalisation Law came to the surface, creating confrontation between the industry and several political representatives in Congress. The relationship between the nationalised oil industry and the government – i.e. the autonomy of the former and the control mechanisms of the latter– were put to the test.

Conclusion

The need to reverse the increasing decline of the oil industry, a favourable international context, and a long-term cumulative process of friction between the oil companies and Venezuelan politicians were among the main factors that fostered the implementation of the nationalisation policy in the mid-1970s.

The result of a negotiated and coherently planned process, nationalisation was implemented in such a way as to avoid conflict with the foreign concessionaires. The action was the logical result of a cumulative past of bargaining between Venezuelan governments and oil MNs. Government policy-makers sought to avoid the mistakes of previous radical nationalisation experiences elsewhere, which resulted in hampering future collaboration with the foreign oil MNs. From the outset, the need to maintain a good working relationship between the newly created oil SOE and the foreign concessionaires was a major concern of the government policy-makers who formulated the nationalisation policy. Both AD and COPEI, government policy-makers and oil MNs, welcomed nationalisation. The government was eager to gain control over the most important sector of the economy and because it would no longer have to include foreign actors in the oil policy-making process. In turn, the oil MNs greeted the policy action with relief and were glad to receive compensation for the assets of an industry that was for the most part obsolete.

Political actors played the leading role in the process of policy-making that preceded the nationalisation of the oil industry. Although various interest groups representing different sectors of society participated in the process of policy formulation, nationalisation was largely the device of political actors. After having consolidated its place in the political system, the political élite set out to gain total control of the oil industry for the state. The nationalisation policy was a crucial milestone in the ascension of the political élite towards an unchallenged position of power.

As in most nationalisation processes elsewhere, in Venezuela the role of the oil industry managers was overshadowed by the active participation of executive officials and political forces. In fact, some of the oil industry managers had been reluctant to regard nationalisation as the ultimate solution to the oil industry's problems, and had shown great apprehensions of a process almost entirely led by politicians and executive officials.

Besides the immediate goal of boosting production and reversing the decline of the oil industry, there was, however, no clear direction as to what were the long-term aims of nationalisation. Significant matters such as the interaction between the industry and the Ministry of Energy or the means the legislature was to implement in order to make the oil SOE accountable for its performance and policy choices were largely neglected. Such unresolved issues came to the surface during the conflicts that stemmed from the adoption and implementation of key policy choices.

The following chapter appraises the industry's formative years and the implementation of its early objectives. It will be argued that the internationalisation policy was a natural outgrowth of the accomplishment of early corporate objectives and that the role of the executive in the process of oil policy-making was to be increasingly challenged by the consolidation and expansion of the nationalised oil industry.

Notes

1   Guillermo Rodríguez Eraso. Former president of LAGOVEN. *Interview.* November 19, 1993.
2   Quoted by George Philip. *Oil and Politics in Latin America: Nationalist Movements and State Companies.* Cambridge University Press, 1982, pp. 307-308.
3   Gustavo Coronel. *The Nationalization of the Venezuelan Oil Industry.* Lexington Books. Massachusetts, 1983. Chapters I-III.

4   The Soviet Union nationalised its oil industry after 1917. In 1951 Iran nationalised the Anglo-Iranian company. Daniel Yergin. *The Prize. The Quest for Oil, Money and Power.* Simon and Schuster. New York, 1992; Philip, *Op. cit.*

5   Yergin, *Op. cit.*; Philip, *Op. cit.*

6   Randall. *Op.cit.,* pp. 4-37; Tugwell. *Op. cit.*

7   *Diario de Debates.* Congress of Venezuela. Caracas.

8   Franklin Tugwell. *The Politics of Oil in Venezuela.* Stanford University Press, 1975; Philip. *Op. cit.,* pp. 293-311.

9   In December 1970 two types of taxes were approved, the substitute tax, which raised the proportion from 52% to 60%, and the 'reference tax' based on the unilateral calculation by the government of the price of oil. Tugwell. *Op. cit.,* pp. 108-116; Toro Hardy, *Venezuela, 55 años de Política Económica.* Caracas, 1992. pp. 74-77.

10   Article by Cayetano Ramírez. 'Se inicia refinación experimental de crudos pesados'. *El Nacional.* April 24, 1983.

11   Rafael Alfonzo Ravard. *Cinco años de Normalidad Operativa.* PDVSA. Caracas, 1981, p. 333.

12   *Petroleum Economist.* Tables.

13   *Series Estadísticas.* BCV.

14   Philip. *Op. cit.,* p. 306; Tugwell. *Op. cit.,* p. 143.

15   Asdrúbal Baptista. *Bases cuantitativas de la economía venezolana, 1830-1989.* Ediciones María di Mase. Caracas, 1991.

16   The service contract policy implemented by the Caldera government, and previously proposed by Pérez Alfonzo, was a way to encourage the companies to further invest in exploratory activities. The no-more-concessions policy had increased the disinvestment trend of the oil MNs: restrictions and unattractive profit margins were deemed discouraging. Tugwell. *Op. cit.,* pp. 105-108.

17   Member of PDVSA's Board of Directors who requested anonymity. *Interview.* August 25, 1993.

18   In 1975, CVP was mandated to take total responsibility for the domestic distribution and sale of petroleum products. Tugwell. *Op. cit.,* pp. 142-143.

19   Wolf Petzall. Former vice-president, PDVSA. *Interview.* September 2, 1993.

20   Philip. *Op. cit.,* p. 305.

21   Luis Pedro España. 'El futuro político de las minorías partidistas'. *SIC.* No. 511, Jan.-Feb. 1989, p. 14.

22   The Punto Fijo Pact will be further discussed in Chapter V. For a full discussion of the Pact and of its implications for the political system that ensued after transition to democracy in 1958, see C. Baena. *Le processus d'apprentissage politique dans la transition vers la démocratie au Venezuela.* M.Sc. thesis. Département d'Histoire. Université de Montréal, 1989.

23   Terry Lynn Karl, 'Petroleum and Political Pacts: the Transition to Democracy in Venezuela'. *Latin American Research Review.* Vol. XXII, N° 1, 1987, pp. 63-94.

24   Quoted from Tugwell. *Op. cit.,* pp. 143-144; Philip. *Op. cit.,* p. 307.

25   It was during this period that the steel, aluminium and electrical industrial complexes were developed. The SOEs created to produce steel (SIDOR), aluminium (ALCASA) and electricity from the Guri Dam (EDELCA) are subsidiaries of the state holding company (*Corporación Venezolana de Guayana, CVG*) that commands the development of natural resources in the country's southern region (Bolívar state).

26   The taxation schemes imposed on PDVSA have been widely analysed by several authors: Randall. *Op. cit.,* p. 117-217; Coronel. *Op. cit.* pp. 159-168; Boué. *Op. Cit.,* pp. 189-192; Bernard Mommer and Ramón Espinasa, 'Venezuelan Oil Policy in the Long Run'. *Energy,* East-West Center, Hawai, 1991.

27   André Giroud and Xavier Boy de la Tour. *Géopolitique du Pétrole et du Gaz.* Technip. Paris, 1987, p. 240. For an economic assessment of the events, *Cf.* Cyrus Bina. *The Economics of the Oil Crisis.* Martin Press, New York, 1985. For a historic and geographic appraisal of the conflict, Georges Duby. *Atlas Historique.* Larousse. Paris. Also, Yergin. *Op. cit.,* Chapter 29, 'The Oil Weapon', pp. 588-612.

28   OAPEC: Saudi Arabia, Iraq, Kuwait, UAE, Qatar, Libya, Bahrain, Egypt, Syria, Algeria and Tunisia. Tunisia's membership was inactivated in 1986.

29   Total embargo was only first imposed on the US and the Netherlands, also considered by the Arab states as a friend of Israel. Total embargo was later to be extended to Portugal, South Africa and former Rhodesia. Also, a partial embargo was multilaterally imposed on all markets, as a general 5% monthly restriction was imposed on all oil shipments from the Persian Gulf area. Yergin. *Op. cit.,* p. 613.

30   Philip. *Op. cit.,* p. 498.

31   Yergin. *Op. cit.,* pp. 660-661.

32   José Toro Hardy. *Venezuela. 55 Años de Política Económica. 1936-1991.* Panapo Edit. Caracas, 1992, pp. 76-86.

33   Mommer and Espinasa. *Op. cit.,* p. 16.

34   Central Bank Tables.

35   The accounts of the consolidated public sector, excluding the oil sector, varied from having a surplus of $4,294 million in 1974 to a deficit of $4,245 million in 1979. *Idem.*

36   The only major problem between the government and one oil MN took place with Occidental Petroleum Company. The conflict, which took almost a decade to be legally settled, was due to the technical and commercial co-operation agreements with the nationalised oil industry and not to the indemnity terms of nationalisation itself. Rodríguez Eraso. *Interview.* November 19. 1993.

37   Although Pérez Alfonzo, 'AD's petroleum philosopher' (Tugwell. *Op. cit.,* p. 33) was Planning Minister (CORDIPLAN) during the Revolutionary Junta during 1945-48, his real influence as an oil policy-maker was exerted when appointed Energy Minister by AD Rómulo Betancourt in 1958, in the first democratic administration after the 10-year dictatorship of Marcos Pérez Jiménez (1948-1958). In the 1970s Pérez Alfonzo was a full advocate of nationalisation of the oil industry, a departure from his early stance.

38   Humberto Peñaloza. Former director of PDVSA. *Interview.* February 2, 1993.

39   In Venezuela commonly known as 'cogollos'.

40   Report. *Comisión Presidencial para la Reversión de la Industria Petrolera.* Caracas, 1974.

41   Susan Johnson. *Organizational Adaptation in the Venezuelan Petroleum Industry.* PhD thesis. MIT, 1987.

42   *Ibid.,* p. 58.

43   The survey is mentioned by Gustavo Coronel. *Op. cit.* pp. 59-60. The study was carried out among over one thousand oil-industry employees, service-company personnel, ministry employees, independent businessmen, students, and housewives. Coronel mentions that 38% of the interviewees answered that they did not have a clear idea of what oil nationalisation meant.

44   *Idem.*

45   *Idem.*

46   Member of PDVSA's Board of Directors who requested anonymity. *Interview.* August 25, 1993.

47   *Idem.*

48   Juan Carlos Gómez. Director, PDVSA. *Interview.* August 31, 1993.

49 *Idem.*
50 *Idem.*
51 Daniel Ramírez. Manager, LAGOVEN. *Interview.* September 2, 1993.
52 PDVSA's member of Board of Directors. *Interview.* August 25, 1993.
53 Among them were FEDECAMARAS, Pro-Venezuela, the student's association from the Central University, directors from the Ministry of Mines and Energy, AGROPET, Association of Professionals from the CVP, Venezuelan Society of Petroleum Engineers, Co-ordinators from the Working Commissions of the Petroleum Reversal Presidential Commission, Venezuelan Chamber of Petroleum, Lawyers Association, CTV (Venezuelan Workers' Union), FEDEPETROL (Petroleum Workers' Union), FENEGAS (Gas Workers' Union), FETRAHIDROCARBUROS (Federation of Hydrocarbons Workers) and the Directory of Graduate courses of the Faculty of Social and Economic Studies of the Universidad Central de Venezuela. The following individuals concerned with petroleum activities participated in the hearings: Leonardo Montiel Ortega, Humberto Peñaloza, Carlos Piñerúa, ex-ministers Juan Pablo Pérez Alfonzo, Manuel R. Egaña and Hugo Pérez La Salvia, and the Republic's Solicitor-General. *Ibid.*, p. 35.
54 *Ley Orgánica que reserva al Estado la Industria petrolera y el comercio de hidrocarburos.* August 29, 1975. Throughout this research, this law will be referred to as the Nationalisation Law.
55 *Official Gazette.* No 1784. December 18, 1975.
56 *Nationalisation Law.* August 29, 1975.
57 *Diary of Congress Debates.* Caracas.
58 Julio César Arreaza. *Diez Años de la Industria Petrolera Nacional, 1976-1985.* CEPET. Caracas, 1986.

Chapter 3
PDVSA's early objectives:
The process of corporate
consolidation

3 PDVSA's early objectives: The process of corporate consolidation

Introduction

One of the main problems facing the nascent oil industry was identified during the transition to nationalisation: the need to create independent channels for crude commercialisation. Besides examining efforts made to tackle this problem, this chapter analyses the first policies implemented by the newly created oil SOE, notably organisational consolidation, across-the-board investment increases, establishment of co-operation and working agreements with the oil MNs. Once these objectives were successfully accomplished, the industry set out to internationalise its activities, on the way to becoming an oil MN. The internationalisation policy was a consequence of the successful accomplishment of many of the industry's early corporate objectives.

With the creation of *Petróleos de Venezuela* (PDVSA) in August 1975[1] the ex-concessionaires came under the umbrella of the newly nationalised holding company. From the beginning, industry policy-makers decided on a structure based on the vertical integration of its affiliated companies, co-ordinated by a mother company, PDVSA, which was to assure the observance of collective corporate and strategic goals. Free-riding and excessive competition among the affiliates were to be minimised through a fixed system of constant consultations and assemblies co-ordinated by the holding company, from where all guidelines directed to the affiliates were to emanate. In order to assure organisational continuity, the new affiliates were shaped to emulate the structure and the corporate culture of the foreign concessionaires. The vertical structure adopted for the nationalised oil industry was somewhat unusual for a SOE, being more typical of a private corporation[2].

Through the establishment of agreements for technological assistance and crude commercialisation, the nationalised oil company managed to maintain its ties with the international oil markets. During the transition to nationalisation, government policy-makers had negotiated with the oil MNs to secure the necessary international links for the nationalised oil company. Subsequent to these efforts, the industry developed its internationalisation policy, enabling direct access to the final consumer through an important refinery network. This policy choice increased the industry's international presence while allowing its managers more autonomy from government controls and from the dynamics of public policy-making.

During its formative phase, PDVSA was given the status of a distinctive SOE, one that had to be kept under the umbrella of the state while being allowed a certain freedom of action. Such freedom was necessary to pursue corporate strategies and to increase efficiency: both objectives would hopefully lead to larger fiscal contributions to the treasury. The need to minimise market uncertainties led PDVSA to seek an independent position in the oil markets. The adoption of the internationalisation policy was a reflection of such a concern. However, becoming an oil MN entailed minimising its subordinate status to both the executive and the legislature. The balance between being the country's most important SOE and the need to become an oil MN contained an inner contradiction which, as will be shown throughout this research, posed numerous political and government policy-making problems. This chapter explores the early efforts of the newly nationalised industry in developing its own links with the oil markets. It is argued that during the industry's formative years the oil industry policy-makers became the most significant actors in the process of oil policy-making. As a result, the Ministry of Energy lost the leading position as policy-maker that it had occupied during the policy process that led to the implementation of the nationalisation of the oil industry.

The first appointments: keeping politics out from the outset

Initially, there was consensus about the need to keep the nationalised industry free from political interference. The appointment of two non-politicians as PDVSA's first president and as Minister of Energy respectively was an example of this ideal. President Pérez appointed a person from outside the oil sector to command over the nationalised industry. Appointed in August 1975 as PDVSA's first president, General Rafael Alfonzo Ravard had accumulated a considerable experience in the public sector, as president of the *Corporación Venezolana de Guayana* (CVG), a large SOE responsible for the development of the iron and steel industries. During his fifteen-year presidency in the CVG, Alfonzo Ravard became acquainted with the complexities of managing a SOE, while gaining a useful insight into the intricacies of politics. Ravard had gained respectability as a solid manager and an independent[3]. An outsider to the oil sector, Alfonzo Ravard remained as head of PDVSA for eight years. At the time when he was designated as president of the newly nationalised industry, there were other people who had more experience in the oil sector than he possessed. But the experience of these oil managers had been acquired under the MNs and doubts arose in political circles as to their true commitment to the goals of the newly nationalised oil industry. The employees of the state CVP were not at the time experienced enough to take up the challenge of managing the new oil industry. An oil policy-maker observed that,

> At that time, we didn't know how they would take the decisions and how they would deal with the nationalised company. The boss was now a politician; before, it was a professional manager in New York[4].

Another outsider to the oil sector, Valentín Hernández from AD, was designated as Minister of Energy in 1974. Although Hernández was a petroleum engineer, the first to graduate in the country, he had been working as a private entrepreneur and diplomat for sixteen years prior to his appointment.

Relative outsiders to the oil sector were also appointed as directors of the first board of the nationalised oil industry. The directors included private businessmen and professionals with limited experience in oil matters. Although far from being party militants, some of the directors were reputed to be close to AD. There was a representative from the labour sector and one from COPEI. Only one of the directors appointed came directly from the oil industry[5]. From the start, government and the oil sector alike made a conscious effort to minimise politicisation within the industry. From the perspective of the oil industry, politics was an external and negative element, one with which industry policy-makers had to grapple in order to impose policy choices.

PDVSA: both a state and a private enterprise

At the beginning it seemed as though PDVSA was to enjoy a high degree of financial autonomy from the central government, as was the intention of some oil policy-makers during the period of transition to nationalisation. However, from an early stage after nationalisation, there were differences of opinion between those who considered the new oil industry more as a private corporation and those who merely regarded it as a SOE[6]. The advocators of the former view, mainly the oil managers who used to work for a private regime under the oil MNs, wanted to confer on the industry the legal embodiments of any private company. In turn, the politicians, the ones who, from different ideological platforms, had advocated nationalisation of the oil industry, were more inclined to keep PDVSA under tight government control. Both sets of policy-makers managed to confer on PDVSA the legal foundations inherent in each of their apparently contradictory conceptions of the oil industry. Thus, PDVSA was conceived as a SOE that is ruled according to the Code of Commerce applicable to private enterprises[7]. This particular status allowed the industry to retain what it needed for its budget and operations, without having to fight over larger cash allocations with the other SOEs and government agencies. As mentioned in Chapter 1, one of the early concerns of PDVSA's policy-makers was to assure the financial autonomy necessary for the industry's operations[8]. Although the budgetary independence of PDVSA has not been free from conflict and government meddling, the industry has managed to keep a much more independent status from government than its SOE counterparts. Such ability to be able to decide over its own budget has helped PDVSA to assert its administrative freedom.

Moreover, the mixed legal status of PDVSA results from the fact that according to Venezuelan law there is no precise legal statute to define a SOE[9]. Contradictory views about the oil industry have been at the core of the numerous tensions between politicians and managers of the oil industry. The ambiguities of interpretation stemming from PDVSA's dual legal standing, and which have been used by various actors at different times to suit vested interests, have exerted diverging influences upon the process of oil policy-making[10]. The industry's first president, Alfonzo Ravard, considered however that there is no ambiguity in the interpretation of PDVSA's legal status.

> PDVSA is not a hybrid company. It is a SOE ruled according to the mercantile code applied to private companies[11].

PDVSA's dual status has been the source of many a conflict in the history of the company's relationship with the executive. From the outset, managers from the oil industry took steps to make PDVSA a company more autonomous from government control. PDVSA was given 'administrative and financial autonomy'[12]. However, lack of a clear definition regarding the industry's autonomy from the executive and the legislature, both financially and in policy formulation issues, has been a constant issue since its creation. As will be shown throughout this study, such a debate lay at the core of the tension, on the one hand, between the executive and the SOE, and on the other, between the legislature and the SOE.

The rationalisation policy: a strategy for organisational consolidation

The operating structure and decision-making process of the new oil industry was simplified and reduced to a manageable size, as well as centralised under the new holding company. The newly nationalised oil company adopted a policy of organisational rationalisation from the beginning. From 1975 to 1976, the thirty-five oil companies operating in the country were reduced to fourteen, including PDVSA. The number was further reduced as the process of rationalisation was consolidated. The Social Christian and future Minister of Energy, Humberto Calderón Berti, pointed out then that,

> It seems hardly convenient to operate with more than 22 state enterprises. We have to rationalise all oil operations in the country. This reduction of the operating companies has to be done based on a series of studies in order to define which are the most efficient ones, which ones operate at the lowest costs, which ones have the highest profits, and which ones the highest technological capacity. Due to these reasons and to other operational considerations, we will organise the rest of the industry around these companies[13].

Table 3.1 describes the significant merging process that took place following nationalisation of the oil industry in 1975.

For the new SOE the structure adopted was a federation of vertically integrated affiliates, each one of them carrying out similar activities. Inspired by the oil concessionaires' period, competition among the new affiliates came to be regarded as a value to strife for. One of PDVSA's former presidents pointed out that 'competition among the affiliates, up until now, has avoided the repetition of administrative vices, common to SOEs all over the world, and of course, in Venezuela'[14]. Nevertheless, a particular negotiation or the implementation of a specific contract can be allocated to just one of the operating affiliates. Under the vertical integration scheme, each affiliate was allowed to negotiate with its clients on the basis of services, delivery, and time. Another PDVSA former president explained why

Table 3.1   The organisational rationalisation of the petroleum industry, 1975-1976

Company	Nationalised company
Creole Petroleum Corporation,	LAGOVEN
Amoco Venezuelan Oil Co.	AMOVEN
Shell de Venezuela NV, Continental Pure Oil Co., Unión Petrolera, Petróleos Bajamar, Tenneco, American Petrofina, Pétrobelge de Venezuela	MARAVEN
Murphy Oil, Venezoil, Ashland Refining, Venezolana Pacific, Venezolana Canadian, Sunny Venez.,Triangler Refineries	ROQUEVEN
Talon Petroleum,	TALOVEN
Mito Juan	VISTAVEN
Mene Grande Oil Co., Gulf International, Guanipa Oil Corp.	MENEVEN
S.A. Petrolera las Mercedes	GUARIVEN
Venezuelan Sun, Charter Pure Oil	PALMAVEN
Venezuela Atlantic Refining Co., Ucar Interam, Sinclair Venez. Oil Corp.	BARIVEN
Mobil Oil Co. de Venezuela	LLANOVEN
Chevron Oil de Venezuela	BOSCANVEN
Corporación Venezolana del Petróleo	CVP
Texas Petroleum Co., Texaco Petrol., Texaco Maracaibo, Coro-Mara Petrol., Texaco Seaboard	DELTAVEN

Sources: Julián Villalba. 'La permanencia de la cultura: la selección de fuentes de asistencia técnica en una empresa nacionalizada', in Janet Kelly (ed.), *Empresas del Estado*, Caracas, 1985; 'Reporte de la Comisión Presidencial de la Reversión Petrolera', Caracas, 1975.

competition over prices is discouraged among the industry's affiliated companies:

> Competition among the operators does not entail fighting over clients, but competition at the production level. There are discussions as to which should be the cost of the barrel price. If a company is, for instance, producing at a cost of a dollar what the other one is producing at two, then something wrong is happening. This [healthy competition] has allowed PDVSA to have [positive] internal levels of productivity. That is why we have wanted to have more than one company[15].

The vertically integrated model adopted for the structure of the oil industry was not in essence a typical SOE model; it echoed more the structure adopted by several private enterprises. Other structures could have been adopted for the nationalised oil industry: horizontal integration, one company-one distinctive activity, or the establishment of only one vertically or horizontally integrated oil company. As the holding company ruling over its affiliates, PDVSA was conceived to co-ordinate, plan and control the petroleum industry. Policy-makers 'never wanted PDVSA to become only one company'[16].

The decision to reduce the operating companies had the full support of the Ministry of Energy, which relied for policy formulation processes on PDVSA's studies and constant feedback. It is the oil company which possesses the most adequate technical expertise to decide over policy orientations. A former PDVSA president remarked that 'PDVSA is in the day-to-day business; the Ministry is farther away'[17].

From an early stage after nationalisation, Ministry officials began following the industry's guidelines for the formulation of oil policy issues. As a result of nationalisation, the Ministry adopted a somewhat subordinate role to that of PDVSA in the oil policy-making process. From having been, along with political actors, the most significant decision-makers during the process that led to nationalisation, the Ministry officials began losing their importance to PDVSA's managers, once the oil SOE consolidated its position.

Table 3.2 shows the rationalisation process undergone by the nationalised petroleum industry after 1976, when the assets of the ex-concessionaires were transferred to the new state company. The merging process deepened as time went on.

As seen above, in the year 1976, there was basically a merging process affecting all former concessionaires, which changed their names to more nationalistically appealing denominations. Highlighting the

Table 3.2   The process of organisational rationalisation of PDVSA's affiliates, 1976-1986

1976	1977	1977	1978	1986
LAGOVEN				
	LAGOVEN	LAGOVEN	LAGOVEN	LAGOVEN
AMOVEN				
MARAVEN				
	MARAVEN	MARAVEN	MARAVEN	MARAVEN
ROQUEVEN				
TALOVEN				
VISTAVEN				
MENEVEN	MENEVEN	MENEVEN	MENEVEN	
GUARIVEN				
PALMAVEN	PALMAVEN			
	LLANOVEN			
BARIVEN				
	LLANOVEN			
LLANOVEN				
		CORPOVEN	CORPOVEN	
BOSCANVEN				
	CVP		CVP	
CVP				
DELTAVEN	DELTAVEN			

Sources: Aníbal Martínez, *Cronología del petróleo venezolano.* Caracas, CEPET, 1986; Gustavo Coronel, *The Nationalization of the Venezuelan Oil Industry,* Lexington, Mass., Heath and Company, 1983; Susan Johnson. *Op. cit.*; Efraín Barberii, *Síntesis de Actividades Relevantes. La Industria Venezolana de los Hidrocarburos.* CEPET, 1989.

beginnings of the rationalisation policy of the oil industry, the financial results of all the affiliates were consolidated in one account in 1976[18]. Other agencies were to be created gradually to meet specific purposes. INTEVEP (*Instituto Tecnológico Venezolano del Petróleo*) was created to carry out research in 1975. The strategy to develop an independent and solid technological basis for the nationalised industry became evident with the early creation of this research agency. The following year in 1976 INAPET (*Instituto de Adiestramiento Petrolero y Petroquímico*) was founded to address the training needs of the working force for the new petroleum industry[19].

An important merger took place in 1978 when the Venezuelan Petrochemical Institute (IVP), the petrochemical complex, became an affiliate of PDVSA under the name of PEQUIVEN. This move reflected the need to merge the petrochemical industry into the nationalised oil industry. BARIVEN was founded in 1980 in order to centralise all the international purchases required by the industry. Soon after, CEPET (*Centro de Formación y Adiestramiento Petrolero y Petroquímico*) was created to improve the industry's personnel in training and specialisation that had formerly been the responsibility of INAPET. In 1985 *Refinería Isla* in Curaçao was acquired under a long-term lease agreement and, due to its geographic proximity, was integrated into the network of domestic refineries. *Refinería Isla* will be given further attention in Chapter VI. The creation of INTERVEN, a special agency responsible for the industry's international network of refineries will also be analysed in Chapter VI. In 1986 MENEVEN and CORPOVEN were merged into one affiliate, keeping the name of CORPOVEN. In turn, BITOR was created in 1989 to attend to the management of the Orinoco Oil Belt region, which contains most of the country's oil reserves and to commercialise Orimulsion™ [20]. More recently, in 1996 PDVSA founded CIED (Centro Internacional de Educación y Desarrollo), conceived as a 'corporate university'[21] to address its personnel training needs, a function previously carried out by CEPET.

The policy-making process between PDVSA and the Energy Ministry

Opposite views on the management of oil by industry and executive policy-makers –'engineers' and 'commissars' respectively– lay at the centre of most oil policy-making issues. Theoretically, there seems to be a set of fixed practices with regard to the way in which the Ministry of Energy and the oil industry should interact and behave in the policy-making process.

Policy guidelines usually emanate from the Ministry, but depending on their nature, they can also spring from the oil industry. Some decisions, such as the designation of the industry's Board of Directors, the fiscal treatment applied to the industry or the fixation of export and domestic prices are determined by the Ministry; such issues are often subject to political controversy. Other issues, however, which at first glance seem to be the sole concern of the industry, such as expenditure levels and strategic investment decisions, may also be subject to executive interference.

PDVSA usually submits to the Ministry a draft of the policy guidelines for the Ministry of Energy to consider. Thereafter, the government agency studies the proposals and makes the necessary amendments. There is usually a considerable exchange of information between the industry and the Ministry at this stage. However, Ministry officials often lack the necessary means and technical expertise required for the different phases entailed in a complex and costly policy-making process. As a former PDVSA president commented:

> The Ministry lacks the financial resources to carry out the necessary studies. Often, the Ministry asks PDVSA for financial help in order to carry out these studies...The poorly-paid Ministry employees pretend to supervise a monster such as PDVSA with more than 10,000 employees. The Ministry assumes responsibilities that it is incapable of meeting. Its employees are public officials who feel they are the ones who control the petroleum industry's policies. They believe they fix the oil policy and that PDVSA's role is only to execute it[22].

For the most part, PDVSA's managers and Ministry officials hold different and often irreconcilable conceptions of the oil industry. For the former actors, oil is a business, a tradable commodity subject to the rationales imposed by the international markets. For the latter, oil is the natural resource whose management determines the country's economic performance and most of the government's margin for action. Many of the industry's directors have had experience working for the foreign concessionaires. This work experience for the oil MNs largely accounts for the continuation of a private work ethic in the industry. Meritocracy, fear of politicisation, and cost-maximisation are, by and large, observed principles in PDVSA. As mentioned in Chapter 2, at the time of nationalisation, some industry policy-makers opposed, if only passively, the state's take-over of the petroleum industry. In contrast, Ministry officials actively worked to bring about the nationalisation action. The government agency was the embodiment of those individuals who brought about the successful and coherently planned nationalisation process and who, furthermore, believed firmly in the convenience of adhering to OPEC, an allegiance often challenged by oil industry managers. In the context of a latent antagonism between the industry and the executive, it is not difficult to affirm that 'there exists a propitious situation for resentment'[23]. It is the very tension between these two sets of policy-makers that characterises the policy-making process in the oil sector.

The Ministry is the government's control arm over the petroleum industry. Contrary to what was proposed by AGROPET during the nationalisation transition, in PDVSA's assemblies the Minister presides over the discussions; the Minister represents the state, the industry's sole shareholder. With the creation of PDVSA in August 1975, the Energy Ministry[24] lost some of the roles it had enjoyed until then. Prior to nationalisation, the Energy Ministry had functioned as the sole supervisor of the oil companies, acting as a sort of state holding agency which regulated the activities of the oil sector then in foreign hands. Upon its creation, PDVSA came to function as an organisational layer between the government Ministry and the affiliated companies of the nationalised industry. Soon after nationalisation, the Ministry was compelled to reformulate its role, as the new oil SOE had assumed a number of its functions.

The power vacuum resulting in the Ministry as a consequence of PDVSA's creation was reflected in an impasse in the process of decision-making between the two policy-making centres. In 1976, 'a grey period, when the Ministry wanted to impose criteria on PDVSA'[25], the newly appointed Board of Directors addressed a letter to President Pérez demanding a clearer definition of roles between the two entities. Pérez and a team of oil experts mainly from PDVSA set out to define distinctive roles for both the government agency and the oil industry.

The draft for the official letter[26] containing the guidelines for the policy-making mechanisms emanated from PDVSA[27]. The preciseness of the document's style and the inclusion of technicalities suggest that it stemmed from PDVSA. This early blueprint on the division of responsibilities between the Ministry and PDVSA in the decision-making process for the formulation of oil policy assigned the industry the authority to decide on its operational activities and its budgetary needs. The official document, signed by President Pérez, also allowed the industry the freedom to establish prices for exported crude, a point that was at the centre of many debates with the Ministry. According to a policy of fuel subsidies that has always constituted an executive prerogative, the Ministry would still define the prices for the internal market[28].

The need to increase investments

Besides the reduction and rationalisation of it operating affiliates explained at the beginning of this chapter, the nationalised oil industry set out to accomplish several immediate objectives: increase investments, transform the refining pattern, and establish agreements for technological assistance and for crude commercialisation with the oil MNs. These objectives reflected the goal of policy-makers to turn Venezuela into a leading world crude exporter. Expectations as to the positive results of the nationalisation process were high and measures to accomplish the industry's objectives were adopted briefly after implementation of the policy.

The first appointed managers of the nationalised oil industry took over a declining industry in urgent need of fresh capital. The realisation by the foreign concessionaires of the imminence of nationalisation led to a significant decrease in their investments in upstream activities. The recovery and maintenance needs of the nationalised industry required large amounts of investment. To render the task easier and provide the industry with more funds, the old tax system applied to the ex-concessionaires was modified in 1976 so as to allow PDVSA to raise investment levels[29]. The rate of rent tax levied on PDVSA was lowered around five percent for the first post-nationalisation year, and was not raised until 1979. From 70.03 % in 1975, it was reduced to 65.13 % in 1976[30].

Table 3.3 shows the extent to which PDVSA increased across-the-board investments for the first five years following nationalisation. For the transition years 1976 and 1977, the industry investment levels grew moderately, increasing impressively thereafter.

Increases in production and proven reserves

One of the first objectives of the nationalised oil industry was to increase production levels and proven reserves. As of 1976 production was 2.3 million b/d and available potential production 2.7 million b/d. The difference of 400,000 b/d was accounted for almost entirely by heavy crude[31]. The industry's goal was to reach a level of 2.8 million b/d of potential production in the medium term, according to the Energy Ministry policy guidelines. Such a goal required new exploratory ventures, the reactivation of inactive wells and the reduction of the depletion rate of many others. Moreover, as the volume of proven reserves increases, the more bargaining power can be exerted when pressing for production quota increases within OPEC. The expansion of exploratory activities and wildcatting was an

Table 3.3   Oil industry operations. Capital spending, 1976-1980 (million $)

	1976	1977	1978	1979	1980
Total	323.5	526.1	1,010.2	1,515.3	2,270.0
Exploration	93.7	96.1	181.6	320.9	510.2
Production	203.0	341.9	506.5	726.5	959.8
Refining	6.5	37.9	172.1	423.3	686.5
Domestic Marketing	4.9	17.7	21.4	27.2	64.4
Other	15.3	32.6	128.6	17.4	49.0

Proven Reserves

	1976	1977	1978	1979	1980
Oil (m/b)	18,228.0	18,039.0	18,228.0	18,515.0	19,666.0
Gas (billion m3)	1,180.0	1,185.0	1,211.0	1,249.0	1,330.0

Sources: Philip. *Op. cit.*, p. 471; PDVSA *Annual Reports*; *Petróleo y Otros Datos Estadísticos* (PODE), MEM.

insurmountable requirement in attaining the objective. Experimenting with state-of-the-art exploratory methods, PDVSA set out to increase its upstream operations[32]. Special attention was paid to exploratory activities in the Orinoco Oil Belt, containing one of the largest reserves of heavy crude in the world. The development of the Orinoco Oil Belt became an early objective of the nationalised petroleum industry[33].

As seen in Table 3.3, significant increases in exploratory activities started in 1978 when spending in this sector literally doubled its previous year equivalent and continued to increase thereafter, eased by the new oil windfall caused by the Second Oil Shock of 1979[34].

Transformation of the refining pattern: adaptation to market needs

In order to change the pattern of refining inherited from the pre-nationalisation period, which was basically aimed at processing light crude, in 1978 PDVSA launched a strategy to adopt recovery techniques to the needs of indigenous production[35]. The idea was to change the existing refining patterns based on the use of light crude to a pattern that would increase the use of heavier crude in the production of petroleum derived products. The goal was to produce and commercialise the country's large reserves of medium, heavy and extra-heavy crude. As of 1976, 35% of Venezuela's oil production was made of light oil, 38% of medium and 27% heavy[36]. The development and eventual exploitation of the Orinoco Oil Belt would modify this balance, largely increasing the proportion of heavy crude.

The 'lightening' of the required slate of products in both the US and Europe increased the demand for lighter crudes relative to heavier ones. In Venezuela the MNs were used to producing residual fuels which required light crude as primary source; this type of fuel found an important outlet on the US East Coast.

As an immediate result of the First Oil Shock of 1973-74, demand for traditional fuels was shrinking while the use of alternative energy sources, such as coal, gas, and nuclear energy was temporarily increasing. The weakening demand for oil affected the refining sector, undermining the need for the construction of new refineries or expanding existing ones.

Another element that justified the transformation of the refining pattern inherited from the pre-nationalisation period was Venezuelan domestic demand, which had been largely neglected by the oil MNs. The internal market required more petroleum-derived products, such as naphtha and gasoline, than residual fuels, the type privileged by the foreign concessionaires[37]. Before 1976, the oil MNs had gradually transferred to *Corporación Venezolana del Petróleo* (CVP) all activities directed towards the domestic market. When CVP came under PDVSA's control in 1975, the reorganised affiliates began to focus part of their activities on attending the needs of the growing domestic market for fuels[38].

From 1977 to 1978 PDVSA increased spending on refining activities from $341.9 to $506.5 million. The strategy to transform refining patterns in order to adopt them to the needs of the domestic market and to upgrade obsolete refineries began in 1978 was already reaping positive results by 1982, when the percentage of derived petroleum products processed in national refineries sharply increased. The volume of residual fuels had in turn decreased. In 1978 the percentage of naphtha and gasoline in all products processed in national refineries was of 19.4% and that of distillates 18.4%. In 1982, it was 24.6% and 25.2% respectively. As for residual products, the percentage decreased during the same period: from 56.2% to 43.7%. As of 1983 this strategy gave further results. Petroleum derived products, especially naphtha and gasoline, increased to 30.8% and distillates to 28.4%. Residual fuel production kept decreasing; in 1983 it was 32.4%[39].

The Agreements for Technological Assistance: continuation of the working relationship with the oil MNs

Another concern of oil policy-makers was to secure the nationalised industry access to needed technology. As shown in the previous chapter, the consensual and planned way in which the oil industry was nationalised allowed the oil industry to maintain working relations with the oil MNs. Thus, a series of *Convenios de Asistencia Técnica* (Agreements for Technological Assistance) were negotiated with the foreign oil companies during the year 1976. PDVSA's new affiliated companies directly signed the contracts with the ex-concessionaires, thereby securing access to technology for upstream operations. The Agreements varied in content. Most of them consisted of a combination of services, such as specialised and constant assistance, corporate organisation guidelines, technological know-how, supervision, licensing, courses, internships, and so on. Some contracts even included assistance to other sectors involved with the oil industry: private companies, engineers, SOEs and university faculties[40].

Under the first Agreements established, the affiliates were not allowed to exchange technology. For instance, MARAVEN, which received assistance from Shell could not have access to the technology used by LAGOVEN, which in turn was being assisted by Exxon. The same was true for MENEVEN, which received services from Gulf Oil[41], and for the other affiliates. In 1978, the bill paid to the various ex-concessionaires involved in these programmes was over $160 million[42].

Such was the importance assigned to these Agreements for Technological Assistance that PDVSA created a separate agency to deal with them and to negotiate more convenient terms with the foreign companies. In 1979 both the terms prohibiting the exchange of technology among PDVSA's affiliates and the form of payment to the foreign companies were modified. Negotiations between PDVSA and the foreign ex-concessionaires involved in the Agreements led to the elimination of the clauses preventing exchanges of technology within the nationalised industry. Regarding payments, the basis for calculations adopted was modified to better reflect the amount of assistance offered, as opposed to the previous method based on royalties calculated according to the production levels of the industry[43].

When the contract terms were renegotiated in 1979, the number of Agreements specifically set up with the ex-concessionaires diminished while the number of other contracts signed with companies which had had no presence in Venezuela during the pre-nationalisation period increased. As time went by the nationalised oil industry achieved an even larger degree of diversification from its traditional sources of technological assistance. After the renegotiation of the contracts, the Agreements made with the ex-concessionaires in 1980 only amounted to 361,579 man/hours, compared to a number of 3 million hours/man from various other companies.

The diversification of sources of assistance was evidence of the changing situation affecting the relationship between the oil MNs and the nationalised companies of oil exporting countries. In 1979, Calderón Berti, the Energy Minister, pointed out that the conditions at the time when the first contracts were established favoured the MNs; however, that situation had changed in favour of nationalised oil companies[44]. As a result of the Second Oil Shock of 1979-80, the oil exporters became the undisputed controllers of the oil markets. In this context, with the bargaining relation favouring the oil exporting companies PDVSA was able to negotiate with 'non-traditional' oil companies and to minimise its dependence on the ex-concessionaires previously operating in the country. PDVSA diversified its working partners, thereby increasing its freedom of action in the international markets.

The Agreements for Technological Assistance were a way to reinforce PDVSA's past tradition as a private corporation, the legacy of its predecessors the oil MNs. Through them, the corporate tradition of private oil companies continued to flow into the nationalised oil industry. The implementation of the Agreements eased the transfer of many organisational patterns from the ex-concessionaires to the nationalised industry, enforcing a peculiar type of work ethic that made PDVSA a distinctive company from other SOEs.

The Agreements for Technological Assistance gradually decreased in number and importance as the oil industry was able to develop its own research centre, INTEVEP, and the research related activities of its petrochemical complex PEQUIVEN.

The commercialisation of crude after nationalisation: beginnings of the internationalisation policy

The problem of PDVSA's crude commercialisation was already identified during the transition to nationalisation. Upon creation of the industry, the need to establish independent means for crude commercialisation became a major concern for industry policy-makers, leading to the creation of the industry's policy of internationalisation. The nationalised oil company faced the problem of creating its own channels to distribute its crude. Loss of the international distribution network of the oil MNs was a source of major concern for policy-makers in the post-nationalisation period. The nationalised oil industry lacked independent downstream mechanisms. In turn, its employees possessed limited expertise to undertake the international sale of its crude. Two months before full nationalisation was implemented, the Energy Minister, Valentín Hernández Acosta, summed up this concern:

> We are consciously aware of the limited experience we have in commercialising our crude. The big transnational companies have had and continue to have almost total control over markets. This is a fact we have to face. We have been clear when stating the necessity to maintain our traditional markets[45].

As early as July 1975 the Pérez administration decided to create a *Comisión Comercializadora* (Commercialisation Commission) largely made up of Ministry and CVP officials in order to secure the sale of crude, after nationalisation. As a result of the work of this Commission[46], different agreements were signed with the ex-concessionaires. The Commission negotiated all phases of the crude commercialisation process, from export volumes to prices. The goal of executive policy-makers was to obtain letters of intent signed and ready for implementation by January 1, 1976 when nationalisation would be implemented. Mobil was the first company to sign a contract with the Venezuelan government to secure crude commercialisation. Shell and Creole soon followed suit. Each operating affiliate was individually assigned responsibility for the implementation of each one of the commercialisation contracts. Most of the contracts were conceived to last for two years starting in 1976, with the possibility of renewal for an equivalent time period. During the early period following nationalisation, price levels were discussed with the buyers approximately one month in advance. After the contract terms were renegotiated in 1979, PDVSA set up prices unilaterally only three days in advance, relying on the buyers' willingness to comply. As PDVSA's clients diversified, and as the bargaining position of the oil producers strengthened, the nationalised oil company increasingly enlarged its margin of action in the area of crude commercialisation.

For at least the first two years of the post-nationalisation period the ex-concessionaires operating in the country continued to carry out the international commercialisation of Venezuelan crude. One of the main successes of the Venezuelan consensual nationalisation process was that it did not sever the nationalised industry from its downstream outlets. The vertical integration of the industry became an early goal of PDVSA's policy-makers. Valentín Hernández Acosta pointed out in 1976 that the country, 'will continue selling oil just as the MNs did'[47].

In January 1976 PDVSA carried out important sales of crude through agreements with the oil MNs for a total of 1.5 million b/d[48]. Implementation of the commercialisation contracts was successful, despite a small drop in sales in early 1976, a tendency that had already been noted in the previous year's fourth quarter. PDVSA proved capable of securing the flow of crude to its traditional clients, achieving the diversification of markets as intended. For the year 1977, 80% of all PDVSA's exports came from sales carried out within the commercialisation agreements with the ex-concessionaires.

Prior to nationalisation, three major companies controlled through their downstream mechanisms the international commercialisation of Venezuelan crude. They were Exxon –in Venezuela, Creole–, Shell and Gulf –Mene Grande–. Most commercialisation agreements had been signed with these companies following nationalisation. By securing crude supplies to its traditional clients, PDVSA had further achieved credibility in the process of oil nationalisation, and had managed to integrate its production into the world markets for oil.

After 1978, when the terms of the contracts were reviewed, oil policy-makers adopted a strategy of diversification for partner companies, both private and SOEs. The objective of diversifying outlets in order to reach a larger variety of markets had also been successfully achieved[49]. The diversification of clients was adopted as a strategy aimed at increasing the industry's market share and minimising dependence on a small number of clients. As of 1985, the number of clients for Venezuelan crudes had in fact doubled compared to that of 1976. Most of the new clients were actually former clients of the foreign ex-concessionaires, a group that PDVSA set out to target from the outset.

Conclusion

The establishment of contracts for technical assistance and for crude commercialisation paved the way for the adoption of PDVSA's internationalisation policy. By strengthening the working relationship with the oil MNs, the nationalised oil industry was able to maintain access to necessary technology and to consumer markets. For the latter objective, after nationalisation PDVSA used the distribution channels of the vertically integrated oil MNs. Through this experience, PDVSA was able to develop its internationalisation policy, mirroring the structure of the vertically integrated oil MNs.

During the transition to nationalisation, both government and industry policy-makers identified the need for the soon-to-be-nationalised oil industry to maintain the necessary channels to distribute crude to the international oil markets. Successful negotiations were held with the oil MNs in order to secure the constant flow of Venezuelan crude to the oil markets. The need to create independent channels from the ones offered by the oil MNs was an important rationale for the adoption of the industry's internationalisation policy. In order to become a fully integrated oil MN itself, PDVSA had to develop its own outlets to access the market.

During its formative years, PDVSA's policy-makers set out to accomplish the corporate objectives it deemed essential for the consolidation of its operations. Mainly due to the consensual character of the nationalisation policy, which allowed the negotiation of many working agreements with the ex-concessionaires, PDVSA was able to reproduce the patterns that characterised the oil MNs: vertically-integrated structure, private work ethic, independent distribution outlets. Short-term corporate objectives such as the increase of production and proven reserves, the transformation of refining patterns, the establishment of Agreements for Technological Assistance, and the commercialisation of crude abroad were successfully accomplished. The internationalisation policy developed as a consequence of the successful accomplishment of the industry's initial corporate objectives. Thanks to the close working relationship with the oil MNs formerly operating in the country, the nationalised oil industry was able to maintain its links with the international oil market. As a result, no rupture was caused between the nationalised industry and key consumer markets.

Furthermore, the accomplishment of the industry's early corporate goals strengthened the position of PDVSA's policy-makers as the set of most important actors involved in the process of oil policy-making. The polarisation of the interests of the two groups of policy-makers directly involved in the oil policy-making process –executive officials and industry managers– which found its origins during the transition to nationalisation, became more evident during PDVSA's formative years, when the first policy guidelines were formulated and implemented. During this period, the ascension of the industry's managers as the most influential policy-makers in oil policy-making contrasted with the decline of executive officials in this process. The position of PDVSA's policy-makers was to be further consolidated with the implementation of the internationalisation strategy, allowing the industry to extend its operations abroad, farther away from government controls.

Notes

1   Decree N° 1,123. August 30, 1975. *Official Gazette* N° 1,170.
2   Johnson. *Op. cit.*, pp. 182-183.
3   Rafael Alfonzo Ravard. First president of PDVSA. *Interview*. November 27, 1993.
4   Petzall. *Interview*. January 7, 1993.
5   Coronel. *Op cit.*, Chapter 3.
6   Arturo Sosa Pietri. *Petróleo y Poder*. Editorial Planeta. Caracas, 1993, p. 61.
7   *Ibid.*, pp. 61-63; Juan Chacín. Former president of PDVSA. *Interview*. January 8, 1993.
8   Philip. *Op. cit.*, p. 477.
9   Enrique Viloria. *Petróleos de Venezuela*. Colección Estudios Jurídicos, N° 21. Caracas, 1983, p. 97.
10   Allan Brewer Carías. *Régimen Jurídico de las Empresas Públicas*. Ediciones del CLAD. Caracas, 1980; Andrés Aguilar, 'Régimen Legal de la Industria y el Comercio de los Hidrocarburos', *Boletín de la Academia de Ciencias Polítcas y Sociales*. N° 66-67. Caracas, 1976; Enrique Viloria, *Petróleos de Venezuela*. Colección Estudios Jurídicos, N° 21. Caracas, 1983; Allan Brewer Carías and Enrique Viloria. *El Holding Público*. Editorial Jurídica Venezolana. Caracas, 1986.
11   Alfonzo Ravard. *Interview*. November 22, 1993.
12   Sosa Pietri. *Op. cit.*, p. 61.
13   Humberto Calderón Berti. *La nacionalización petrolera. Visión de un proceso*. Caracas, 1978, p. 67.
14   Sosa. *Op. cit.*, p. 100.
15   Juan Chacín. Former president, PDVSA. *Interview*. January 8, 1993.
16   *Idem*.
17   *Idem*.
18   Alfonzo Ravard. *Annual Report*. PDVSA. 1976.
19   Barberii. *Op. cit.*
20   Orimulsion is a fuel mainly consisting of 70% Orinoco extra-heavy crude (bitumen) and 30% water, along with an emulsifying agent that stabilises the mixture. The fuel has many of the best features of both heavy fuel oil and coil, without its main disadvantages.
21   Article by Ana Díaz. 'Universidad corporativa. Nueva filial de PDVSA forma profesionales del siglo XXI'. *El Nacional*. May 14, 1996.
22   Chacín. *Interview*. January 8, 1993.
23   *Idem*.
24   Then called the Ministry of Mines and Hydrocarbons.
25   Chacín. *Interview*. January 8, 1993.
26   The existence of this document is also reported by Sosa Pietri. *Op. cit.*, p. 16. The letter was dated March 17, 1977 and sent to PDVSA's first president, Rafael Alfonzo Ravard by President Pérez.
27   For the redefinition of the roles of the Ministry and those of the industry no presidential commission was appointed.
28   Chacín. *Interview*. January 8, 1993.

29 For a detailed explanation of the taxation schemes applied to PDVSA, see Randall. *Op. cit.*, Chapter IX, especially p. 172.

30 Petróleo y Otros Datos Estadísticos (PODE). Ministry of Mines and Energy (MEM), 1991. The imposed fiscal rate on PDVSA rose again in 1977 to 67.03%. In 1981 it was reduced to 65.70%. In 1995 it was raised again to 67.7%.

31 *Annual Report.* PDVSA, 1976.

32 Alfonzo Ravard. *Cinco Años de Normalidad Operativa.* PDVSA Edit. Caracas, 1981, p. 27.

33 The development of the large heavy-crude reserves available in the Orinoco Belt region became an early goal for the nationalised industry. This area, an extension of 42,000 Km^2 full of heavy and extra-heavy crudes, is considered to be one of the world's largest. In 1977, PDVSA implemented a programme to develop this change crude reservoir.

34 Martínez. *Cronología.* Table 1, 'Exploration in Venezuela', p. 215; *Annual Reports.* PDVSA.

35 Barberii. *Op. cit.*, p. xii.

36 Philip. *Op. cit.*, p. 470.

37 Alfonzo Ravard. *Op. cit.*, p. 313.

38 *Ibid.*, p. 340.

39 *Petróleo y Otros Datos Estadísticos.* MEM; Barberii. *Op. cit.*, p. xxxii.

40 Julián Villalba. 'La permanencia de la cultura: la selección de fuentes de asistencia técnica en una empresa nacionalizada', in Janet Kelly, (ed.). *Empresas del Estado en América Latina.* IESA. Caracas, 1985, p. 317.

41 *Petroguía.* PDVSA Publications. Caracas, 1987, p. 154.

42 Villalba. *Op. cit.*, p. 318.

43 *Idem.*, pp. 318-320.

44 'Humberto Calderón Berti. Intervención ante la Comisión Delegada'. *El Nacional.* September 27, 1979.

45 Valentín Hernández Acosta. *Apuntes sobre la Nacionalización de la Industria Petrolera.* PDVSA Publications. [Not dated], p. 22.

46 The Commercialisation Commission was made up by Félix Rossi Guerrero, Alirio Parra, Hernán Anzola, Manuel Ramos and Alberto Flores. A first-hand account of the Commission's work was given by one of its members, Félix Rossi Guerrero, *Diario de un Diplomático Petrolero. Los Años de Washington (1972-1979).* Ministry of Foreign Affairs. Caracas, 1978, pp. 202-239.

47 *Petroguía. Op. cit.,* p. 152.

48 *Idem.*

49 Thaís Barrios. *La Diversificación de los Mercados Petroleros: el Caso de Venezuela.* B.Sc. thesis. UCAB, Faculty of Economics. Caracas, 1979, pp. 157-179.

Chapter 4
The first phase of policy implementation: The Veba Oel contract

4 The first phase of policy implementation: The Veba Oel contract

Introduction

The successful accomplishment of objectives such as the development of independent commercialisation channels for crude and the diversification of markets found a natural continuation in PDVSA's internationalisation policy. During its formative years, the goal to tackle corporate problems became clear policy orientations. The internationalisation policy had its antecedents in the commercialisation and the technological assistance agreements established with the oil MNs formerly operating in the country. The first fruitful negotiation in PDVSA's efforts to acquire downstream assets abroad was established with Veba Oel in April 1983. In a context of financial adversity, the internationalisation strategy was given special attention by industry policy-makers, as it provided them with a mechanism to minimise the risks imposed by both the domestic and the international contexts.

In order to gain legitimacy for their policy choice, industry policy-makers sought to obtain executive and legislative approvals. The Ministry of Energy agreed from the start with the internationalisation of the industry, soon granting it executive legitimacy; thus, the policy became part of the government's agenda. Legislative legitimacy was a more complicated matter. Seeking to gain legitimacy for the SOE's policy choice, the Energy Minister decided to consult the Republic's Solicitor General, whose advice is often sought by the executive regarding public administration matters, in special concerning natural resources[1]. The Republic's Solicitor General did not think that the Veba Oel contract should be considered according to the terms specified by Article 5 of the Nationalisation Law, and therefore it did not require Congress approval for its signing. However, political actors in Congress thought otherwise and were not willing to grant legislative legitimacy to the industry's policy choice.

PDVSA's efforts to become a MN took place in adverse conditions, which imposed immediate constraints on the industry. The joint-venture agreement with Veba Oel was the industry's response to a combination of short-term demands imposed by the oil market and the government's financial situation. The dramatic plunge in the price of oil in 1982 had resulted in a financial crisis for the government: between 1982 and 1983 contributions to the treasury were sharply reduced. In 1982 the industry was forced to transfer to the Central Bank a significant amount of its reserves placed abroad. Furthermore, in an effort to stop the decline of the price of the barrel, in 1983 OPEC members decreed a sharp reduction in production. Venezuela was particularly affected by this measure which forced it to reduce a significant part of its production levels.

After the windfall effects of the Second Oil Shock had worn off, the economic policy implemented by the Herrera Campins administration reflected the desperate needs to minimise the impact of the crisis affecting OPEC members. Falling prices and a loss of presence in the international markets did nothing but reveal the government's structural dependence of the oil sector's fiscal contributions.

The purpose of this chapter is twofold. First, to identify the international and the domestic contexts to the formulation of PDVSA's internationalisation policy leading to the signing of the contract with Veba Oel. Second, to analyse the decision-making process that characterised the negotiation. The establishment of the first contract in the industry's internationalisation strategy was partly the result of an attempt to enlarge market share in the context of a difficult oil market.

The Second Oil Shock: impact on OPEC and OECD countries

As another conflict broke out in the Middle East, the international oil market situation turned once again in favour of the exporting countries. When the Shah of Iran was ousted in 1979 and as events in the Iranian Revolution began to unfold, affecting the contribution of that country's oil to the world markets[2], the price for the Arabian Light (API° 24), OPEC's mark barrel, rose to unprecedented levels.

From the first to the last quarter of 1979, the Arabian Light barrel in the spot market went from \$13.48 to \$38.17. Until the end of 1980, the price of the barrel went on increasing[3]. In Venezuela, the average price for the export of crude and products increased from \$13.77/b in 1978 to \$38.21/b in 1981, representing a hike of 280%. The sudden rise in the price of oil improved the country's balance of payments and its current account which went from a deficit of \$5,735 million in 1978 to a surplus of \$350 million in 1979[4]. Table 4.1 shows how the increases in the Venezuelan crude basket were translated into higher levels of fiscal contributions to the treasury between 1978 and 1983.

Table 4.1 Barrel price and income from PDVSA, 1978-1983

	Average prices ($/b)	Fiscal income from oil sector (Million $)
1978	13.77	6,003
1979	19.88	7,746
1980	32.69	10,542
1981	38.21	16,484
1982	34.73	11,679
1983	31.64	9,429

Source: Petróleo y Otros Datos Estadísticos (PODE), MEM.

The financial situation of most oil exporting countries improved with the new flow of petrodollars and the offer of fresh loans from international financial institutions. In the beginning of the 1980s medium and long-term economic projections for the oil producers were highly encouraging. Most analysts and banks believed that the price for the oil barrel would go on increasing; estimates of $100 per barrel were not unusual. Credit institutions based their policy of loans to many oil companies and governments of producing countries on this scenario[5].

The period that followed the Second Oil Shock was one of economic recession for most OECD countries. Between 1981 and 1982, the average GDP for the industrialised countries decreased. In the US, for example, GDP had fallen by 2.5% and the balance of payment's current account had plunged from $4,640 million in 1981 to a deficit of $11,200 million in 1982. By 1983, it had decreased to an alarming deficit of $40,840 million. The UK economy was showing even more alarming signs: GDP plunged 4.4% between 1980 and 1981. In turn, (West) Germany's GDP decreased 1.1% during the same period[6].

Economic recession resulted in shrinking oil demand. Energy consumption has been historically very sensitive to economic upheavals. Usually reinforced after a major oil crisis, policies implemented to develop non-oil energy sources were reaping results. For the first two quarters of 1982 oil consumption in the OECD region was of 34.4 million b/d, which represented a 3.2% decrease compared to the previous year and 16% lower than in 1979[7].

A significant feature of the oil market situation during the early 1980s was the release of large inventories acquired during the Second Oil Shock.

At the end of 1981, the inventories acquired during the 1979 crisis started to be released. The result was a reduction in demand for OPEC oil and a decline in the barrel price. In this context, OPEC could no longer control supply: prices spiralled downwards. In 1982 the average release of oil from inventories amounted to 1.4 million b/d. This amount increased for the first quarter of 1983, when the inventories released reached 4.5 million b/d. Crude oversupply and shrinking demand pushed down the barrel price. OPEC could no longer maintain the price of $43 for its marker crude. In turn, the Organisation's production level was reduced to 15.6 million b/d for the first quarter of 1983, after having been 31.7 million b/d during the same period in 1979[8].

Another important element that contributed to the reduction of OPEC's oil share in world markets was the increase in the level of exports from non-OPEC producers, especially the UK, Norway, Mexico, Egypt and Malaysia. After the price hikes of the First Oil Shock, significant developments in exploration and production in the non-OPEC countries between 1973 and 1983 resulted in the penetration of 5 million b/d of new production into the oil market. Excluding oil from the centrally planned economies of the time, OPEC's oil contribution in global oil supply had decreased to 49% in 1982. This decrease meant that OPEC's market share had shrunk to 64%, compared to 90% in 1960, the year of its creation[9].

During most of 1982 OPEC was in virtual crisis, as consensus over production quotas could not be reached. Notably Saudi Arabia, but also Qatar, Kuwait and the UAE threatened to reduce prices unilaterally if other members did not respect production quotas and ceased selling at lower prices than agreed. OPEC's efforts to control markets had until then proved disappointing. Lack of confidence and disobedience among members deterred the successful implementation of strategies aimed at reversing the decline of OPEC oil in the market[10].

The London Agreement: an attempt to control the market

In its extraordinary meeting on March 14, 1983 in London, OPEC agreed to bring stability to the market, through controlling production and cutting prices. The London Agreement represented a turning point in OPEC's history, largely because it was the first time since the 1974 First Oil Shock that members reached consensus in attempting to gain control of the market by reducing both production levels and prices. It was also the first time that OPEC contacted oil exporters outside the Organisation in order to reach some level of understanding regarding global production and prices.

Although a global production level was decided a year earlier in Vienna, the Organisation had failed to agree on the allocation of individual quotas. In London, member countries took some key decisions. First, they reduced the official selling price of the marker crude by $ 5/b to $29/b in compliance with the unilateral reduction of $5/b announced by Nigeria. Second, they established a ceiling for total OPEC production of 17.5 million b/d with individual quotas allocated to each member, except for Saudi Arabia which remained as swing producer to meet the changing requirements of the market[11].

The immediate market reaction after the London Agreement seemed favourable to the Organisation's strategy. For the months following the adoption of the quota production system in March 1983, the Arabian Light marker crude went from $29/b to $33.60/b in May. Non-OPEC producers adjusted their production levels to OPEC's new quotas and price reduction. Soon after the London Agreement, Mexico brought down its production levels, averaging 1.5 million b/d for the year 1983. Mexico also announced that it would co-operate with Venezuela to work out a convenient price structure. In turn, British National Oil Company (BNOC) brought down the prices for its Brent crude in line with the Nigerian crude. This atmosphere of accommodation, however, was to prove temporary and elusive, as OPEC members soon failed to stick to their production quotas. As conflict settled in among OPEC members and their inability to control markets became evident, prices dropped, leading to the drastic price drop of 1986[12].

As a result of the terms of the London Agreement, Venezuela's production was reduced by 150,000 b/d, the highest production cut accepted by an individual member[13]. PDVSA interpreted the measure as a constraint to its decision-making freedom, an obstacle to the implementation of its corporate goals[14]. The acceptance by the executive of the new production quota limited PDVSA's investment and expansion plans. A former PDVSA director even suggested that the Minister of Energy at the time of the London Agreement, Calderón Berti, should have been brought to trial for accepting OPEC's quota and reducing production, 'making the nation lose millions of dollars'[15].

The reduction of production resulting from the London Agreement came to worsen PDVSA's financial situation. In fact, since the beginning of 1982 the industry had been registering a significant decline in its production of residuals and in the sale of its heavy crude. With a reduction of 150,000 b/d in March 1983, PDVSA found it more difficult to satisfy the demands of its clients, let alone expand market share. The reduction, 40% below its peak level of 1970, meant that Venezuela's production average for 1983 was 1.79 million b/d, the lowest level in thirty-two years[16].

For the year 1983, PDVSA was forced to reduce its budget by more than 10%. The plan to develop the Orinoco Heavy Oil Belt had to be rescheduled. From a goal to produce 1 million b/d for the year 2,000, the industry reduced its target to 500,000 b/d. The DSMA (Development of the heavy-crude area in the Monagas state region) project, whose cost had originally been calculated at $5,000 million, was dropped[17].

As shown in Table 4.2, for the year 1983 the level of investments by the oil sector shrank significantly, reversing for the first time the upward trend it had managed to sustain since nationalisation.

Table 4.2   Oil sector net investment, 1978-1983

	(% of GDP)
1978	1.7
1979	2.3
1980	3.3
1981	4.4
1982	5.4
1983	3.5

Source: Central Bank, *Anuario de Cuentas Nacionales.*

The economic policy of the Herrera administration: responses to the oil market

For the general elections of December 1978, both AD and COPEI candidates did not differ significantly in their economic programmes. Both stressed the need to curb corruption and to redress unfair income distribution policies. In a political system dominated by two main parties, popular discontent often means casting votes to the opposition candidate. In 1978 Social Christian candidate Luis Herrera Campins won the presidential elections with a very small margin over AD, which still managed to keep a majority representation in Congress. COPEI obtained 38.59% of votes; AD received 38.47%. The proportion of deputies in Congress favoured AD, 44.22% against 42.21% for COPEI[18]. However, the composition of Congress in favour of AD would make difficult the adoption of policies proposed by the COPEI government.

Upon assuming the presidency in February 1979, President Luis Herrera Campins said in Congress that he was receiving a 'mortgaged country', much to the outrage of the AD opposition and the bewilderment of many observers. The legacy of the Pérez administration (1974-79), characterised by massive subsidies, price controls, huge public spending and large-scale foreign indebtedness was the result of a period in which the government had enjoyed the benefits of the 1974 oil windfall and had expected even higher oil prices in the future.

Despite the evident improvement of the national accounts as a result of the 1979 oil windfall, the Herrera administration, perhaps drawing on past experiences, decided in the beginning to implement an austere economic policy based on monetarist precepts. As of early 1979 the economy was showing alarming signs, as the windfall effects of the 1974 First Oil Shock had dwindled. By 1978 oil prices were already on the decline; the economic policy applied attempted to minimise the adjustment effects on the new oil situation which had reduced government income levels. In 1978 government current revenue had dropped to 23.2% of GDP, from the previous year's level of 26.8 %[19]. The oil exports bill had dwindled from $9,180 million in 1977 to $8,660 million in 1978[20]. The consolidated accounts for the public sector posed a real financial concern for the government. For the year 1978, the consolidated public financial accounts, excluding the oil sector, had reached a deficit of $4,232 million, which represented 10.6% of GDP.

When policy-makers of the Herrera administration set out to diagnose the economy, they did it based on the scenario presented during the last year of the Pérez administration. At the end of August 1979, the administration implemented a set of austerity policies aimed at decreasing government consumption and expenditure levels. As a result, the central government consumption levels fell from 8.3% of GDP in 1978 to 7.2% in 1979 and to 7.1 % in 1980. Its levels of savings went from 7.9% of GDP in 1978 to 8.3% in 1979 and to 9.0% in 1980[21].

Initial austerity measures were abandoned as the government began using the petrodollars resulting from the oil windfall. The effects of spending domestically the revenues originated abroad had a clear impact on the economy. Venezuela has traditionally suffered from the Dutch disease, a term usually used to describe the economic distortions caused by oil windfalls. The most evident consequences of this syndrome are twofold: excessive appreciation of the real exchange rate and high levels of government expenditure on services. Perhaps more than other economic activities, oil revenues are more likely to produce Dutch disease effects because they represent a rent[22]. Governments have problems minimising the adverse consequences of the economic distortions caused by oil revenues. As Noreng explained:

For governments, oil revenues represent easy money. Thus, they can use oil revenues to create a comfortable position for themselves. The problem is, however, that within a complex industrial economy, the ability to absorb a sudden influx of easy money is limited, so that oil revenues tend to become a substitute for other income rather than a supplement. Consequently, the net short-term gain may be less than large oil revenues indicate in a dynamic perspective; the short-term use of rentier income may compromise the long-term generation of other forms of income[23].

Noreng's words fit perfectly well the Venezuelan case. When the treasury began registering the 1980 oil windfall effects, the initial policies of contraction were softened. It seemed politically too costly for the government to justify such a set of policies when there was no apparent need to do so, at a time when many analysts were betting on a price of $80/b for the coming years. Hence, after 1980 the early policies of fiscal austerity were reversed and new economic policies were adopted to stimulate demand. The economic policy of the Herrera administration during the first couple of years had been consistently implemented, and was dropped once the oil price situation changed favourably. However, when the government decided to increase its expenditure levels and put aside its previous austerity plans in the light of a new oil windfall, public support for government performance had withered and lack of confidence in the economy and in the government's ability to redress it was widespread.

The Herrera administration relied on the incoming high oil revenues and set out to spend unrestrictedly, carrying out numerous projects and reproducing expansionist policies that were the trademark of the previous administration. Despite the new oil windfall and a temporary reduction in government spending, the public sector –as Table 4.3 shows– continued experiencing large deficits, reflecting the poor performance of many SOEs.

Table 4.3   Fiscal performance of the consolidated public sector, 1979-1983 (million $)

1979	1980	1981	1982	1983
434.4	-381.6	-1,474	-3,670	-3,018

Source: Central Bank.

For the year 1983, the oil sector's consolidated contribution to the central government was $9,400 million, a sharp decline from the previous year's amount of $11,400 million. In 1981, reaping the fruits of the Second Oil Shock, PDVSA had contributed the sum of $16,400 million to the treasury[24]. In 1983, with a production average of 1.5 million b/d, Venezuela's crude exports had declined to almost half its 1973 levels, when its production had averaged 3.36 million b/d[25].

Capital flight

During the period 1980-81, OECD interest rates had achieved historic heights in the midst of recession, but the Venezuelan Central Bank insisted on maintaining a policy of low interest rates. Whereas in the US interest rates for investment were around 20%, in Venezuela the Herrera administration decided to stick to a low 12%, stimulating the transfer of capital to banks abroad[26].The maintenance of low interest rates was accompanied by a policy of free currency convertibility and fixed exchanged rate at an impressively strong parity for the bolívar (Bs 4.30 = $1). As a result, the private sector massively changed its bolívar assets into dollars. The balance of payments' current account consequently declined. Massive capital flight from 1980 onwards was a crucial element in deteriorating Venezuela's debt situation from 1978 to 1983.

In order to stop capital flight, domestic interest rates were elevated to competitive international levels by the Central Bank in the last quarter of 1981. However, the private sector kept steadily purchasing dollar assets abroad for most of 1982, encouraged by a fear of massive currency devaluation and as confidence in the government's economic policies eroded. The oil windfall income had definitely done away with the government's early contractionist economic policy, creating once again an illusive scenario of bonanza that, misinterpreted by economic policy-makers, contributed to the depletion of the country's foreign reserves. With the inconsistent implementation of economic policies, the government had alienated most private sector support for its command of the economy[27].

The debt problem

At the end of the Pérez administration in 1978 there was no real debt problem since the country had accumulated sufficient foreign assets to secure payments. In turn, the private sector, including banks and financial entities, had amassed foreign assets of over $25,000 million[28]. However, the public sector was in net terms heavily indebted abroad, with a debt of $27,500 million. The acquired foreign liabilities of the public sector were not backed up by assets abroad as these were being used to feed the massive capital flight of the private sector. The VIF and PDVSA were bearing the weight of such an enormous transfer of wealth. The VIF's assets had shrunk by almost half from 1981 to 1982, from $2,400 to $1,500 million[29]. In late 1982, the government, using PDVSA's recently transferred assets, sold $800 million worth of government bonds to the private sector, a measure that helped finance this sector's massive capital flight.

By implementing policies aimed at strengthening the national currency and keeping interest rates at levels lower than the international average, the private sector increased its purchases of dollars and foreign assets. With this policy, the Herrera administration favoured key groups of the private sector and the high middle class to which it was closely linked. This policy had devastating regressive income distribution effects. An important factor in creating the country's foreign debt problem, this policy affected the majority of the population, government finances, and SOEs, in particular PDVSA. During the oil windfall caused by the Second Oil Shock, the enormous net external debt acquired by the public sector had, thus, contributed to finance the acquisition of foreign assets by the private sector.

As table 4.4 shows, by 1983 Venezuela's public external debt was $27,500 million, 52% of which had been acquired on a short-term basis.

Table 4.4   Public external debt, 1979-1983
(1,000 million $)

	Long and medium term	Short term	Total
1979	8.2	6.8	15.0
1980	97	7.0	16.7
1981	9.5	9.4	18.9
1982	12.1	7.7	19.8
1983	13.2	14.3	27.5

Note: The data until 1982 do not include the net debt acquired by government financial entities. This debt is included in the year 1983.
Sources: Central Bank and Ministry of Finance.

As a result of the oil windfall caused by the Second Oil Shock, the debt payment scheme had been automatically renewed during the Pérez administration. However, when the oil situation worsened and petrodollars became scarce, creditors started to pressure for a prompt agreement on payment formalities. Debt rescheduling and fresh loans were aligned to the International Monetary Fund austerity plan. In the early 1980s the IMF became an important player in the Latin American economic scene. The IMF austerity plan was similar for most Latin American debtors, especially for oil exporters such as Mexico, Ecuador and Venezuela, all of which were affected by an unfavourable oil market[30]. In the case of Venezuela, the plan included a reduction of the government budget by more than 15%, a unified currency exchange rate, restriction of monetary liquidity, higher interest rates and regulatory controls of non-essential imported goods[31].

With the obvious decline in oil exports, analysts from international financial institutions feared that the Herrera administration might stop disbursements, as a way to pressure for better payments conditions. The international financial community had clear reasons to worry. The example provided by the Mexican debt crisis had created profound apprehensions among international creditors who feared the extension of such a situation to other Latin American countries[32]. Many US banks that had loaned unrestrictedly to Latin American governments were foreseeing imminent bankruptcy if payments were halted[33].

When the first negotiations to settle terms for debt payment began in early 1983, Venezuela encountered a harsh attitude among international financial creditors. Support for Argentina in the Falkland Islands' conflict had strained relations with the UK, and consequently with most of its OECD counterparts. Thus, access to jumbo loans and favourable payments became difficult. Venezuela owed $27,500 million and international reserves totalled only $11,200 million; 52% of the country's external public debt had to be paid by 1983. Figuring out the real amount and the composition of the debt was a difficult task, since many SOEs had acquired most of it without authorisation from any central co-ordinating agency. For the most part, government policy-makers had to rely on figures submitted by the international financial creditors. Seeking to minimise potential domestic and government policy-making problems, the Herrera administration recognised the debts acquired by the government's decentralised entities, after having allowed them a large degree of autonomy and freedom of action[34]. Government failure to keep a tight control over its large public sector and to implement effective accountability mechanisms for their policy choices had a devastating impact on government finances. Reaching a satisfactory rescheduling plan to service debt payments was going to be a major concern for the following administration of AD's Jaime Lusinchi.

Currency devaluation

In 1983 economic policy-makers were confronted with the necessity to act quickly in order to reverse the depletion of the balance of payments' account. In other Latin American countries at the time, massive capital flight had only stopped once the national currency had suffered major devaluations: in Mexico the currency had been devalued by 1,000% and in Chile by 200%[35]. On February 18 the Central Bank announced a major devaluation of the bolívar: the dollar went from Bs 4.30 to Bs 7.50[36]. Soon after, economic policy-makers applied two instruments to reduce the negative effects of the devaluation of the bolívar on the national economy. The instruments applied were the *Sistema Administrado de Precios* (System for Administered Prices), consisting of severe controls aimed at preventing the transfer of production costs to consumer prices; and the *Régimen de Cambios Diferenciales* (Regime for Differentiated Exchange)[37] aimed at providing special dollar rates for certain producers and entrepreneurs.

Transfer of PDVSA's assets: loss of financial autonomy

Not only were the high expenditure levels of the central government after 1980 financed by the rise in oil prices, but also by increasing PDVSA's fiscal contribution to the treasury and by transferring to the BCV the industry's foreign assets. At the end of 1980, the executive increased the 'reference tax' applied to the industry from 17% to 20%[38]. Desperate for cash to keep government finances afloat and to settle the bill of some money-losing government financial agencies, the Herrera administration opted to seize PDVSA's foreign currency holdings in 1982, as well as those of other government agencies[39]. The measure was interpreted by the industry as a clear sign of political interference, directly threatening its financial autonomy and, thus, its expansion plans. Envisaging the major devaluation the bolívar was soon to suffer in the light of the massive capital flight, the government decreed that PDVSA's financial assets abroad be transferred to the Central Bank. During 1981 and 1982, PDVSA's president, General Alfonzo Ravard, resisted pressure from the national government to provide cash to the accounts of the Central Bank.

Despite the outcry from PDVSA's representatives, in September 1982 the industry was forced to transfer $5,000 million of its foreign currency assets to an account in the Central Bank. The funds were placed in the International Reserves' Account in national currency. Soon after, in an extraordinary shareholders' meeting summoned by the executive, PDVSA was instructed to use a large portion of the funds just transferred to acquire public debt bonds in order to alleviate the treasury's lack of liquidity. When a major devaluation occurred in February 1983, PDVSA had lost more than half the remaining amount it had been forced to transfer to the Central Bank. As a result, the industry's development plans were seriously affected[40]. With the reduction of the overall export bill, PDVSA also reduced its fiscal contributions to the central government from 22.2% to 14.6% of GDP from 1981 to 1982[41].

The transfer of PDVSA's assets demonstrated the antagonism between the objectives of the petroleum industry and the government. The objectives of government policy-makers, as budget-maximisers concerned with short-term financial objetives, clashed with those of PDVSA: its expansion plans were reformulated as a result of meeting the government's cash demands. In this context, PDVSA's decision-makers set out to accelerate the process that led to the first contract in the internationalisation strategy, a policy whose implementation would allow the industry to minimise government interference, as well as a means to increase its market share.

PDVSA's responses to the 1983 financial crisis

In 1983 PDVSA's financial situation was critical. With the price of the oil barrel steadily decreasing since 1981, PDVSA's sources of income were being consequently curtailed. In 1981, the average price for the basket of Venezuelan crudes had been $38,21/b; in 1983 it had been reduced to $31,64/b. The oil industry's income had been cut down from $17,293 million in 1981 to $10,845 million in 1983. Consequently, the industry's rent tax contribution to the treasury dwindled from $12,135 million in 1981 to $7,540 million in 1983[42].

Talks about the shortage of PDVSA's cash flow were common among oil analysts and industry managers in 1983. The industry's reserves, including bonds, amounted to $3,999 million at the end of 1982. In 1983, the industry spent an estimated $1,513 million from that sum for its operations. PDVSA's forecasts calculated operation costs at $1,627 million yearly thereafter. In 1983 PDVSA's deficit was calculated at $1,600 million[43]. Taken into account that it needed $697.6 million a year for its functioning and in the context of decreasing income levels, the industry was bound to encounter serious cash flow limitations in the short term[44].

Access to sources of finance had been a constant concern of PDVSA's policy-makers since 1983. Among the schemes more frequently contemplated for improving PDVSA's financial situation were the reduction of the government's fiscal imposition and the ability to gain access to loans from several financial sources and capital markets. In October 1983, soon after his appointment, the Energy Minister, José Ignacio Moreno León, explained that one of the objectives of the Bicameral Commission for the Revision of the Hydrocarbons Law was the creation of a new fiscal system, less detrimental to the oil industry's investment plans. Around the same time, Calderón Berti, recently appointed PDVSA's president, supported the executive's position by declaring that the oil industry suffered from 'excessive fiscal imposition'[45].

The executive's 1983 proposal to implement an urgent plan to supply the oil industry with fresh cash was originally frustrated. The plan entailed the sale of $395 million in mortgage bonds and $1,046.5 million of public debt bonds held by PDVSA to public and private financial institutions. From the outset, the plan met with the resistance from Central Bank decision-makers who mistrusted PDVSA's financial estimates and underestimated the industry's financial crisis. Another option envisaged by government policy-makers to ease PDVSA's financial situation was that the Central Bank acquired PDVSA's future receipts. A similar formula had been rejected by Central Bank authorities at the end of 1982, when PDVSA demanded provisional compensation after its external assets, $5,000 million, had been transferred to this financial institution[46].

Finally, an across-the-board reduction in PDVSA's expenditure levels and the implementation of the initial financing scheme proposed by the executive were able to avoid a cash flow crisis in the short term. As a result, the oil industry was able to begin the year 1984 with a balance account that enabled it to carry out a level of investment similar to the previous year[47]. Moreover, the executive approved in November 1983 a rescheduling for the outstanding payment of $4,580 million in public debt bonds held by the BCV and that the industry had been forced to acquire a year earlier[48]. According to the new payment terms, a part of the bonds (about $1,064 million) was to expire on a monthly basis during 1984, allowing the industry some space to manoeuvre by avoiding paying the entire debt by November 1983. As a result, the cash flow crisis had been temporarily postponed[49]. The plan helped to alleviate the shortage of cash in the short term, but did not change the chronic problem of excessive taxation about which the industry has traditionally complained.

PDVSA as a SOE subject to the dynamics of the government's decision-making structure is caught between several and diverging decision-making centres. Not only did PDVSA have to cope with the demands coming from Congress, but also from other government decision-making centres such as the Ministry of Energy, the Finance Ministry, and the Central Bank. How well the company deals with such demands determines its performance and the accomplishment of its policy objectives. The critical financial situation in which PDVSA found itself in 1983 was largely a consequence of the defeats it had suffered in its conflicts with government agencies. Notably significant in damaging the industry's cash flow situation had been the measure imposed by the Central Bank in 1982 to transfer its international reserves. Having scored little success in fending off the demands of the Central Bank for asset transfers and in minimising tax impositions, the industry increasingly saw its financial situation weaken.

The conflicts among Congress, the executive, and the oil SOE lay at the centre of the dilemma inherent in oil policy-making processes. PDVSA has frequently been at odds with political forces in Congress and/or with other government institutions delivering policy decisions. The Veba Oel controversy would only make some of these latent antagonisms rise to the surface. The arm's length relationship between PDVSA's policy-makers and political actors was, then, put to the test. In turn, the Veba Oel conflict revealed the tensions between those who considered oil as essential for the creation of public goods, both material and political, and those for whom it was a commodity subject to the international market. A major source of tension with government's policy-makers was PDVSA's need to assert a higher degree of administrative freedom and financial autonomy, thereby minimising government interference.

The refining context in the consumer markets

The favourable context for the acquisition of refineries in Europe at the beginning of the 1980s was an important factor in helping PDVSA's policy-makers to expand the industry's vertically integrated activities abroad. The oversupply of refineries in Europe was accompanied by the difficult financial situation of OPEC members. A constantly declining barrel price and a loss of market share were largely the result of crude oversupply, due to the increasing competition from non-OPEC producers. As previously mentioned, OPEC attempts to control the market had brought about the London Agreement, which entailed quota and price reductions for its members.

During the 1980s such was the level of competition among the producer countries seeking to purchase refinery assets abroad that a high-level executive of a European oil company reported the following:

> Let's leave the OPEC countries the chance to purchase our exceeding refinery capacities, so that they have to bear the costs of closing them later[50].

When PDVSA signed the joint-venture contract with Veba Oel there was a clear surplus in the refining capacity of Western European refineries, due to OECD economic stagnation, decline in oil consumption, and crude oversupply. 'In the US as well as in Europe, refineries were losing money'[51]. In the US, the changes brought about by the Reagan administration rendered the purchase of refinery assets more advantageous. Several measures that had regulated the refinery market during the Carter administration were lifted[52]. In the US refining capacity fell by 4.9% for the same period and oil consumption by 4.2%. In Western Europe, the decline in refining capacity, particularly acute in 1982, marked the end of a period of unrestricted economic growth. Between 1981 and 1982 the decline in refining capacity was of 9.9%, whereas the decline in oil consumption totalled 4.4%. In 1982 redundant refineries had slowed production by almost 2 million b/d, notably in Belgium, France, (West) Germany, Italy, the Netherlands, and the UK. Overall European refining capacity was brought down to 14.2% from its 1976 level, when refineries processed a peak of 21 million b/d[53]. European refineries were in a difficult position as returns from downstream products had dwindled due to oversupply of oil products[54].

Despite the large refinery closures in the countries with more regulated oil markets such as Belgium and France, the refiners' situation seemed to be less dramatic than in regulation-free (West) Germany. Refiners and distributors operating in (West) Germany experienced losses of over $2,000 million in 1982 and did not herald major improvements for 1983. The situation for the first quarter of 1983 did not improve[55]. In 1983 Klaus Marquardt, chairman of the German National Oil Industry Association, reported the following:

> European toll refining for OPEC producers and competition from state-subsidised refiners in other European countries are further dangers for refineries operating in the German free oil market[56].

In (West) Germany there had been several closures and the Veba Oel refinery was on the list. If Veba Oel had continued to experience negative financial results the German government would perhaps have proceeded to its closure. For the government the closure of the refinery in the Gelsenkirchen area, with a high concentration of industries, would have entailed high political and social costs. The charcoal and steel industries had been experiencing substantial losses in the Ruhr area and were only able to continue thanks to substantial government subsidies[57]. The government wanted to prevent this area from becoming 'a ruin of industries'[58]. Veba Oel's case was different from other refineries operating in (West) Germany and which belonged to large vertically integrated companies. Veba Oel was not an integrated oil company, but 'simply a net crude purchaser'[59]. It was used to buying oil from its competitors, a situation that clearly limited its strength in the refining market. For Veba Oel the solution was to secure supply, by coming into association with a net crude producer, which in turn would not be fully integrated either. When proposing the association to PDVSA, Veba Oel was allegedly 'desperate'[60].

Antecedents to the Veba Oel contract

The history of the relationship between PDVSA and the German government dates back to the early post-nationalisation period and the Agreements for Technological Assistance. The first Pérez administration had signed a co-operation agreement with the German government, allowing three German companies –Lurgi, KWU and Veba Oel– to co-operate with PDVSA in its process of consolidation as an oil industry. Known as the German-Venezuelan Agreement, this technological co-operation agreement was intended to facilitate the upgrading of heavy and extra-heavy crudes from the Orinoco Belt area. The joint-venture contract between Veba Oel and PDVSA was rooted in this early working relationship[61].

As stated in the previous chapter, since its creation PDVSA had undertaken efforts to gain reliable access to downstream channels in different markets. Along with the early negotiations undertaken with Veba Oel since 1980, PDVSA had simultaneously been carrying out conversations with Elf Aquitaine representatives in order to establish a joint-venture association that would include gaining access to the refining and marketing system in France[62]. Discussions envisaged the construction of a new plant to process between 35,000 b/d and 50,000 b/d of Venezuelan heavy crude[63]. However, nothing concrete came out of the negotiations with Elf, on the one hand because the costs of building a new refinery in

France were excessive (about $600 million) and, on the other, because of the French price controls imposed on the domestic market for fuels. PDVSA was not interested in building a new refinery plant there or anywhere else, since upgrading one of the refineries in Venezuela was less costly. When a new socialist administration took office in France in 1981 implementing further price regulations for oil products in the domestic market, PDVSA halted the negotiations with Elf. In this context, the deal with Veba Oel, which operated in an open market, became a more attractive option for PDVSA[64].

The partner: Veba Oel AG

As mentioned above, the first internationalisation contract was established with a company with which PDVSA had been working since its creation. German Veba Oel had an important stake of state ownership: in 1983 the German state still owned 44% of Veba Oel's shares. The remaining 56% shares were held by about 650,000 private shareholders. In 1965, following the (West) German government's policy of extending ownership of most SOEs, Veba Oel sold 56% of its shares to 1.2 million private shareholders. Veba Oel was a well-integrated energy group whose interests ranged from oil refining and electricity generation to marketing networks. Veba Oel marketed its petroleum products under the ARAL network, which was 56% owned by Veba Oel and which possessed 11,000 petrol stations in Germany and in neighbouring countries. Veba Oel marketed its products through its totally owned Raab Karcher subsidiary, which at the time accounted for roughly 1/6 of all oil products sold in Central Europe[65]. Furthermore, Veba Oel owned 56.30% of DEMINEX, a company dedicated to upstream activities, as well as a totally-owned research company.

Veba Oel had important technological experience and installations for processing and refining heavy crude, an obvious attraction for Venezuela. The Lurgi process to turn coal or heavy crude into lighter distillates had been successfully developed in Germany during the Second World War. Veba Oel improved this conversion technology and developed 'Veba Combi Cracking' (VCC) which at the time was considered one of the most advanced methods of processing the type of heavy crude abundant in Venezuela[66].

In 1982 the company accounted for 15% of all oil products sold in the (West) German market, representing about 300,000 b/d; 80% of Veba Oel's crude came from different suppliers. For the first quarter (January-April) of 1983, the most important oil supplier to the (West) German market was the UK, followed by Libya, Saudi Arabia and Nigeria. Venezuela came fifth with 125,000 b/d, of which only 20,000 b/d were sold to Veba Oel. This was, however, an important increase in comparison to the previous year, when Venezuela had supplied an average of 30,000 b/d to the (West) German market[67]. This increase was the result of the new agreement with Veba Oel, whose implementation began in January 1983[68].

The decision-making process leading to the joint venture

Between 1980 and April 1983 numerous contacts and visits took place between PDVSA and Veba Oel representatives. If decision-making is the work of individuals, the origin of the process that led to the establishment of the joint-venture agreement between Veba Oel and PDVSA can be largely attributed to the efforts of two men, Fritz Oschmann and Wolf Petzall. The former was at the time the president of Veba Oel and had worked as superintendent in one of Venezuela's oil fields, Anaco, before nationalisation. 'Charmed with the country'[69], Oschmann had numerous contacts in Venezuela and had, once in Germany, followed events in Venezuela with a keen interest. In turn, Petzall was a Venezuelan of German origin and a PDVSA vice-president at the time when negociations took place[70]. Petzall was known as a Social Christian and his affiliation with COPEI had allegedly allowed him to develop a close working relationship with Humberto Calderón Berti, Minister of Energy during the Herrera administration and full supporter of the joint venture with Veba Oel[71].

Based on the existing working relationship between Veba Oel and PDVSA since 1978, Oschmann submitted in 1980 a concrete proposal to PDVSA's president, Rafael Alfonzo Ravard in 1980. Oschmann mentioned the intention to extend the existing working experience 'to other areas such as that of heavy and extra-heavy crudes'[72]. Soon after, Alfonzo Ravard answered the Veba Oel proposal by admitting PDVSA's intention to continue negotiations in order to implement the long-term project concerning the commercialisation of heavy crude and the 'building in German territory of the installations to process such a crude'[73]. A supply contract was then signed with Veba Oel in January 1982, according to which PDVSA agreed to sell Veba Oel 20,000 b/d of light crude[74].

A meeting proposed by Veba Oel officials with the intention of further discussing the project took place in March 1982 when Energy Minister, Calderón Berti, visited OPEP's headquarters in Vienna. Veba Oel offered PDVSA a 45% equity participation in its 200,000 b/d Gelsenkirchen refinery with a 90,000 b/d conversion plant and a major petrochemical complex located in the Ruhr area. Also, Veba Oel proposed to market PDVSA's products in the German market. Such an arrangement would provide PDVSA with an outlet for about 100,000 b/d of crude as well as with the added value resulting from the upgrading process in the new refinery and petrochemical plant[75]. PDVSA was also offered participation in the 140 b/d-pilot plant under construction in Gelsenkirchen using the Veba Combi Cracking technology supposed to come on line in 1987, which could convert Venezuelan heavy oil and residues[76]. Veba Oel also offered to provide technological know-how and training assistance at cost levels[77].

Upon his return to Venezuela, Minister Calderón Berti, enthusiastic about the meeting in Vienna, sent a communication to Veba Oel's president ratifying his interest 'in seeing that Veba Oel AG send a concrete proposal to PDVSA based on the scheme discussed in [the previous] meeting'[78]. As the negotiations progressed during the year 1982, PDVSA and the Energy Ministry assessed Veba Oel's proposal. Under Petzall's direction, a group of analysts from PDVSA's commercial, refining, planning and legal units was constituted to study all aspects of the joint-venture association.

The form of PDVSA's participation, benefits and amount of heavy crude to be processed in the German refinery were discussed when Veba Oel's representatives paid a visit to Caracas in July 1982. There followed months of consultations and analyses of the financial and legal mechanisms for a joint-venture association in the Gelsenkirchen refinery. In July, PDVSA hired the services of a German firm of auditors, Deutsche Treuhand Gesellschaft AG, in order to evaluate the financial assets of Veba Oel's refining complex in the Ruhr area. Also, Davy McKee, an international engineering firm, was hired by PDVSA's subsidiary MARAVEN to carry out a technical evaluation of the refinery[79]. In November, PDVSA agreed to sign a letter of intent with Veba Oel, demonstrating its willingness to go ahead with the joint venture on a 50-50-equity basis[80].

The terms of the contract were to be implemented upon authorisation from the industry's Board. The meeting of the Board of Directors[81] took place on December 2, 1982. Petzall gave a presentation on the association agreement with Veba Oel, pointing out that 'the negotiations corresponded to the premises and guidelines approved for the period 1983-88 and to the industry's commercialisation strategies'[82]. The Board voted unanimously in favour of the agreement which included the acquisition of 50% of the Ruhr Oel refining plant and the right to send 100,000 b/d of a combination of crudes, 'heavy and extra-heavy or, alternatively, light and medium'[83].

There was the commitment by Veba Oel to distribute through its marketing channels the products resulting from the refining process. Thus, PDVSA's Board approved the joint venture with Veba Oel and concluded that the industry's legal experts and the executive had to provide opinions on the contract. The company's legal advisor, Andrés Aguilar, had been at the December Board meeting and had been in favour of the contract. Soon after, Minister Calderón Berti proceeded to seek the opinion of the Republic's Solicitor General regarding the association with Veba Oel[84].

The evaluation from the Solicitor General was developed around three fundamental aspects: PDVSA's Constitutional Act, the Budget Law for year 1983, and the Nationalisation Law. First, according to the industry's legal guidelines, the Solicitor General concluded that,

> There is no impediment for PDVSA, by itself or through its subsidiaries, to proceed with the acquisition of the proposed assets. The company's shareholders' meeting should however approve this operation[85].

Second, regarding the Budget Law for Fiscal year 1983, the Solicitor General considered that, according to Article 21, if PDVSA had acquired credits authorised by this Law, then the company was compelled to inform Congress about the contract it intended to establish. However, since this was not the case, the Solicitor General did not deem it compulsory to keep Congress informed of the negotiations[86].

Third, the Solicitor General considered that, after evaluation of the Nationalisation Law, especially Articles 5 and 126, there was no objection to the proposed association. This conclusion was based on two premises: that the company with which PDVSA was entering in association had an important state participation, and that the deal was not going to take place in Venezuela where the state had the monopoly over oil activities.

The process of decision-making had been accomplished: consultation with all bodies whose approval was considered necessary by PDVSA's policy-makers had taken place and the consent of the Solicitor General had been obtained.

PDVSA's president, General Alfonzo Ravard, was prevented by other commitments from signing the contract in Düsseldorf on April 20, 1983. Instead, PDVSA's Board of Directors authorised Petzall to sign. Minister Calderón attended the signing ceremony as a guest as he happened to be in Europe on OPEC-related matters[87]. Although the contract was dated January 1983, as specified in the letter of intent signed in December 1982, the actual signing took place in April. Payments received by the sale of refined products resulting from PDVSA's daily deliveries of 100,000 b/d to the Gelsenkirchen refinery during a period of over three months since January 1 had been deposited in an interest-earning account abroad. The money was not intended to reach PDVSA's account in the Central Bank until the contract was finally signed[88].

From an early stage of the decision-making process, the executive, through the Energy Minister, had conferred legitimacy to the joint-venture contract. Minister Calderón Berti had been one of the contract's main promoters. 'Engineers' and 'commissars', in accordance with the modification brought upon this distinction in Chapter 1, agreed with the establishment of the Veba Oel contract. There was no contradiction between PDVSA on one side, and the executive on the other. The Energy Minister had been as much a supporter of the association deal with Veba Oel as PDVSA's managers. As will be further discussed in the next chapter, the controversy created by the deal came from factions of the opposition in Congress who were critical of government performance.

The decision-making process that led to the establishment of the Veba Oel contract was largely worked out between PDVSA, the Energy Ministry and Veba Oel. The private sector did not have any noticeable participation in the formulation of the internationalisation policy[89]. In turn, although the Sixth National Plan (1981-1985), drawn up by CORDIPLAN, the government's planning agency, did not mention internationalisation of the oil industry as such, it did specify the need to increase outlets for Venezuelan heavy crude[90].

Features of the joint-venture contract

The contract was based on the creation of a new 50-50 equity refinery, Ruhr Oel, located in Gelsenkirchen with a capacity to refine over 200,000 b/d. The PDVSA-Veba Oel contract minimised the degree of market vulnerability of both companies. On its way to becoming an oil MN, PDVSA became a vertical-integrated company: it managed to diversify downstream outlets by gaining access to the final consumer in a highly competitive regulation-free market. In turn, Veba Oel became an upstream-integrated company, securing access to crude supplies.

Key differences distinguished the PDVSA-Veba Oel contract from the more usual netback arrangement, instead making it similar to production-sharing agreements. In netback contracts, the refiner is guaranteed a minimum profit, regardless of the final selling price of the product: the producer gets the rest, minus the costs incurred. In order to obtain further profits, the refiner has an interest in placing larger volumes of products[91].

In such netback contracts, the minimum crude price for the refiner is set by the producer at whatever price seems appealing enough to persuade the partner to refine[92]. The extended establishment of netback deals launched by Saudi Arabia was a key factor in the price collapse of 1986, after the country ceased to be OPEC's swing producer. Saudi Arabia began striking netback deals in 1985, when it had sought to enlarge its market share by dropping prices and increasing export volumes. This policy shift led to the major price collapse of 1986, as other OPEC exporters imitated Saudi Arabia in a bid to regain market share. As larger quantities of crude began flooding the markets, prices inevitably spiralled downwards.

The PDVSA-Veba Oel contract was a joint venture where both companies were owners of the refinery. Determined by market price upheavals, losses and/or profits were to be equally shared by the two partners. Apart from a minimum and negotiable sale price, the refiner was not guaranteed a fixed payment for every barrel refined. Besides, in contrast to typical short-term netback deals, the joint-venture contract with Veba Oel was more binding in time, with an extendible limit of 20 years. Furthermore, the level of crude supply was established at 100,000 b/d and not more, at least in the immediate future. Veba Oel, as the distributing company, did not have great incentives to distribute more products at lower prices, since PDVSA was not assuring it an unlimited supply of crude. The joint-venture contract was not, in this sense, part of an aggressive policy aimed at bringing about dramatic price falls in the market for oil.

Despite these differences, the Veba Oel contract shared with netback deals the objective of allowing the producer direct and eventually larger access to consumers. In this sense, PDVSA became a pioneer in a trend that was to dictate the relationship between many companies from exporting countries and those from consuming ones. By implementing the Veba Oel contract in early 1983, PDVSA's policy-makers had in a way foreseen the scenario that was to characterise the oil market in the medium term. When most exporting countries began defending their share of the market in 1985 following Saudi Arabia's policy reversal, since 1983 PDVSA had already been implementing a strategy to enlarge market share with the Veba Oel contract.

It is precisely the acquisition of refinery assets, in the form of joint ventures, that allows us to talk about a policy of internationalisation in PDVSA's attempts to fully integrate its operations. Purchasing refinery assets is an obvious form of DFI, commonly used by oil MNs. However, the establishment of netback deals, limited in time and excluding asset ownership, does not mean that a company has internationalised its operations, at least not on a permanent basis. Neither do netback deals secure a long-term platform for asserting corporate freedom and enlarging the company's decision-making powers. As will be further discussed in Chapter 7, netback deals have commonly been implemented by various companies seeking to enlarge their share of the market, without necessarily entailing the internationalisation of their operations.

Cost of the joint-venture operation

The total value of the Ruhr Oel assets was calculated at $ 531 million (DM 786 million)[93], to be owned in equal parts by Veba Oel and PDVSA. It included the refineries in Sholven and in Horst, the port at Bottrop, and tanks for oil storage in Duisburg-Ruhort. Along with those assets, Ruhr Oel was inheriting some liabilities as a result of the transfer operation from Veba Oel. Allegedly, the debts amounted to $ 590 million (DM 874 million)[94] .The existence of such liabilities was later to be used as an argument by critics of the PDVSA-Veba Oel agreement.

Taking into consideration 50% of Veba Oel's crude and products in inventory and pending liabilities, PDVSA estimated that the initial price of $149 (DM 220) asked by Veba Oel for 50% of the equities deserved a substantial reduction. The final price was agreed at $121 million (DM 179 million) for 50% of the refinery. PDVSA paid $63 million (DM 93.24) in cash for the purchase and obtained financing for $58 million (DM 85.84) from several German banks[95]. According to PDVSA and to *The Monthly Report*, the cost to acquire 50% of the refining plant and the subsequent expansion would have been far cheaper than upgrading similar refineries in Venezuela[96].

Conclusion

The establishment of the first contract in the international expansion of PDVSA's operations took place at a time when the government lacked parliamentary majority, making the adoption of the policy choice more difficult. Furthermore, the contract was signed in a context where the industry was facing the demands of a highly competitive oil market and a government in financial disarray. The result was a critical situation in its cash flow and the postponement and reformulation of several of its investment plans. Finding it increasingly difficult to adjust to the exhaustion of the Second Oil Shock windfall, the government imposed further fiscal demands on the industry. Such a measure hampered domestic expansion plans and cash flow availability: in 1982 the industry had been required by the government to transfer a significant amount of its deposits abroad to the Central Bank. Moreover, in 1983, seeking to increase market share and to reverse the decline in oil prices, OPEC decreed a substantial reduction of its production. In this context of financial crisis featured by the convergence of numerous demands, PDVSA set out to enlarge its share of the market through the establishment of a joint-venture contract with Veba Oel which entailed the ownership of half the assets of its Ruhr Oel refinery. The first international joint-venture contract stemmed from an existing co-operation with Veba Oel. Both partners sought to consolidate their working relationship and fulfil their respective needs. PDVSA would provide a constant flow of crude. In turn, Veba Oel would contribute with marketing channels in the German market and with state-of-the-art refining technology.

The joint venture with Veba Oel was the first of its kind, a cornerstone in PDVSA's plan to become an oil MN. The contract was conceived as a purely corporate matter, which counted on the support of the executive. From an early stage of the policy formulation phase, executive legitimacy was granted: the internationalisation of the oil industry became part of the government's agenda. Fearing adverse political reaction to the international expansion of the industry's operations and to the association with a foreign partner, PDVSA and the Ministry of Energy sought the advice of the Republic's Solicitor General, regarding the need to consult Congress prior to implementation of the contract. Upon evaluation, the Solicitor General advised that Congress approval was not necessary. As will be shown in the next chapter, Congress had a different view and considered that the contract did need its consent prior to implementation. A conflict among the most important government decision-making bodies ensued, highlighting the main tensions inherent in oil policy-making issues.

Notes

1   The Republic's Solicitor General is appointed by the President and ratified by Congress. In principle, he acts as an independent legal counsellor for the executive; Allan Brewer-Carías. *Instituciones Políticas y Constitucionales.* Vol 2. Universidad Católica del Táchira. Caracas-San Cristóbal, 1985, pp. 251-255; *Official Gazette,* No. 27.921, 'Ley Orgánica de la Procuraduría General de la República'. December 22, 1965; *Constitución de la República de Venezuela,* 1961.

2   In 1979 Iran reduced its production to 3.16 million b/d from 5.24 b/d in 1978. The rest of OPEC members –except Algeria, Gabon and Indonesia– increased their production in 1979. *Petroleum Economist.* Tables.

3   *Petroleum Intelligence Weekly*.Tables.
4   *BCV*. Tables.
5   For instance, Exxon built Exxon Oil Town in Utah based on the projections that oil prices would steadily increase. Petzall. *Interview.* September 24, 1993.
6   'International Financial Statistics'. IMF.
7   Christopher Brogan. *The oil crisis in Ecuador: The search for an external solution, with special reference to the period 1979-1983.* PhD thesis. LSE. London, 1990, p. 184.
8   Fadhil J. Al-Chabali. 'El desarrollo del mercado petrolero durante 1982 y 1983. Las condiciones que influyeron en la producción de precios de la OPEP'. *Boletín Mensual.* MEM. July-December. Caracas, 1984.
9   *Idem.*, pp. 39-40.
10   Ramón Juan Espinasa Vendrell. *The Long Term Dynamics of International Petroleum Production and Price Formation.*PhD thesis. University of Cambridge. December, 1984.
11   *Ibid.*, pp. 162-163; Brogan. *Op. cit.*
12   Brogan. *Op. cit.*, pp. 195-196.
13   *Annual Report*. PDVSA, 1983.
14   Peñaloza. *Interview*. February 2, 1993.
15   A PDVSA executive who requested to remain anonymous. *Interview*.
16   *The Oil and Gas Journal;* Boué. Op. cit., p. 47.
17   'Inversiones de PDVSA'. *Veneconomía.* April 13, 1983.
18   'El futuro político de las minorías partidistas'. Luis Pedro España. *SIC.* Centro Gumilla. N° 511, January-February, 1989, p. 15.
19   'Informe Económico. 1979'. *BCV.*
20   'PODE. 1979'. *MEM.*
21   'Anuario de Cuentas Nacionales'. 1981. *BCV.*
22   Oystein Noreng. *The Oil Industry and Government Strategy in the North Sea.*ICEED. Boulder, 1980; for the concept of rent applied to the Venezuelan case, *Cf.* Mommer. *Op. cit.*, 1990.
23   Noreng. *Ibid.*, p. 195. Quoted by Boué. *Op. cit.*, p. 180.
24   'Anuario de Series Estadísticas'. *BCV*, 1983.
25   *Petroleum Economist*. Tables.
26   'Anuario de Series Estadísticas'. BCV. Judged devastating, this policy has been criticised by many economists. *Cf.* Pedro Palma, *Op. cit.*, p. 186, and Miguel Rodríguez, *Op. cit.* , p. 44.
27   'Empresarios Exigen Políticas Coherentes', in *Veneconomía*, March 23, 1983. The article underlines that FEDECAMARAS, the representative body of the entrepreneurial sector, was eager to see an end to the differences between the Central Bank president and the executive. The lack of confidence in the ability of economic policy-makers had reached unprecedented levels when both parties AD and COPEI demanded the immediate resignation of the Central Bank's president. By then, President Luis Herrera Campins was about his only supporter. *Veneconomía*. March 16, 1983.
28   'Anuario de Cuentas Nacionales'. BCV; and William Cline, 'Estructura, orígenes y administración de la deuda pública externa de Venezuela'. *La economía contemporánea de Venezuela.* BCV Publications. Caracas, 1987: Rodríguez, *Op. cit.*, pp. 43-44.
29   'Anuario'. BCV, 1983.
30   Brogan. *Op. cit.*, p. 192.
31   'Venezuela vs. Banqueros Extranjeros'. *Veneconomía*. March 29, 1983.
32   Yergin. *Op. cit.*, pp. 730-732.

33   'Moratoria de Deuda'. *Veneconomía*. March 16, 1983.
34   Toro Hardy. *Op. cit.*, p. 113; 'Moratoria de deuda'. *Veneconomía*. March 16, 1983.
35   'Fuga de Capitales'. *Veneconomía*. March 16, 1983.
36   'Informe Económico'. BCV, 1983.
37   Commonly known as RECADI.
38   The 'reference tax', a legacy from the concessionaires' period, constitutes a tax applied to the sales of oil abroad independent of the actual amount of the transaction. The tax can vary from 15% to 20% of the price of the oil barrel; Chacín. *Interview*. January 8, 1983.
39   The case of the Banco de los Trabajadores (The Workers' Bank) is but an example. The situation of this government bank worsened when the government decided in 1981 that it should acquire large quantities of bonds, which the Central Bank authorities refused to pay in due course. The BTV went bankrupt and was closed soon after. *Veneconomía*. December, 8. 1982. Vol. 1, No 4.
40   Letter of PDVSA's president, General Alfonzo Ravard. *Annual Report*. PDVSA. 1982.
41   Miguel Rodríguez. 'Public sector behaviour in Venezuela, 1970-1985'. IESA. Caracas, 1987, pp. 34-36.
42   BCV data; Strategic Planning Unit, PDVSA.
43   'El déficit de PDVSA es más grave que la renegociación'. *El Diario*. June 16, 1983.
44   *Veneconomía*.Vol. 2-1. November 16, 1983.
45   *Ibid.* Vol. 1-48. October 26, 1983.
46   *Ibid.* Vol. 1-50. November 9, 1983.
47   'No han desaparecido los factores críticos que afectaron en 1983 el mercado petrolero', article by C. R. Chávez. *El Universal*.April 3, 1984. Besides, for the first time since its creation in 1956 the petrochemical industry, merged in the oil industry, gave positive results in 1983. The gains for that year totalled $6.7 million; 'El gobierno pidió a PDVSA reducir gastos de operación'. *El Universal*. March 31, 1984.
48   Decision adopted in PDVSA's extraordinary assembly of November 13, 1982.
49   From speech by Brígido Natera, 'No han desaparecido los factores...'. *Op. cit.*
50   N. Sarkis. 'La réintégration de l'industrie pétrolière: mythes et réalités'. *The Future of National Oil Companies*. International Seminar. Université Paris-Dauphine. Paris. May 26-27, 1994.
51   Gómez.*Interview*. August 31, 1993.
52   *Idem.*
53   'Gathering pace of plant closures'. *Petroleum Economist*. October, 1983.
54   *PIW*. July 18, 1983.
55   *PIW*. March 21, 1983.
56   *Platt's Oilgram News*. N° 50. March 14, 1983.
57   Plans to rationalise and reduce the operations of Deutsche BP were taking place during 1982, after company officials assessed the performance of the British-owned refinery in (West) Germany. In 1982, the losses totalled DM5,500 million (£1,280 million). 'Deutsche BP announced major re-organisation'. PDV-UK reports. Archive material; Bonse-Geuking. *Interview*. October 11, 1995.
58   Petzall. *Interview*. February 23, 1993.
59   *Idem.*
60   *Idem.*
61   *La Industria Venezolana de los Hidrocarburos*.Vol. II. CEPET. Caracas, 1989, p. 271. Also, Cayetano Ramírez, 'El Convenio Veba-PDVSA (II)'. *El Nacional*. July 12, 1983; 'Intervención del Ministro Humberto Calderón Berti en la Cámara de Diputados', May 1983; 'Cronología-Relaciones con Veba'. Document. Archive material.

62   Eda Fabro-Fuad. Commercial attachée. *Interview*.French Embassy, London. March 15, 1992. Since 1980, within the terms established by the technological assistance contracts, the Institut Français du Pétrole had been providing technological know-how to INTEVEP, the research affiliate of PDVSA. *La Industria Venezolana de los Hidrocarburos*. Vol. II. CEPET, p. 272.

63   Humberto Calderón Berti. 'Intervención en la Cámara de Diputados'. May 1983, p. 6.

64   *Idem*.

65   Also, 'Intervención del Ministro Humberto Calderón Berti en la Cámara de Diputados'. May 1983. Archive material.

66   Robert Bottome's draft paper for *The Monthly Report*; and 'PDVSA y Veba Oel. Socios del Complejo de Refinería de Gelsenkirchen, Alemania'. Archive material.

67   DPA (German Federal Office for Commercial Activities). May 19, 1983. Archive material.

68   Petzall. *Interview*.February 23, 1993.

69   Peñaloza. *Interview*. February 2, 1993.

70   *Idem*.; also Andrea Salvadore. Former director, LAGOVEN. *Interview*. January 4, 1993. Petzall's visit to Veba in 1981 was covered by the German press, which highlighted the importance allotted to the possible consolidation of the association Veba Oel-PDVSA. 'Venezuela Verhandelt mit Veba Oel'. *VWD*, March 2, 1981; 'Venezuela: Oelkunden bleiben gleich' VWD, March 2 1981; 'Deutsche Konzerne sollen mitmischen'. *Wirtschaft und Finanzzeitung*. March 2-3, 1981; 'Venezuela sucht technische Assistenz'. *Börsen-Zeitung*, Düsseldorf, March 3, 1981; 'Besuch aus Venezuela'. *Suerfche Zeitung*, March 28, 1981; 'Besuch aus Venezuela bei Veba'. *Ruhr Nachrichten*, March 3, 1981; Möglicherweise mehr Öl aus Venezuela'. *Borkener Zeitung*, March 3, 1981; 'Deutsche Partner für die Ölgewinnung am Orinoco'. *Süddeutsche Zeitung*, March 3, 1981; 'Engere Öl-Kontakte'. *Die Welt*, March 3, 1981. Archive material.

71   Calderón mentioned that Petzall was an independent, although a follower of COPEI's Rafael Caldera; H. Calderón Berti. *Petróleo y Opinión Pública*. Fondo Editorial Oro Negro. Caracas, 1986, p. 440; Petzall denied ever having been a COPEI militant. *Interview*. February 23, 1993.

72   Quoted from letter by Fritz Oschmann, former president of Veba Oel AG. Schloven, Germany, August 28, 1980. Archive material.

73   Letter by General Alfonzo Ravard, former president of PDVSA. Caracas, February 17, 1981. Archive material.

74   'Cronología-Relaciones con Veba'. Document. Archive material.

75   Telex addressed to Hans Rheinheimer, Veba Oel's representative in Caracas. Document reported by Rafael M. Guevara. *Petróleo y Ruina. Veba-PDVSA*. Ediciones de Instante. Caracas, 1983, pp. 33-34.

76   However, at the time Veba Oel only had a small demonstration plant for this process. No commercial scale plant has been built so far using the VCC process. Petzall. *Interview*. February 23, 1993.

77   Guevara. *Op. cit.*, pp. 33-34.

78   Letter from Humberto Calderón Berti, Energy Minister, to Fritz Oschmann, president of Veba AG. March 31, 1982. Archive material.

79   Guevara. *Op. cit.*, p. 42.

80   'Cronología'. *Op. cit.*

81   The Board of Directors comprised PDVSA's president, General Rafael Alfonzo Ravard, Julio César Arreaza, Antonio Casas González, Enrique Daboín, Gustavo Gabaldón, Alirio Parra, Humberto Peñaloza, Manuel Peñalver, Pablo Reimpell, Nelson Vásquez, and Wolf Petzall. Alternate directors were Francisco Guédez, Raúl Henríquez, Edgar Leal and Manuel Pulido. The industry's legal consultant was Andrés Aguilar.

82 Act N° 372. Meeting of the Board of Directors. December 2, 1982.
83 *Idem.*
84 Letters addressed to Carlos Leáñez, Solicitor General. February 2, 1983 and April 6, 1983. Archive material.
85 *Idem.*
86 *Idem.*
87 Act N° 394. Board of Directors' Meeting. April 14, 1993.
88 Petzall. *Interview.* February 23, 1983.
89 Agustín Amaro. Strategic Planning Unit, PDVSA. *Interview.* February 5, 1993; Humberto Alcántara. Director, Petroleum Chamber. *Interview.* February 3, 1993.
90 Petzall. *Interview.* February 23, 1993.
91 *Idem.* Netback deals will be further discussed in Ch. VII.
92 Juan Carlos Boué. *Venezuela. The Political Economy of Oil.* Oxford University Press. Oxford, 1993, p. 167.
93 Calculated at DM1 = $1.48.
94 Guevara. *Op. cit.*, pp. 67-68.
95 *'La internacionalización de PDVSA'.* PDVSA, July 1992.
96 *The Monthly Report.* Cited in article by Robert Bottome. *Op. cit.*

Chapter 5
The Veba Oel case: The impact of politics over oil policy-making

5 The Veba Oel case: The impact of politics over oil policy-making

Introduction

After obtaining the advice of the Solicitor General, who concluded that the contract did not require Congress approval prior to its implementation, PDVSA's policy-makers went on to implement the Veba Oel contract. Many Congress members, however, considered that the Veba Oel contract was of the utmost importance to the 'national interest' and that therefore it should have required legislative approval. Thereafter, an impasse in the government's policy-making structure originated as Congress members set out to determine the legitimacy of the contract.

The industry's policy-makers and the Ministry of Energy on the one hand, and the legislative on the other, showed opposite views regarding the industry's internationalisation policy. PDVSA sought to become vertically integrated oil MN, thereby increasing its corporate freedom and minimising government interference. On the contrary, Congress was concerned with making sure PDVSA was complying with short-term government demands, as is the lot of a SOE.

Control and accountability are two of the means of interaction between Congress and a SOE. The former seeks to exercise its means of control over the latter in order to verify the accomplishment of objectives, which usually are an ill-defined set of goals comprising economic, political, and social targets. In turn, the SOE is accountable to Congress for its performance in attaining such goals. As representative of the people, Congress wants to get adequate information on the SOE: disclosure of many key and confidential negotiations is requested. Usually, there are no fixed rules for the exercise of control. Forms and procedures vary according to the specificity of the policy case and to the nature of the SOE. The more a SOE grows in importance and size, the more the legislature finds its supervisory functions curtailed. When the SOE is powerful, as in the case of PDVSA, Congress efforts to control it are limited.

A delicate balance exists between the legislature and the SOE: the spaces allowed by the exercise of control are used by the SOE to display various degrees of administrative and corporate autonomy. A vertically integrated SOE with DFIs abroad is even more difficult to control. Often, Congress feels threatened by the freedom of action exercised by the SOE's policy-makers. A way of coping with the weight of control over the SOE is to adopt a scheme whereby accountability to Congress becomes a means to gain legitimacy for performance and policy implementation.

The issue of accountability to the legislative body became the major source of conflict during the initial implementation phase of the industry's policy choice. This chapter explores the ways in which Congress exercises its control over PDVSA and the extent to which the latter is accountable to the former for its performance. Congress was a key policy actor in the outcome of the internationalisation policy.

In the confrontation between Congress and industry policy-makers over the Veba Oel case the major opposing issues at the centre of oil policy-making sprang to the surface. The short-term political concerns of the legislature came up against the long-term corporate policy objectives of the industry. This chapter argues that although the confrontation was significant between, on the one hand Congress and, on the other, the executive and the oil SOE, the implicit conflict-avoidance principle which characterised the political system in Venezuela was not challenged by the dispute. The policy-making impasse created within the state's structure –as depicted in the confrontation between Congress and the executive– was characteristic of the bargaining dynamics typical of public policy-making processes in democratic systems.

As political criticism of the Veba Oel contract amounted to challenging government performance, opposition to the industry's internationalisation policy was silenced once AD won the elections and a majority representation in Congress. In such a context it made less sense to continue finding faults with a policy carried out by the oil SOE.

Another feature of the process of oil policy-making is the opposition between politicians and industry policy-makers over OPEC. Politicians often regard the Organisation as an effective platform allowing members to control the oil market. In turn, most industry policy-makers are sceptical of OPEC's capacity to influence the market effectively; they tend to argue that oil is a commodity unquestionably subject to the uncertainties of an international market more influenced by competition and exogenous variables than by OPEC's devices.

In 1986 the combination of three independent variables –government finances, political context, and the oil market– contributed to the unhindered continuation of PDVSA's internationalisation policy. Further internationalisation contracts were not established until 1986, when a government financial impasse, a different political context and a difficult international market fostered a new phase of policy implementation. In this second and more in-depth phase of policy implementation, both sets of policy-makers –political actors and oil industry managers– agreed on the basic principles regarding the benefits of PDVSA's downstream expansion. This chapter argues that this agreement was more the result of contextual factors and pressing demands than of a definite and settled agreement over oil policy. For the most part, the perceptions of the two groups of oil policy-makers have remained basically antagonistic.

PDVSA's legacy as a private company and accountability to Congress

Since their creation, many SOEs, especially those modelled on private companies, contemplated the inclusion of means to minimise parliamentary control over their operations. For example, in the case of PDVSA dependency on government budget allocation practices was overruled from the outset. As mentioned in Chapter 3, the policy-makers who devised the company's structure and decision-making guidelines sought to guarantee its budgetary autonomy from government.

During the pre-nationalisation period, PDVSA's policy-makers were largely unfamiliar with being accountable to the legislature. For years before nationalisation, oil managers had practised a kind of pulling and hauling dynamic with the Ministry of Hydrocarbons –later the Ministry of Mines and Energy– in a constant bargaining for more concessions and less government control over their operations. Throughout that process oil managers kept a very low profile: aloofness and silent retreat were common responses to fierce criticism. Many oil managers met the new era opened by nationalisation with uncertainty and suspicion. One researcher of the transition to nationalisation of the oil industry in Venezuela wrote that,

> Industry managers had very little experience of dialogue with other sectors of Venezuelan life, of assessing the depth and direction of criticism, of responding in different ways. These skills fairly common to the world of the public administration, still had not been learned by the oil people[1].

As argued in Chapter 3, one of the salient elements that ranks the oil industry as an unusual type of SOE is its tradition as private enterprise. PDVSA's affiliates were private enterprises during fifty years before nationalisation. Having an organisational cultural past as a private and foreign enterprise singles out the oil industry from the rest of domestically born SOEs. PDVSA's policy-makers had been learning the oil business for a considerable number of years already when the company was nationalised. Suddenly, the oil managers found themselves working in a SOE without exactly knowing how much of their behaviour needed to be modified. From the outset government policy-makers who implemented the nationalisation policy had wanted to preserve certain characteristics of the private way of operating the industry. Financial autonomy, fiscal payments to the treasury, high scale of salaries, the principle of meritocracy, and a vertically-integrated structure were traits that government policy-makers sought to preserve for the nationalised industry. The Veba Oel controversy provided a way of assessing how much of that private character oil policy-makers should retain in their performance[2].

Conflict between political actors and oil policy-makers

Legislative reaction to the implementation of PDVSA's internationalisation policy was initially hostile. Opposition parties had strongly opposed the Veba Oel contract. So strong was their reaction to it that the industry's plans to extend the internationalisation policy were temporarily halted. Various contracts in negotiation were dropped. Because of the uproar in Congress around the Veba Oel contract other negotiations that were simultaneously being held between PDVSA and other foreign oil companies were rescheduled or virtually abandoned. A PDVSA manager commented that,

> During a three-year period after the Veba Oel case, no other contract went to Congress. In fact, PDVSA could have bought Citgo and Champlin three years before it did[3].

Already advanced plans to enter into an association with Kuwait in order to acquire a considerable number of Gulf's assets consisting of refineries and petrol stations resulting from the merger with Standard Oil of California (SOCAL) were abandoned[4]. Allegedly, the negotiations were halted when news spread suggesting the possibility that Congress in Venezuela was proposing the reversal of the Veba Oel contract[5]. A news article cited Gulf sources as follows:

> There was not much assurance in making a joint venture with Venezuela, if afterwards Congress was to question its legality or write it off[6].

At the centre of the controversy that followed the initial implementation of the Veba Oel contract lay the fact that the oil industry's policy-makers had not sought the approval of the legislature in a deal with apparent implications for the national interest, according to Article 5 of the Nationalisation Law. Heated congressional debates ensued once political forces learnt about the joint-venture contract.

Dismayed by the fact that PDVSA's policy-makers and the Ministry of Energy had overlooked the legislature in such a crucial deal, opposition forces in Congress considered that the industry's policy choice lacked legitimacy. In electoral year 1983 the Veba Oel contract became a political issue. Congress and the media provided the battleground. The Veba Oel–PDVSA contract became a subject of common discussion in the press during the years 1983 and most of 1984. The media, perhaps weary of PDVSA's usually low profile, amply covered the controversy. Political criticism of the oil industry's policy choice was harsh. Opposition Congress members voiced their concerns about the industry's attacks on the vague concept of 'national interest' and about the excessive freedom of action exerted by the industry's policy-makers with the implementation of the Veba Oel contract. Not only was political criticism aimed at the industry, but also at the executive, as the Ministry of Energy had given full support to the policy choice. Political opponents in Congress used the Veba Oel issue to downplay government performance.

PDVSA's policy-makers and the Minister of Energy were frequently summoned to Congress and were asked to justify the industry's policy choice. The polarisation of stances was not between the executive and the oil industry, since the Energy Minister was a prominent advocate of the internationalisation policy. Conflict sprang up between Congress and the executive: COPEI found few supporters in an AD-dominated Congress, even less so in the context of an electoral year.

With the crucial implications of oil for the country's economy and government performance, many Congress members were reluctant to accept the increasing commercial risks involved in the establishment of a contract abroad, where market uncertainties were greater and where government controls over the industry were more difficult to exert. Politicians, many of them fervent nationalists, had brought about the nationalisation of the oil industry. Any attempt to change the status quo installed by this action, and which had the effect of limiting the overall control of oil by the state, engendered hostile reactions from political forces. In turn, the oil industry's policy-makers were in general more sceptical of OPEC's capacity to influence the market effectively: oil was a commodity unquestionably subject to the uncertainties of an international market more influenced by competition and exogenous variables than by OPEC's devices. On the contrary, OPEC provided oil nationalists with a comfortable umbrella under which to entertain hopes to control the oil market. As mentioned earlier, a conceptual discrepancy regarding oil lay at the centre of the confrontations triggered by the Veba Oel case between political actors and PDVSA's managers. Not only did the controversy over the Veba Oel contract generate a conflict between these two sets of policy-makers, but also among the state's key decision-making centres: the executive, the legislature, and the Solicitor General.

Even though the legislature periodically receives a considerable amount of information –e.g. annual reports, questionnaires, quantitative data, and special reports– on the performance of SOEs, legislators normally lack the necessary expertise to fully understand the technical intricacies involved in their management and the multiple demands that weigh upon their decision-makers. Rarely do legislators possess the necessary skills to discuss strategic or highly technical policy issues. Capacity and readiness to process specific information are frequently absent. Policy decisions requiring parliamentary approval are more often subject to delays and political meddling than to objective technical scrutiny.

Congress decision-making in Venezuela

As a result of the heterogeneous composition of political forces that fought side by side to overthrow the last dictatorship in 1958, the political system installed after the transition to democracy sought to avoid majority rule and to respect minority rights in the legislative decision-making process. These were common concerns for most Latin American governments following the disintegration of military dictatorships. In principle, decisions would not only be the result of the minimum majority, but also of the outcome of bargaining among all the forces in Congress. The goal was to legitimise the decision-making process in Congress by enlarging the scope of political participation. However, two negative elements could result from this type of decision-making structure: the excessive tendency to form coalitions or the simple overruling of the minority. In order to achieve the enlargement of the basis for participation in congressional decision-making and to minimise the pervasive emergence of the two elements mentioned, the Venezuelan post-1958 political system adopted three explicit characteristics: bicameral Congress, proportional representation, and separation of powers.

The reason why the legislative power is made up of one or two chambers usually depends on the legal and political decision as to whether or not to favour minorities. The rationale behind having a second chamber –the Senate in the Venezuelan case– is to allow Congress representation for certain minorities[7] which might find themselves under-represented in or totally absent from the Chamber of Deputies due to the proportional representation system of vote counting. In Venezuela, all the states have a right to be represented by two senators. In this way, small states with low populations have equal representation to more populous ones. The existence of the Upper Chamber or Senate stemmed from the idea of fostering a federal system, in an attempt to circumvent the centralist tendency of the state. However, in the absence of a federal political structure, the Senate in Venezuela has in turn helped to reinforce the power of the two most important political parties. States' representatives have been, until recently, from either AD or COPEI, according to the system that allocates two senatorial seats to the parties that obtain the highest proportion of votes. Such a system does not allow representation to the parties that come next, even if their percentages might closely follow those of the two winners. Until the 1993 elections, whose results challenged the bipartisan system and the traditional representation scheme in both chambers, the Senate in Venezuela has been largely dominated by the two majority parties, AD and COPEI. Initially conceived to make up for the weakness of territorial minorities, in practice the bicameral division of Congress in Venezuela has come to reinforce the power of the majority.

The electoral system based on proportional representation aims to reflect the political choices of the regional states in the Chamber of Deputies. Limited minority representation is assured by applying the method of D'Hondt[8] and by using a system of closed lists[9] in which candidates are nominated by the parties' highest decision-makers[10]. Mainly derived from the application of the D'Hondt formula[11], the slight tendency to favour majority parties in Congress increases when the votes are concentrated between two parties. In the case of the traditionally two-party-dominated Venezuelan Congress, the characteristics of the proportional representation system applied further minimised the action of minority parties in the legislative decision-making structure.

One way of assuring the power division structure between the President and Congress members is by holding separate, often simultaneous elections for each of them. The result of these elections is that often the President and Congress majority are of different political tendencies. In Venezuela, following the overthrow of the last military regime in 1958, coalition governments were the norm. In order to secure a solid transition to democracy, the search for consensus characterised congressional decision-making between 1958 and 1968. During those years when AD

Presidents governed with AD-dominated Congresses, decision-making was mostly a process of consensual bargaining devoid of radical positions. There was a tacit agreement between the two main political parties –AD and COPEI– regarding governance and economic policy issues.

As a result of the rules of the game drawn up in the Punto Fijo Pact signed between AD, COPEI and URD during the transition to democracy in 1958, a conflict-devoid process of bargaining has traditionally characterised the means of reaching policy decisions in Congress. As explained in Chapter II, the Punto Fijo Pact narrowly defined the rules of the political game in the new democratic regime[12]. Between 1960 and 1968 there was a tendency to form coalitions around AD and COPEI. After the first COPEI government of Rafael Caldera in 1968 this situation changed and government policy-making processes began to reflect the bargaining dynamics of various challenging political forces that had made their appearance in the legislature. As a consequence, AD and COPEI felt increasingly threatened by the increasing presence of minority forces in legislative decision-making processes. Seeking to minimise the action of the new political forces in Congress, AD and COPEI signed a new pact in order to reinforce the principles of the 1958 Pact. In 1970 AD and COPEI signed the Institutional Pact to reinforce the terms of the former Punto Fijo Pact. This tendency to create pacts between the two major parties has surfaced whenever minorities have contested their objectives or conceptions of democratic practice. In a context where minorities declined to enter into coalitions with the two main parties, AD and COPEI have sought to reinforce their control over Congress policy-making processes. The pact-centred mechanism in Venezuela has been a recourse to minimise the impact of decisions sprang from outside the two main parties. Traditionally, the tendency towards the concentration of power around AD and COPEI initiated with the Punto Fijo Pact and reinforced with the Institutional Pact, besides highlighting the traditionally strong bipartisan character of Venezuelan democratic practice, fostered the exclusion of minorities from congressional decision-making processes.

With the advent of the minority government of Rafael Caldera in 1968 congressional discussions over oil policy became more vehement. Before, oil policy had been the main concern of the Energy Ministry, caught up in various battles with the foreign oil companies. Due to the more diverse correlation of political forces in the legislature and to the unwillingness of minorities to form coalitions with the two major parties, after 1968 Congress became a key centre for debates over oil policy matters. In that context, Caldera could not rely on the support of any of the minority parties, which in turn used oil policy as a platform to contest executive decisions. The Caldera administration lacked the necessary support for implementing many key oil policy decisions. Oil policy became a battleground for political bargaining during this period, with the two major parties, AD and COPEI, seeing their command on the decision-making process challenged by the action of minority political forces. The need to nationalise the oil industry concentrated most of the debates over oil policy during Caldera's administration. As soon as AD's Pérez took power in 1974, his administration set out to implement the nationalisation policy[13].

In Venezuela, the three schemes previously described –bicameral Congress, proportional representation and separation of powers– conceived to encourage minority participation have in practice tended to minimise the action of minority groups in the decision-making processes at the executive and legislative levels. Furthermore, the tendency of the two main parties to form pacts has traditionally contributed to the exclusion of minorities from the key government decision-making processes. Often, minorities avenge their exclusion by attacking government performance. In this context, the Veba Oel contract was used as a target not only by AD but also by the nationalist forces of minority parties.

Political reaction to the Veba Oel contract

In a popular television programme usually featuring political figures as guests, AD's former deputy Celestino Armas publicly uttered his criticism of the Veba Oel contract:

> The Veba Oel contract is absolutely illegal. I take this opportunity to denounce it officially. This contract violates the Constitution, the Nationalisation Law, and even the Law for the Safeguarding of the Public Patrimony. The action was adopted without Congress knowledge of it; the Nationalisation Law explicitly forbids this. It is clearly stated that Congress approval was needed. I will officially ask the CEN (National Executive Committee) of AD to open an investigation of the multimillion contract signed with Veba Oel[14].

Although Armas was not a Congress member at the time, his complaints were to open the long and tortuous series of debates that confronted, on one side, the industry's representatives and the Ministry of Energy, and on the other, Congress, following the joint-venture agreement with Veba Oel.

As requested by Armas, the Veba Oel case was taken to AD's National Executive Committee, the party's highest decision-making group.

The CEN, after appointing a commission presided by Armas himself[15], decided to propose that Congress open a thorough investigation of the oil industry's policy choice. AD raised the issue in Congress and managed to gain the support of the parties of the left. Congress accepted the proposal of Arturo Hernández Grisanti, AD's deputy and future Minister of Energy for the Lusinchi administration (1984-89), to form a bicameral commission to 'consider all judicial, economic, and technical aspects of the contract signed between PDVSA and Veba Oel'[16]. Admitting its limited understanding of the negotiations, the congressional commission agreed to seek the opinion of several technical and legal experts, as well as to summon the main policy-makers responsible for the formulation of the internationalisation policy.

From the outset, most members of the bicameral commission expressed their distrust of the way the negotiation had been carried out. In turn, the claims of PDVSA's policy-makers concerning the transparency involved in all the phases of the policy-making process leading to the Veba Oel contract encountered the scepticism of many Congress members. Terms such as financial embezzlement, violation of the Constitution, and loss of sovereignty permeated the discussions in Congress and the series of questions posed to the industry's managers responsible for the Veba Oel contract. The main task of the bicameral commission was to determine whether the contract with Veba Oel should be deemed of 'national interest'[17]. Congress had not been duly informed of the negotiations, and politicians demanded justification for such an omission.

During the initial discussions about the Veba Oel contract in the Chamber of Deputies, the left complained that PDVSA's policy-makers had not consulted either the political parties or Congress regarding a negotiation with undeniable implications for the 'national interest'[18]. Jesús Angel Paz Galarraga, leader of MEP, referred to the Veba Oel deal as a 'national interest' contract according to both the Constitution and Article 5 of the Nationalisation Law. 'Any negotiation of this magnitude must be previously debated by Congress, the body responsible for discussing and approving contracts of this nature'[19]. Based on similar legal assumptions, Radamés Larrazábal from the Communist Party (PCV) went as far as to demand, in a letter to the Solicitor General, penal sanctions against the Minister of Energy for 'having carried out an action in violation of the law'[20]. After deploring PDVSA's recourse to foreign capital through 'various associations abroad'[21], Larrazábal overtly manifested his suspicion of PDVSA's management: 'high cost autocratic methods, heavy technocracy and corruption without punishment continue their course unhindered'[22].

Not surprisingly, COPEI tried to defend the performance of the executive and the industry's managers. Placing the contract in the context of the oil market situation, COPEI's Godofredo González estimated that PDVSA had the right to establish the joint-venture contract with Veba Oel; PDVSA was 'acting in defence of oil markets for Venezuela. Countries such as Saudi Arabia and Kuwait have established [similar] contracts with European refineries to secure markets for their crudes'[23]. Regarding the Veba Oel issue, COPEI's highest decision-making body achieved consensus. COPEI's leader, Luis Enrique Oberto, summoning up the party's official position, considered that for the negotiation with Veba Oel,

> Congress approval was not necessary; but since it was a negotiation abroad, what we have to look at is under what conditions the operation was carried out. If the operation is so favourable to the country, as we truly believe it is, what we have to ask ourselves is why we haven't carried out more operations of this type[24].

Oberto considered that part of the misunderstanding that arose in Congress around the PDVSA-Veba Oel negotiation was due to the fact that at the same time the government was going through a difficult period in the negotiation and rescheduling terms of its foreign debt[25]. Politicians in Congress were under considerable pressure, coping with different government decision-making centres, such as the Ministry of Finance and the Central Bank. Furthermore, elections were approaching. The Veba Oel case had entered the Congress agenda at the wrong time, making its understanding more difficult. As a result, Congress members' distrust of oil policy-makers became the order of the day. Had the timing been less strenuous, perhaps Congress would have considered the contract with Veba Oel as a more transparent operation.

Reactions to the Veba Oel contract however were not all negative, former President Carlos Andrés Pérez praised the contract and analysed its 'favourable implications'[26] for the industry. He placed the Veba Oel association on a level with the post-nationalisation policy of establishing technological exchanges between the oil industry and companies from the US and Europe. Therefore, Pérez did not consider the Veba Oel contract opposed to the national interest. Nevertheless, he expressed his doubts as to whether or not oil policy-makers were supposed to have consulted Congress in due time. This issue, Pérez admitted, refers to the most discussed aspect of the Nationalisation Law, included in Article 5[27].

Most of the arguments put forward by the political forces in Congress opposed to the internationalisation policy were so permeated by nationalist elements that soon the debates became nebulous digressions used to show one's patriotic values, often removed from the essential issues of the internationalisation policy. Political actors in Congress set out to determine whether the Veba Oel contract had been a 'national interest' contract or not. If so, Congress could proceed to its revocation, considering that according to Article 5 of the Nationalisation Law the oil industry should have consulted the political forces in Congress about the contract.

AD's Celestino Armas, one of the main assailants of the contract, deplored that 'the first significant investment made by Venezuela abroad in all of its republican history is going to be administered by another state'[28]. Armas also criticised the fact that new technological devices were to be developed in the Gelsenkirchen plant to process heavy and extra-heavy crudes. This fact was to increase Venezuela's technological dependence on the industrialised countries, a tie that the industry had already tried to loosen with the policy of the Agreements for Technological Assistance implemented during the industry's formative years explained in Chapter 3. Armas considered that with the Veba Oel contract PDVSA was increasing Venezuela's dependence on the industrialised countries, 'while forcing the country to supply crude to those countries while our industry falls into abandonment and backwardness'[29]. Implicit in Armas's argument was the fear that the Venezuelan state and thus its political élite were losing their monopoly over the management of oil resources, a right fully acquired with nationalisation in 1976.

Furthermore, the opposition political parties reckoned that the oil industry was compromising the natural resource by signing a contract whereby it was committed to supply up to 100,000 b/d of crude to a refinery abroad for a period of twenty years[30]. To the eyes of political actors, the oil resource could not have any other owner than the state. In the management of this resource, both the executive and oil industry policy-makers were accountable to the legislature. Accountability of the oil industry was deemed more imperative in the case of the Veba Oel contract, in so far as PDVSA was investing important sums abroad by purchasing refinery assets, establishing a joint venture with a foreign company and compromising the supply of daily quantities of oil.

The cost of the operation as a source of criticism

Another major concern of the congressional commission appointed to investigate the Veba Oel contract was the financial aspect of the negotiation. How could PDVSA acquire half the assets of a refinery abroad if its investment plans had been curtailed by $1.3 million and its major development programmes subsequently postponed?[31]. The financial situation of the country hardly allowed the industry to undertake such a venture abroad, commented Hernández Grisanti, AD's spokesman. He cited the cases of Saudi Arabia and Kuwait, which, having implemented a similar policy of downstream expansion, enjoyed by contrast a better financial situation than Venezuela[32]. Hernández Grisanti showed his preoccupation for the example that such a deal could create for future international deals the industry might implement. He warned that potential buyers might want to impose on PDVSA the condition to carry out similar associations in their refineries and marketing facilities[33]. If that was the case, he added, PDVSA's financial situation, and therefore the government's, would be further impaired, as new expenses would have to be added to the commercialisation of crude. With the Veba Oel experience, Hernández Grisanti argued, 'Venezuela could be conditioning the placement of its oil abroad to the possibility of carrying out such investments'[34].

By carrying out refining activities abroad, all the value-added economic benefits related to this operation would be lost. This argument arose from the concern with the neglect of domestic refinery projects. Politicians wondered if PDVSA's intention when seeking to expand its downstream activities abroad entailed abandoning the industry's plans to improve the refining installations in the country. If this was the case, Venezuela 'will continue to be a net exporter of natural resources, since its crude will be processed and upgraded abroad'[35].

In turn, some Congress members were concerned that with the Veba Oel contract PDVSA was increasing its exposure to market risks. In the regulation-free German market, both partners were going to share both the projects and the risks of distribution and sale of oil derived products. Politicians were at odds with the idea that the commercialisation of the products processed in the Gelsenkirchen refinery was to be carried out by the distribution channels owned by the foreign partner. Hernández Grisanti deplored the fact that with the joint-venture association with Veba Oel, 'PDVSA does not sell its oil and does not receive payments immediately. It has to wait for its partner to refine and sell'[36]. In such a scheme, payments and prices would be subject to further market uncertainties.

The idea of exposing the commercialisation of oil to further market uncertainties was met with reluctance by Congress members, more persuaded of OPEC's controlling powers over the market than PDVSA's policy-makers. Once again, conceptual differences regarding the management of oil resources were at the root of the tension between industry policy-makers and political actors. In a Congress speech, Hernández Grisanti mentioned the following:

> The deal seems to contradict the declarations of official representatives, since in 1982 and now in 1983, when OPEC fixed Venezuela's quotas in lower export volumes than those that the country was producing. It was said that after reducing the export levels the country would not have great difficulties in placing larger amounts than the ones it was already producing. If [the country] has an assured clientele willing to buy more crude at known prices, why does PDVSA have to invest important amounts abroad to secure markets?[37].

In turn, Armas regretted PDVSA's incapability to set prices in the deal, which he considered as a blow against OPEC's collective action principles and a lack of solidarity with other producing countries.

> With this agreement, we are not fixing any export price for crude. The income to be perceived by the nation will be subject to the results of the operations in German territory. The fact that we are incapable of fixing export prices is already significant of Venezuela's internationalisation policy in comparison to other exporting countries that have always struggled to adjust the price of the natural resource to the growth of inflation, which we import from the industrialised countries[38].

The oil sector's defence of the joint venture contract

PDVSA's president, Rafael Alfonzo Ravard, explained to the Senate's Energy Commission that negotiations such as the one carried out with Veba Oel, where another company shares with PDVSA the cost of the operation, were needed. Budgetary reductions for the year 1983 and a difficult oil market required the establishment of joint ventures abroad in an attempt to enlarge market share and gain direct access to consumers[39].

Humberto Calderón Berti, Energy Minister, complained about having been called to Congress 'thirty-one times, three of them before both chambers and twenty-eight before commissions'[40]. Convinced that none of his predecessors had been so frequently called before Congress, Calderón corroborated his position regarding the alleged need to seek Congress approval for the Veba Oel negotiation.

> It is not mandatory for the executive to seek previous authorisation from Congress in order to sign association contracts. The judicial analysis by

[jurist] Melich Orsini and by the Republic's Solicitor General is focused on the territoriality of the laws. They affirm that because this venture takes place outside the national territory there is no objection to be made[41].

Calderón explained to Congress members that the operation had been a sound investment; PDVSA had obtained a considerable discount from the initial price asked by Veba Oel. According to the Minister of Energy, PDVSA was aware that with the joint venture operation it was inheriting some financial liabilities, but Ruhr Oel, the company created with the association, would be able to service them[42]. Calderón further explained to Congress how PDVSA, after carrying out economic and policy analyses, had agreed that going into partnership with Veba Oel was the best policy option.

The Minister of Energy explained to the critics of the joint-venture contract that, for instance, to change the refining pattern of Amuay's refinery for a processing capacity of 105,000 b/d of heavy crude, an investment of $11,800 per processing capacity barrel was needed. In the case of the Veba Oel contract, with a heavy crude capacity of 42,000 b/d, only an investment of $6,000 was required for each processing capacity barrel. Moreover, this amount was in fact substantially lower than the investment required in the deal proposed by Elf Aquitaine[43].

By the time the contract with Veba Oel was signed in April 1984, the Central Bank had not registered the amount PDVSA was due to be receiving for supplying the Gelsenkirchen refinery. Congress accused the industry's policy-makers of lack of financial transparency in the implementation of the contract with Veba Oel. According to some Congress members, the Central Bank had not been receiving the money resulting from the joint-venture contract implemented since January 1983. However, it had been agreed with Veba Oel that the sums paid to PDVSA for the supply of oil would be accumulated in an account abroad, awaiting the creation of a definite scheme for regular payments[44]. The lost battle against the government measure to centralise the industry's international reserves in the Central Bank in 1982 explained in Chapter IV was still fresh in the minds of industry's policy-makers who sought to prevent this situation from happening again.

In September 1983, only a few months before the end of his term, President Herrera Campins appointed Calderón Berti as president of PDVSA[45]. Soon after his appointment, Calderón Berti commented as follows regarding the accusations of financial mismanagement of the contract:

The double billing of which PDVSA is accused by AD and parties of the left stems from the industry's compliance with Venezuelan law which requires the company to register as sales any outflow of oil from the country. To comply with this law, PDVSA makes a preliminary bill for these products which must still be transported, refined and sold as products in Germany. Once the sale takes place, then the definitive bill is made. However, in the Veba Oel case it is not a real sale but a shipment of raw materials to our refinery abroad[46].

PDVSA's new president further argued that the difference between the $1,022 million the company reported as income resulting from the contract and the $750 million the Central Bank had reported receiving was due to the fact that PDVSA had not received payments for some of the crude that had already left the country, even though its accounts registered them. The crude for which PDVSA had not received payments was mainly crude on board tankers in transit to Germany, crude inventories in the plant at Gelsenkirchen, crude in the process of being refined and stored products[47].

Wolf Petzall, PDVSA's second vice-president and one of the main precursors of the Veba Oel deal was also called to Congress on various occasions. His defence arguments reiterated those explained by Calderón Berti. As to the accusations regarding the sum paid for the purchase of 50% equities of the refinery, Petzall pointed out that,

> PDVSA can expect to receive its initial investment (about $121 million) in four or five months. The gains are close to the cost of the complex: more than $100 million[48].

During the first quarter of 1983, PDVSA shipped an average of 70,000 b/d. At an average price of $25/b, shipments to Ruhr Oel refinery amounted to approximately $157 million, more than the amount paid for the acquisition of 50% assets: $121 million, of which $63 million were cash and $58 million from loans. Concerning the liabilities acquired with the operation, Petzall mentioned that PDVSA did not have to pay those debts: on the initial balance sheet of the Ruhr Oel refinery there was sufficient money to service them[49]. He argued further that the investments required to upgrade domestic refineries exceeded the industry's cash flow availability. Petzall placed the Veba Oel contract within the industry's policy to develop the marketing of its heavy crude. He explained that operations such as the one established with Veba Oel offered incentives to current and potential clients by assuring them long-term crude supplies. Moreover, PDVSA could process its abundant heavy crude[50].

The heavy crude rationale

According to oil policy-makers the joint-venture deal with Veba Oel was to provide an opportunity to process Venezuela's abundant heavy and semi-heavy crudes, which made up at the time 'about 64% of the country's oil reserves'[51]. When summoned by the Energy Commission of the Chamber of Deputies, Calderón Berti defended the Veba Oel deal arguing that 'Venezuela has been consistently developing a policy for the commercialisation of heavy and medium crudes'[52]. In this sense, oil policy-makers were following the guidelines of the Sixth Plan, in whose section allotted to Hydrocarbons there was a mention about the commercialisation of heavy crude[53]. Calderón insisted that heavy and extra-heavy crudes have played an increasingly important role in PDVSA's policy orientations. Calderón pointed out that,

> In order to secure markets for heavy crude, it is mandatory that Venezuela continue to look for contracts and negotiations similar to the Veba Oel one[54]. There should be continuity in the country's policy to market heavy crude[55].

Calderón's defence arguments refuted the accusation put forward by AD's Celestino Armas and the Communist Party regarding the type of crude that was being sent to the Gelsenkirchen refinery since the implementation of the joint-venture contract with Veba Oel. According to Armas's evidence, PDVSA had been sending light crude to Germany, in overt contradiction to one of the rationales alluded to by PDVSA's policy-makers[56]. In the period between December 1982 and May 1983, 27.3 million barrels or 52% of the crude sent to the Gelsenkirchen refinery were light, 4.1 million barrels or 8% were medium, 10.1 million barrels or 19 % were heavy, and 2.8 million barrels or 5 % were distillates. During that period, the Gelsenkirchen plant had also processed 6 million barrels of Soviet crude[57], corresponding to 11% of its output, and 2.6 million barrels, from other sources. In defence of the accusations that it had sent a package of light crude, PDVSA argued that the variety of crudes sent to the Ruhr Oel refinery emphasised the flexible character of the agreement; it was not an intention to violate the goal of eventually supplying and processing increasing amounts of heavy crude[58].

In turn, Pablo Reimpall, a key PDVSA policy-maker, defended the joint-venture operation based on its technological benefits, as it allowed access to a better know-how to refine heavy crude.

> The technological exchange component that allows PDVSA access to the Veba Oel technology without paying royalties far surpassed other technology-transfer agreements[59].

Interest groups and the Veba Oel contract

As mentioned in Chapter 4, the private sector was largely absent from the decision-making process that led to the establishment of the Veba Oel contract. Once the joint-venture contract was signed, groups of the private sector, represented by the Petroleum Chamber and FEDECAMARAS, voiced their opinions about the deal. Initially the Petroleum Chamber, the lobby group that assembles private sector companies involved in petroleum related activities, was somewhat reluctant about the PDVSA-Veba Oel contract. As a pressure group representing the interests of the private sector, the Petroleum Chamber voiced its opinions through periodic publications[60], meetings with government, industry managers, journalists and various representatives from different sectors of society. The Chamber also participates in the largest representation group for the private sector, FEDECAMARAS.

The Chamber's president, Edgar Romero Nava, initially disagreed with the Veba Oel contract, arguing that in the context of reduced levels of its overall investment projects, the oil industry should be concentrating its operations on the domestic market[61]. The transfer of PDVSA's funds to the national treasury in 1982 and the maintenance of a preferential value for the dollar (Bs 4.30= $1), limiting the industry's access availability of local currency in a context of massive devaluation, jeopardised its domestic investment plans. Fiscal crisis and the constantly declining value of the oil barrel threatened both the government's expenditure levels and the oil industry's investment plans. As mentioned in Chapter IV, the downsizing of the industry's investment budget from $20,000 million to $15,000 million for the year 1983 compelled PDVSA to postpone many of its projects[62]. Romero Nava explained that according to data from FEDEPETROL, the petroleum workers' union, the failure to accomplish planned programmes domestically caused 6,000 redundancies of petroleum workers during the first five months of 1983. The multiplying effect on the economy produced by the upgrading of an existing refinery or the construction of a new one in Venezuela was lost as a result of the association with Veba Oel[63].

Not surprisingly, union leaders criticised the joint-venture agreement because it prevented the implementation of certain projects domestically. Leaders of the *Confederación de Trabajadores de Venezuela* (Venezuelan Workers' Confederation) visited (West) Germany in 1984 invited by the Friedrich Ebert Foundation. There, they commented upon the controversy that the joint venture had generated in the Venezuelan Congress and media. Although considering the deal positively in general terms, Carlos Castañeda, one of the union leaders visiting Germany, pointed out that some of its terms had to be reviewed and clarified. The union leaders' concerns ranged from the composition of the crude supplied to (West) Germany to the compromise of the country's reserves[64].

In turn, FEDECAMARAS' opinion regarding the PDVSA-Veba Oel contract was favourable from the start[65]. This lobby group representing the entrepreneurial sector openly defended the contract and the benefits of the internationalisation policy in general. During 1984 and 1985 FEDECAMARAS took an active part in the defence of the internationalisation of PDVSA[66], expressing its views through press statements and documents addressed to the government[67]. At the time, Guillermo Rodríguez Eraso, president of FEDECAMARAS' Petroleum Commission remarked that a country only becomes a true oil exporter 'when it participates in all the aspects of the commercialisation chain from the port to the final consumer'[68].

The contact's immediate economic impact on PDVSA

Venezuela's oil exports to (West) Germany increased significantly as a result of the implementation of the Veba Oel contract. From being a rather marginal crude supplier to (West) Germany, Venezuela came to occupy the fifth place during the first quarter of 1983, following the implementation of its association with Veba Oel. As a result, LAGOVEN, PDVSA's subsidiary in charge of supplying the Ruhr Oel refinery, was able to maintain its 600,000 b/d export level from 1982; this, in a context where its general crude exports had fallen by 4%[69].

If the contract with Veba Oel contributed to increasing Venezuela's market share in (West) Germany, it did not however reverse the tendency towards a general reduction of PDVSA's export and income levels. Despite the implementation of the contract with Veba Oel Venezuela did not register significant gains from its overall oil exports. Average crude production was 1.79 million b/d for the year 1983, in comparison to 2.16 million b/d for 1980. In March 1983 in London, OPEC decreed a reduction of Venezuela's quota of 150,000 b/d. As a consequence, Venezuela's crude oil exports, including derivatives, were reduced to $13,857 million in 1983, from a level of $15,659 million in 1982. PDVSA's fiscal contribution to the treasury consequently dwindled from $12,077 million in 1982 to $9,910 million in 1983[70].

In a context of declining exports and income levels, the implementation of the Veba Oel contract was PDVSA's anticipated response to the strategy of output reduction that OPEC was soon going to implement in London in March 1983. Moreover, by establishing the contract with Veba Oel PDVSA was also anticipating OPEC's 1985 policy reversal, when the Organisation dropped its quota system as a means to enlarge market share. A price war ensued. At the time, many companies from OPEC members were compelled to establish netback deals with refiners in order to strengthen their market position and curb competition. PDVSA did not have to resort to such arrangements the way that other producing companies did: the joint venture with Veba Oel already allowed the possibility to increase market share.

Veba Oel's response to the political controversy in Venezuela

As a result of the joint-venture agreement with PDVSA, Veba Oel had strengthened its position in the German market by gaining access to the upstream sector. When the reaction of the Venezuelan Congress against the negotiation began to make its way into the German newspaper headlines[71], Veba Oel's president, Rudolf von Bennigsen reiterated his company's satisfaction with the agreement and praised it as an example for potential contracts between producer and consumer countries[72].

As the controversy over the terms of the contract mounted in Venezuela, making its revocation by Congress likely, the German Bundestag sent a deputy to Caracas to analyse the contract[73]. SDP (Social Democratic Party) deputy Ulrich Steiger, after meeting with top government and Congress representatives felt 'confident that if the [Congress] commission looks closely at the contract it would conclude that it is as good a deal for Venezuela as it is for Germany'[74]. In the German Congress, consensus had not been unanimous about the joint venture between Veba Oel and PDVSA. After all, Veba Oel was partially a SOE and it was accountable to the legislature, just as PDVSA was[75]. Steiger admitted that the contract was initially attacked by some extreme right legislators in (West) Germany who questioned the wisdom of selling part of the company's operations to a SOE of a foreign nation. However, such concerns gradually diminished and political consensus on the issue was reached[76].

In the light of continuing criticism from political forces, the president of Veba Oel AG Holding, Rudolf von Bennigsen admitted to a group of Venezuelan journalists visiting Düsseldorf that, if PDVSA demanded, the terms of the contract signed could be reviewed and, if necessary, subject to possible modifications. Von Bennigsen claimed that the allegations of

Venezuelan politicians regarding Veba Oel's financial losses, were unfounded. He contended that the losses experienced in 1982 were due to a difficult situation affecting most refineries in Europe. German refineries lost a total of $2,000 million that year, a situation that was aggravated during the first quarter of 1983. The 1982 losses registered by Veba Oel AG had been, nevertheless, lower than in the previous year. Positive results in other areas of the Veba Oel complex such as crude oil, natural gas, petrochemicals and marketing activities from Raab Karcher could not compensate for the losses in the refining sector. *Petroleum Intelligence Weekly* reported that in the case of Veba Oel 'partial release of the price increase reserve had to be made to prevent the balance sheet from showing a loss'[77]. Veba Oel's president explained that both PDVSA and Veba Oel had profited from the joint venture. Von Bennigsen explained that for the first quarter of 1983 Veba Oel's total sales increased to $8,628 (DM 12,770 million) from the previous year $8,181 million (DM 12,110 million). Net profits were $109.46 million (DM 162 million) for the year 1983, compared to $62.17 million (DM 92 million) in 1982[78].

The Venezuelan journalists visiting Germany also inquired about the allegations of deliveries of light crude, in apparent contradiction with the terms of the contract that contemplated the supply of heavy crude to the Gelsenkirchen refinery. Von Bennigsen replied that although it was true that the crude sent by PDVSA had mainly been medium and light, this was a response to the energy situation in 1983: oversupply and plummeting oil prices rendered the sale of heavy crude difficult[79].

As mentioned, PDVSA had begun sending crude to Gelsenkirchen some time before the contract between the two partners had been actually signed; this had caused confusion when political actors in Venezuela appraised the negotiation. According to von Bennigsen:

> The rules of international commercialisation do not admit supply to remain subject to the expectation of signing a contract. PDVSA, at the end of 1982 and beginning of 1983 was interested in starting to supply Veba Oel because there was a situation of oversupply in the international market, and it was looking for clients like crazy[80].

Both partners were anxious to establish a joint venture association, because as reported in Chapter IV, Veba Oel was also in a desperate situation to find a crude supplier. Veba Oel sought to secure a steady supply of crude and to share the operating costs of the refinery, in a context where refineries were experiencing major losses. In turn, PDVSA wanted access to a new market through the distribution channels provided by the new partner[81], thereby minimising oil market uncertainties. Moreover, the possession of assets abroad would increase the company's administrative freedom, thus minimising goverment interference in its corporate affairs. In order to make the deal more attractive for PDVSA, Veba Oel obtained from the German government an exception clause for the new Ruhr Oel plant in order to minimise tax impositions. Thus, a non-profit agreement was negotiated and approved by the German government for the new operations of the Ruhr Oel plant to be jointly owned by Veba Oel and PDVSA[82].

Furthermore, von Bennigsen rejected the allegations of financial mismanagement raised by Venezuelan politicians, who argued that Veba Oel had not paid anything for the supply of 100,000 b/d between the implementation of the contract in January and its signing in April 1983. Von Bennigsen remarked that 'every 10th, 20th and 30th, [Veba Oel] had been making its payments for the past 16 months'[83].

Political settlement of the Veba Oel controversy: a partial legitimacy

With the triumph of AD in the elections of December 1983, political opposition to the internationalisation policy began to diminish. The electoral results had given AD a majority representation in Congress. AD members such as Armas and Hernández Grisanti, who had formerly criticised the Veba Oel contract, found it politically unwise to continue attacking the government's policy –as embodied in PDVSA's internationalisation strategy–, especially after President Jaime Lusinchi had given it his support[84]. Thus, soon after being appointed by President Lusinchi as head of the oil industry, Brígido Natera stressed PDVSA's commitment to pursue the internationalisation policy, and condemned the 'misinformation campaign and the systematic criticism'[85] addressed at PDVSA during the Veba Oel controversy.

President Lusinchi designated a bicameral commission entirely made up of AD members to finally settle the controversy over the Veba Oel contract[86]. In its report to the President, the commission criticised the violation of Article 5 of the Nationalisation Law, the disrespect of Congress, the supply of light crude instead of heavy one, and the financial irregularities entailed in the contract's implementation. The commission recommended 'to modify the contract with Veba Oel and to reduce its duration'[87]. The commission agreed that Congress should have been consulted and asked for approval. The report produced by the commission condemned the actions of the Minister of Energy and Mines, Calderón Berti, and of the Solicitor General, Carlos Leáñez[88]. The consultation with the Solicitor

General by the Minister of Energy was not a sufficient means to secure accountability for the SOE's policy choices[89].

Both Congress Chambers decided that the Supreme Court was the body that should have the final word in determining whether or not the Veba Oel contract had violated the terms of the law[90]. Eventually, the case did not become the subject of proper inquiry by the Supreme Court and the case was not pursued. President Lusinchi had intervened to silence political opposition and gain support for a policy that in the context of an AD-dominated Congress was not difficult to obtain. Political legitimacy was granted as a result of a decision taken at the highest level: legitimacy did not reflect political consensus over the industry's policy choice. The result was a partial legitimacy, one that hardly reflected the bargaining dynamics that had characterised Congress debates over the issue. In government policy-making processes, impasse over policy decisions or failure to reach an agreement are often settled by the intervention of a high political figure, e.g. the President. Thanks to such an arrangement, a policy can be allowed to continue, postponed or revoked. In the case of PDVSA's internationalisation, the policy was allowed to continue and, in turn, gathered further momentum in its next phase of implementation. However, as a result of the outcome that reflected a partial legitimacy, legislative opposition to the industry's policy of internationalisation remained latent.

Conclusion

During the controversy in which key government policy-making centres were confronted, Congress functioned as a forum where the fundamental tensions inherent in oil policy-making were exhibited. Congress was largely concerned with the short-term benefits of the deal. Attacking PDVSA's policy was a way of criticising government performance. In turn, industry policy-makers defended principles of administrative freedom and long-term corporate goals. Congress reaction to the policy for a moment broadened the number of groups concerned with oil policy, a matter which had usually attracted little attention from the non-oil sectors. Unions, the media, and different private interest groups suddenly focused their attention on the affairs of the oil industry.

PDVSA's freedom of action exerted with the establishment of the joint-venture contract with Veba Oel challenged Congress' position within the process of oil policy-making: PDVSA had not sought legislative legitimacy prior to implementing the contract. Once the conflict broke out, it was not clear to Congress what were the exact short-term benefits of the deal.

Not only did the Veba Oel controversy antagonise the oil industry against Congress, but also against the former and other government decision-making centres seeking to meet the cash requirements of the treasury, notably the Ministry of Finance and the Central Bank.

At the same time that it was implementing its policy of international expansion, PDVSA was compelled to meet the treasury's demands. The need to minimise the impact of such demands on the industry's corporate goals and its freedom of action provided further rationales for pursuing the internationalisation policy.

Too much freedom of action from the industry's policy-makers proved to be, in the short term, detrimental to policy implementation. Accountability to Congress was a crucial issue in the implementation of the Veba Oel contract. As a SOE, the oil industry had to grapple with being accountable to the legislature. The practice of control as a system of checks and balances over the SOE's performance proved to be clearly influenced by variables such as political context, government finances and oil market situation. In the implementation of the Veba Oel contract and in the conflict that followed with Congress, the political context variable proved to be of great significance for the course of events. The origin of the conflict was largely political. And so was the settlement that ended the controversy: political opposition to the Veba Oel contract dwindled once the political context was modified. In the absence of a final Congress decision over the industry's policy choice, political legitimacy was granted as a result of a decision taken by the President. The uneventful way in which the controversy was appeased hinted at the fact that it had partly taken place as a political strategy to criticise the government's performance, a scheme common to the dynamics of public policy-making processes in a democracy. Minority parties, even though strongly critical of the deal, did not participate in the settlement. Even though this outcome emanated from the highest political level, it failed to reflect the plurality and the bargaining dynamics that the controversy had generated in Congress: partial legitimacy followed the absence of a clear decision over the industry's policy choice. Thus, political opposition to the industry's internationalisation policy remained latent.

Despite its attacks, Congress did not revoke the contract with Veba Oel: PDVSA succeeded in implementing its policy choice. As a result, PDVSA was on its way to becoming a vertically integrated oil MN. The industry was also able to assert its position as main policy actor within the oil policy-making process: the executive and Congress had followed the course dictated by the industry. The equation Congress-Ministry-SOE that rules the decision-making process in most public policy issues makes little sense in the case of PDVSA. The Ministry is weak and lacks the necessary means to impose policy orientations over the SOE. In turn, Congress finds it difficult to counteract industry-emanated corporate policies and exercise its means of controls over a powerful and ever-expanding SOE.

PDVSA's policy-makers were given freedom to continue implementing the internationalisation policy as early as 1984. Between 1984 and 1986, they assessed the first phase of policy implementation and the lessons learned from the Veba Oel experience. However, it was only in 1986 that a new and more aggressive phase in the implementation of the policy was launched. In 1986, a difficult market and, consequently, a government financial crisis became pressing demands for policy change. In this context, PDVSA found a favourable context to further pursue the implementation of its internationalisation policy. A more detailed analysis of the factors that fostered the second phase of policy implementation will be undertaken in the following chapter.

Notes

1   Johnson. *Op. cit.*, pp. 362-363.
2   *Idem.*
3   Juan Pulgar. Strategic Planning Unit, PDVSA. *Interview.* August 16, 1994.
4   The US Securities Commission, whose authorisation is required when a company is seeking to merge with or sale a substantial number of its shares to a foreign one, had already given its approval for the deal.
5   'Se frustró la negociación de Venezuela con la Gulf'. *El Diario*. May 7, 1984; 'Petróleo y Congreso'. *El Diario*. May 8, 1984; *Veneconomia*. Vol. 2, N° 24, May 9, 1984.
6   'Se frustró...'. *Ibid*. At the end, Kuwait entered alone in the deal.
7   For example, territorial minorities (e.g. the southern states in the US Senate) or class-oriented minorities (e.g. the hereditary-nobility in the UK House of Lords). *Democracies. Patterns of Majoritarian and Consensus Government in twenty-one Countries.* Yale University Press. USA, 1984, p. 35.
8   Liphart. *Ibid.*, p. 153. The D'Hondt formula consists of dividing the total number of votes in each party in each state by 1,2,3...n., and so on (n+the number of deputies to be elected). Then, it is necessary to order the obtained coefficients from larger to smaller, accordingly allocating seats for each party; Luis Pedro España, 'El futuro político de las minorías partidistas'. *SIC*. Centro Gumilla; No. 151, Jan.-Feb. 1989, p. 15.
9   Data from the Electoral Supreme Council, 'La estadística evolutiva de los partidos, 1958-1978'; L.P. España, *Op. cit.*
10 Challenged by many, this system of deputy allocation according to closed lists was partially modified in 1992. A new scheme was applied in the presidential and congressional elections of December 1993. Fifty per cent of deputies are now elected through this system; the other fifty per cent by direct vote, or uninominal vote. The argument used against the outright abandonment of the closed lists' system is precisely the need to protect minorities.

11   According to Lijphart, the application of D'Hont method favours large parties. *Op. cit.*, p. 35.

12   After having fought alongside the political forces of the centre, the left was excluded from the process of defining the rules of the political game for the democratic period. The parties which signed the Punto Fijo Pact in 1958 were AD, COPEI, and URD (a centre-oriented party whose importance has been increasingly reduced to near insignificance). Alienated from this process the left found recourse in the armed struggle, opening one of the bloodiest periods in the country's contemporary history. Subsequently, the government and the military defeated the radicalised left. The Caldera administration of 1968-1973 conferred an amnesty on the last group of insurgents.

13   During Caldera's administration various political forces put forward different projects for the nationalisation of the oil industry. Also, an AD-proposed fiscal reform, including the elimination of reference prices for crude, was implemented. COPEI, in turn, proposed the nationalisation of the gas industry, a policy that was implemented in 1970 and that served as a learning ground for the major nationalisation of oil in 1975. Also during the Caldera administration, it was decided that the executive should unilaterally fix export values, in order to avoid further discussions with the oil MNs; J.A. Giacopini. Former consultant to PDVSA's presidents. *Interview*. October 14, 1993; also, Tugwell. *Op. cit.*

14   'Buenos Días', T.V. programme presented by Carlos Rangel and Sofía Imber. May 13, 1983. Archive material.

15   Besides Armas, the commission was made by deputies Gustavo Mirabal Bustillos, Guillermo Altuve Williams, and Arévalo Guzmán Reyes; Alvaro Vilachá was appointed secretary. *Ultimas Noticias*. May 17 and 23, 1983.

16   The proposal was adopted on May 24, 1983 by the Chamber of Deputies. 'Diputados aprobó estudiar todos los aspectos jurídicos de negociación la PDVSA-Veba Oel', article by Carlos Villegas. *Ultimas Noticias*. May 25, 1983.

17   Article by Alirio Bolívar. 'Se constituyó Comisión Bicameral de Energía y Minas'. *El Universal*. May 26, 1983.

18   'AD y la izquierda coinciden en llevar al Congreso contrato PDVSA-empresa alemana'. *Ultimas Noticias*. May 15, 1983.

19   *Idem.*

20   'PDVSA se burla de la nación con su último informe'. *El Universal*. January 7, 1983.

21   *Idem.*

22   *Idem.*

23   'AD y la izquierda coinciden en llevar al Congreso contrato PDVSA-empresa alemana'. *Ultimas Noticias*. May 15, 1983.

24   Article by Elena Block. 'Luis Enrique Oberto. No era indispensable la opinión del Congreso para efectuar la operación'. *El Nacional*, [not dated].

25   'Tough line on loan to Venezuela'. *Times*, June 16, 1983.

26   'CAP y el contrato con la Veba. Creo conveniente este tipo de negociaciones'. *El Nacional*. May 5, 1983.

27   *Idem.*

28   Article by Alirio Bolívar. *El Nacional*. May 30, 1983. 'El interés nacional no se puede comprometer en secreto'.

29   Article by Mario Villegas. 'Algunos aspectos del contrato no convienen al interés nacional'. *El Nacional*. June 26, 1983.

30   Article by José de Córdoba. *The Daily Journal*. May 19, 1983. 'Is it wise to tie ourselves to 20 years without asking anyone's opinion? Petroleum is too serious a matter to leave it in the hands of the oilmen'.

31 Energy Minister Calderón Berti declared that the reduction in PDVSA's investment plan totalled only $697,000; the plan was reduced from $4,070 million to $3,372 million. *Idem.*; 'Reducidas en tres mil millones las inversiones petroleras', article by Cayetano Ramírez. *El Nacional.* April, 14, 1983; Bernardo Fisher. 'Postergado proyecto central para el desarrollo de la Faja del Orinoco'. *El Nacional.* May 24, 1983; 'Postergado proyecto central para el desarrollo de la Faja del Orinoco'. *El Nacional.* May 24, 1983.

32 Article by Alirio Bolívar. 'La negociación con la Veba puede crear un peligroso antecedente'. *El Universal.* May 25, 1983.

33 *Idem.*

34 *Idem.*

35 Article by Mario Villegas. 'Hernández Grisanti: algunos aspectos del contrato no convienen al interés nacional'. *El Nacional.* June 26, 1983.

36 *Idem.*

37 'La negociación con la Veba Oel puede crear un peligroso antecedente'. *Op. cit.*

38 'Problemas financieross de la Veba Oel refuerzan argumentos de la oposición'. *El Universal.* June 16, 1983.

39 'Finanzas y Valores'. *El Universal.* May 29, 1983.

40 Article by C.R. Chávez. 'Explica el Ministro de Energía y Minas'. *El Universal.* June 16, 1983.

41 'El jurista José Melich Orsini y el caso Veba Oel'. *El Universal.* June 26, 1983.

42 'Hechos y cifras de la semana'. *El Universal.* May 29, 1983.

43 *Idem.*

44 In the meantime, PDVSA's policy-makers were looking for a suitable legal scheme that would make the two partners pay fewer taxes to the German government. Finally, following the advice of fiscal advisors, the scheme adopted was the establishment of a legal intermediary company, PROPERNYN B.V., to avoid excessive tax payments. All subsequent internationalisation contracts would be managed according to that formula; Petzall. *Interviews.* February 23 and August 6, 1993.

45 Many analysts called the decision a political appointment, the beginning of the industry's politicisation. Barely six months after his appointment, when the new administration of AD Jaime Lusinchi was inaugurated in February 1984, both Calderón Berti and Moreno León –appointed Energy Minister were not confirmed in their positions. President Lusinchi appointed Brígido Natera as head of PDVSA and Arturo Hernández Grisanti as Minister of Energy. The issue of PDVSA' politicisation will be further developed in Chapter VI.

46 'PDVSA refutes charges of irregularities in contract'. *The Daily Journal.* July 14, 1984.

47 *Idem.*

48 *Idem.*

49 *Idem.*

50 *Idem.*

51 Article by José de Córdoba. 'In 1982 Venezuela produced 692 billion oil barrels'. *The Daily Journal.* May 19, 1983.

52 *Idem.*

53 As explained in Chapter IV, in the Sixth National Plan (1981-1985) the internationalisation policy of the oil industry was not specifically mentioned. The Plan did mention, however, that special attention should be given to fostering the export and process of heavy crude.

54 'Nada tiene de extraño que una refinería petrolera independiente pierda dinero'. *El Universal.* May 16, 1983.

55   Article by José de Córdoba.'Is it wise to tie ourselves...'. *Op. cit.*
56   Article by Mario Villegas. 'Algunos aspectos del contrato no convienen al interés nacional'. *El Nacional.* June 26, 1983.
57   At the time, there were negotiations to reactivate an agreement for the exchange of crude between Venezuela and the former USSR. The original agreement, that contemplated the supply of Venezuelan crude to Cuba while the former USSR sent crude to Spain and Portugal through PETROGRAL, was implemented between 1978 and 1982. The swap agreement ceased when the price difference between the lower priced Soviet crude and the Venezuelan crude marker made the offer unattractive. Since OPEC's price reduction policy adopted in March 1983, the price of both crudes –Soviet and Venezuelan– was about $29/b, rendering the implementation of the swap feasible again. The negotiations for the renewal of the exchange agreement with the Soviets were based on the condition that Venezuela send 10,000 b/d to Cuba while the USSR send the same amount to the Ruhr Oel plant. Fleet costs would thereby be saved. *Veneconomía.* Vol.1- N° 37. August 10, 1983; Vol. 1- N° 22, April 27, 1983; 'Venezuela-Soviet oil swap would involve 10,000 b/d'. *The Daily Journal.* April 23, 1983; 'Estudian acuerdo con la URSS'. *El Nacional.* April 21, 1983; *The Daily Journal.* April 23, 1983.
58   'PDVSA refutes charges of irregularities in contract'. *The Daily Journal.* July 14, 1984; 'Ha dado ganancias y no pérdidas el convenio con la Veba Oel'. *El Nacional.*July 14, 1984.
59   'PDVSA defends Veba Oel contract'. *The Daily Journal.* May 24, 1983.
60   *Barriles* is the Chamber's bimonthly magazine.
61   'Cámara Petrolera. Dramática situación del sector petrolero'. *El Diario.* May 1, 1983.
62   'El convenio trinacional. Compartir el mercado petrolero en EE.UU.' *El Universal.* June 6, 1983.
63   'La Cámara Petrolera. Inconveniente y contradictoria la negociación con la Veba Oel'. *El Nacional.* May 21, 1983.
64   'Sindicalistas venezolanos en Bonn critican acuerdo petrolero firmado entre Venezuela y Veba Alemania'. *El Universal.* June 7, 1984.
65   'Guillermo Rodríguez Eraso. Es sano internacionalizar la industria petrolera'. *El Nacional.* April 16, 1984.
66   Rodríguez Eraso. *Interview.* November 19, 1993.
67   The most coherent of Fedecámaras' documents addressed to the government on the defence of the internationalisation of PDVSA bore the title 'Sugerencias y posibles acciones en el sector petrolero' ('Suggestions and possible actions in the oil sector'). The internationalisation of PDVSA was a crucial topic in the group's extraordinary assembly of January 1984. Rodríguez Eraso. *Ibid.*
68   Newspaper article. April 16, 1984. Archive material:
69   'Lagoven scrapes through a tough year, but at least exports stay at the 1982 level'. *The Daily Journal.* May 23, 1984.
70   *Oil and Gas Journal;* Boué. *Op. cit.,* p. 47; BCV, *Informe Económico,* 1970-1991; OCEI, *Anuario del Comercio Exterior de Venezuela; Petroleum Economist* data; *PODE.*
71   'Debatte um Veba-Vertrag mit Venezuela'. *Süddeutsche Zeitung.* May 25, 1983. Mentioned in press reports gathered by the Venezuelan Consulate in Munich and sent to the Ministry of Foreign Affairs in Caracas. Received on July 26, 1983. Archive material.
72   'Veba Oel no interviene con controversia venezolana'. *Ultimas Noticias.* May 5, 1983.

73   'El Bundestag y la Veba Oel. Objeciones al contrato conoció diputado alemán'. *El Nacional*. April 6, 1984.
74   'Bonn oil minister finds Veba support'. *The Daily Journal*. April 15, 1984.
75   'As mentioned in Chapter 4 the German state owned 44% of Veba Oel's shares.
76   Interesting enough, in Germany the right used the same nationalist rhetoric to criticise the association Veba Oel-PDVSA as the left in Venezuela.
77   *Petroleum Intelligence Weekly*. March 21, 1983, p. 6. Reported by PDVSA-UK; based on press reports. Archive material.
78   'Si PDVSA lo solicita estamos dispuestos a revisar el contrato de asociación'. *El Universal*. May 25, 1984.
79   'Si PDVSA lo solicita estamos dispuestos...'. *Op. cit.*
80   Comments attributed to von Benningsen. *Idem.*
81   Petzall. *Interview*. September 24, 1993.
82   W. Bonse-Geuking. President, Veba Oel. *Interview*. October 11, 1995.
83   'La Veba sí le ha pagado a Venezuela'. *El Diario*. May 24, 1984.
84   Rodríguez Eraso. *Interview*. November 19, 1993.
85   'PDVSA president alleges smear campaign'. *The Daily Journal*, [not dated].
86   The commission was made up of Celestino Armas, Reinaldo Leandro Mora, Carlos Canache Mata, Isidro Morales Paúl, Manuel Peñalver, David Morales Bello and the new Minister of Energy Arturo Hernández Grisanti, all of them AD members. Article by C.R. Chávez. 'El Gobierno pidió a PDVSA reducir gastos de operación'. *El Universal*. March 31, 1984.
87   'Comisión de AD entregó informe al Presidente'. *El Nacional*. August 23, 1984; 'Entregado al Presidente Informe sobre la Veba Oel'. *El Universal*. August 23, 1984.
88   'Condena al Ministro de Minas y al Procurador aprobó la Comisión Parlamentaria'. *El Universal*. July 22, 1983. COPEI's official reaction to the report of the commission was a dismissal of the arguments put forward for the condemnation of the PDVSA-Veba Oel deal; COPEI labelled the report a 'judicial non-sense and a political intrigue with detrimental effects for the interests of Venezuela'. 'Disparate jurídico el informe sobre convenio PDVSA-Veba Oel', *El Nacional*. July 23, 1983.
89   'La mayoría llegó a la conclusión de que el Ejecutivo debió enviar al Congreso el contrato con la Veba Oel'. *El Universal*. July 23, 1983.
90   'El Congreso no quedó convencido'. *El Nacional*. May 5, 1983; article by Cayetano Ramírez. 'El Congreso no echará atrás el convenio de PDVSA con Veba'. *El Nacional*, [not dated].

Chapter 6
The second phase of policy implementation: Corporate strategy unhindered

6 The second phase of policy implementation: Corporate strategy unhindered

Introduction

Despite fierce opposition from Congress to the Veba Oel contract and the standstill to which the policy was brought during a three-year period, its implementation continued virtually unmodified. Opposition to PDVSA's internationalisation policy was silenced after President Lusinchi gave his support to the industry's policy-makers. Partial political legitimacy was conferred as a result of a presidential decision. The outcome was more the result of a high-level political decision than of a clear position regarding the industry's intention to acquire DFIs in the form of refinery assets allowing it to become a vertically-integrated oil MN. Between the signing of the Veba Oel contract in 1983 and the second phase of policy implementation in 1986, no new joint ventures were established; PDVSA's policy-makers used that period to assess thoroughly the first phase of policy implementation that corresponded to the Veba Oel contract. Industry policy-makers evaluated the first phase of policy implementation and its implications for the establishment of further contracts. PDVSA's policy-makers had won the battle against Congress, which in the end declined to exercise its veto powers to reverse the contract's implementation.

The pattern of acting as if Congress approval for a policy choice had been granted –the *fait-accompli* approach– was used more consciously after assessing the experience of the contract with Veba Oel. Going ahead with policy implementation without prior Congress approval proved a valuable instrument for the industry, a way of coping with the uncertainty and risks of eventual opposition.

The cost of reversing a policy already being implemented are usually higher than allowing it to follow its course. PDVSA has used this logic to its advantage, and Congress, however reluctantly, has tended to follow behind. Not surprisingly, this pattern of action has often triggered the animosity of the various political actors who judge the industry as an insubordinate and rebellious sibling among the SOEs.

This chapter explores the background to the continuation of PDVSA's internationalisation policy. A combination of political, strategic and economic factors facilitated the implementation of a new phase of internationalisation after 1986. Not only had the political context changed in favour of a new policy continuation, but also the oil market context. In 1986 oil prices collapsed stressing OPEC's limitations in controlling the market. As a result, PDVSA's contribution to the treasury declined sharply. This context provided the industry's policy-makers with further motivations for continuing with the acquisition of DFIs in the form of refinery assets. Furthermore, this chapter argues that the victory over political obstacles and the use of oil market difficulties into its advantage during the first phase of policy implementation were two significant factors in stimulating the launching of a more aggressive and diversified implementation phase.

The *fait-accompli* approach to policy-making

Often, Congress reacts when there is an impending crisis. By taking advantage of the situations of crisis which demand quick policy responses, PDVSA's policy-makers succeeded in making the political forces go along with their policy orientations. With varying degrees of conflict, the *fait-accompli* approach to decision-making has been applied in several of the industry's policy choices: the internationalisation policy is but one case. From the Veba Oel experience, PDVSA's policy-makers realised the advantages of the *fait-accompli* approach to policy-implementation as it enabled them not to miss out on deals considered crucial to the industry's expansion and policy guidelines. The following comments by PDVSA's policy-makers shed light on the industry's approach to being accountable to Congress:

> [Acting before obtaining legislative legitimacy] is a way of always behaving without waiting for the government –Ministry and Congress included– to approve the policy. After the decision has been taken, and often even implemented, PDVSA drags the government behind its decisions. PDVSA goes in front of the political establishment[1].
>
> The industry has long-term strategies. It is a few years ahead of the state. The industry is the tail that moves the dog, and it should be careful that the dog does not bite its tail[2].

The basic tension between industry managers and the political leadership over the management of oil also lay at the centre of the controversy over the implementation of the internationalisation policy. Short-term political objectives are often opposed to long-term corporate goals.

The political background: a favourable context to policy continuation

The 1983 elections were won by AD. It was the first time that AD had won an election by such a large margin over its rival COPEI. For the coming presidential period the decision-making powers of the executive and the legislature were to be concentrated on AD, and, as with the previous election, minority parties saw their importance diminished. The bipartisan political system remained unchallenged by the electoral results of 1983[3].

When AD won the presidential elections in 1983, the old combatant against the internationalisation strategy, Celestino Armas, allegedly wanted to continue with his crusade against the industry's policy choice. By then, however, both the government and the Minister of Energy were from AD. His party peers told Armas, to 'stop the nonsense, because now we (AD) cannot maintain a power confrontation if we have the majority in Congress and in the executive'[4].

Having been forced to stop his attacks on the oil industry, Armas was no longer able to use his 'instrument of confrontation'[5] and was allegedly put aside. Armas' story is an interesting one of political manoeuvring and perseverance which enabled him not to fade from the political arena. Peñaloza depicted this period of Armas's political career as follows:

> I think Armas was left with the resentment caused by his failure to be part of AD's highest decision-making centre, CEN. That affected him, the fact that he could not continue to exploit his gold mine once AD was in control of the executive and Congress. In the next electoral round for the CEN, Celestino Armas was left out. Of course, President Lusinchi rescued him as Minister for other things. But the truth is that opposition to the internationalisation of PDVSA had a boomerang effect on him. After that, I do not know through which mechanism, maybe direct election within the CEN, he was finally elected, but not with the base support of the party, bruised as he was from the attitude he took regarding the Veba case[6].

As mentioned in Chapter 5, before stepping from power President Luis Herrera Campins appointed Calderón Berti to replace Alfonzo Ravard as PDVSA's president in 1983. The non-political career of the leaving president sharply contrasted with the highly political image of the new one. The designation of the former Minister of Energy as PDVSA's head was immediately considered a political action that enraged most of the industry's managers, who feared the politicisation of the industry. By moving Calderón from Minister to president of the oil industry, President Herrera had trampled on the oil industry's principle of seniority. Without the strong political support enjoyed throughout his career, it was unlikely that Calderón would have reached this position in such a relatively short time. As one of the industry's policy-makers pointed out:

Calderón was a relatively young man, who in a normal career in the industry would have never reached that post at such a young age. He was a politician as well as an oil person. In Exxon or in Shell, he would have only reached high posts in a short period of time had he proved to be extremely brilliant. That would have been very odd, very unlikely[7].

The principles of professionalism and meritocracy had been violated with the appointment of Calderón Berti. As Sosa Pietri, PDVSA's president from 1990 to 1992, put it:

The appointment of a political militant as maximum head of PDVSA did not leave any doubts as to the intention of the political leaders to keep reducing, more and more, PDVSA's autonomies, and to assume the roles that had been attributed to the company[8].

Usually, industry managers look down upon politically appointed positions. What F.M. Marx called 'the economic of small chances' (1957: 97, cited by Ham and Hill, 1993: 137) in the public administration holds true for PDVSA more than the rest of government entities.

Meteoric rise of the outstandingly able individual is therefore discouraged, quite in the same way as favouritism and disregard of rules are. Advancement, if it is not to attract suspicion or unfriendly eyes, must generally stay in line with the 'norm'. Exceptions call for too much explaining. All this tends to make reward for accomplishment something that comes in small packages at fairly long intervals[9].

During the presidential campaign of 1983, both candidates, AD's Jaime Lusinchi and COPEI's Rafael Caldera, had made it clear that if elected presidents they would immediately remove Calderón as PDVSA's head. Soon after being elected, Lusinchi carried out his electoral promise: Calderón Berti's short-lived career as president of PDVSA had lasted only three months. President Jaime Lusinchi appointed Brígido Natera, who had a long career in the oil industry. Natera's period as president of PDVSA was however characterised by frequent confrontations with the Minister of Energy, then Arturo Hernández Grisanti[10]. The disputes with the Minister of Energy became so frequent and irreconcilable that, allegedly, 'Brígido [Natera] very soon wrote his resignation letter and always carried it with him. Soon after his second year of mandate, he resigned from his position'[11]. From the beginning, Natera was confronted with attacks from the executive against the industry's freedom of action. Natera was constantly reminded to observe OPEC's quota and to sell crude according to the prices mandated by the Ministry. Development programmes in the Orinoco Belt and in the Cardón refinery were postponed during Natera's presidency. Moreover, the industry was forbidden to continue with new internationalisation ventures[12].

The balance shifted in favour of PDVSA when President Lusinchi appointed his half-brother, Juan Chacín, to replace Brígido Natera as its president. Chacín was an industry man and his appointment, despite his kin relationship with President Lusinchi, was not used as an argument against the politicisation of the industry. During his five-year-period 'Lusinchi always kept oil career employees'[13] in the industry. Chacín enjoyed the utmost confidence of President Lusinchi. This tacit empathy helped to improve the relationship between the industry and the executive, providing the 'possibility to recover the industry's autonomies'[14].

The oil market context: the 1986 price collapse

Even though the period initiated with the appointment of Juan Chacín as head of PDVSA in 1986 helped to improve the relationship between the industry and the executive, it was also the government's critical financial situation that fostered the continuation of PDVSA's internationalisation. Sosa Pietri explained this context as follows:

> The small respite of the industry during that period was the direct result of the spectacular plunge in prices and, certainly, of the ability of the oil management to take advantage of the moment to launch PDVSA towards more sound policies, plans, and programmes[15].

In a context of low barrel prices and high competition in the oil markets, PDVSA's policy-makers set out to purchase new refinery assets and consolidate existing ones. The crisis provoked rapid and more aggressive policy responses. PDVSA's response to the 1986 price collapse was to launch once again its internationalisation policy as a way to enlarge market share and minimise market uncertainties. As mentioned, the initial establishment of joint-venture partnerships required few cash disbursements. A shortage of cash flow as a result of the price plunge of 1986 did not pose a major obstacle to the expansion of DFIs in the form of refinery assets. On the contrary, a situation that at first hand looked disadvantageous proved to be encouraging for continuing the establishment of joint ventures abroad. Faced with the pressing need to defend market share and maintain contributions to the treasury, the industry found no obstacles from Congress or the executive in pursuing its international expansion.

To understand the main causes of the price collapse of 1986, it is necessary to look at the variables that affected the oil market during the first half of the 1980s. At the beginning of the 1980s, the events of the Iranian Revolution brought about a supply shortage that caused prices to soar temporarily. OPEC producers had been experiencing a steady loss of market share. Overall, OPEC's total production fell by about 45% between 1979 and 1985[16]. Table 6.1 highlights this evidence.

Table 6.1 OPEC's data, 1980 and 1985

	1980	1985	Level of decline (%)
Total production	26.9	15.6	42
Level of exports	24.9	13.2	47
Revenues (1,000 million $)	282	132	53.2

Sources: World Tables, 1991, IBRD; Petroleum Economist Tables.

Three independent factors had contributed to OPEC's overall market decline. First, the change in the transformation of the production structure towards the less energy intensive service sector. Second, the implementation of fiscal policies aimed at decreasing oil consumption. Third, the constant increases in non-OPEC oil production, as the following data in Table 6.2 show.

Table 6.2   Non-OPEC production, 1981-1986. Selected countries (million b/d)

	1981	1982	1983	1984	1985	1986
US	10,181	10,199	10,247	10,509	10,580	10,231
Mexico	2,547	3,003	2,946	3,013	3,018	2,767
UK	1,831	2,118	2,358	2,574	2,610	2,602
Norway	505	523	648	745	815	906
Canada	1,616	1,587	1,665	1,899	1,813	1,798
Non-OPEC*	21,080	21,886	23,044	24,355	24,945	24,836
OPEC	22,694	19,287	17,759	17,529	16,365	18,694

* Includes US, Canada, Mexico, Brazil, Argentina, Australia, Oman, UK, and Norway.

Source: Petroleum Economist Tables.

Despite GDP improvements between 1983 and 1985, demand for OPEC oil in the OECD countries had failed to rise. In fact, between those years the relation between net oil imports and GDP indicators went in opposite directions. This unequal balance was particularly noticeable in the year 1985, even though prices for oil had dropped. Only in the year 1986, when prices collapsed, did the level of exports catch up with the rise in GDP figures.

Although its overall production had decreased by 15% in comparison to the previous year, the year 1985 was crucial for OPEC. It had to come to terms with the inefficiency of the quota system to achieve the desired control of the market and with the continuing advance of challenging competitors outside the Organisation. In the UK and the US significant measures to regulate the energy market were implemented. BNOC was abolished in the spring of 1985 by the Thatcher administration in an attempt to minimise the government's involvement in the oil sector. In the US the deregulation of the energy market implemented by the successive Reagan administrations added more strength to the logic of the free market[17]. Around the same time, and in outright violation of OPEC's quotas, Nigeria adopted its policy of 'Nigeria first' in an effort to increase output and to meet the demands of its treasury[18]. In fact, Nigeria was only being outspoken on an issue that most OPEC producers had been consistent: the need to fulfil government financial needs was more pressing than allegiance to OPEC's collective action precepts.

OPEC members were basically left with two choices in order to reverse their accrued loss of market share; to reduce prices or to influence the market through price or quota fixation instruments, a strategy that had resulted in the implementation of conservationist and energy-substitution policies by consumer countries. Recovery in non-OPEC areas and a failure to control the market left the Organisation with few viable options. However, OPEC's largest producer, Saudi Arabia, finally brought about the policy change. This country, which due to its sheer importance and large reserves enjoys the strongest bargaining role within the Organisation, in 1983 agreed to take on the role of swing producer in an effort to modify its production levels in order to support the OPEC price. However, for Saudi Arabia the cost of sticking to its role as swing producer soon proved to be too high, especially in the light of decreasing market presence and its corollary the enormous fall in revenues. Ever-fiercer competition from non-OPEC producers and the constant violation of the quotas assigned by its OPEC counterparts pressed the Saudi government to embrace in 1985 a radical policy shift. When Saudi Arabia abandoned its role as swing producer and adopted a strategy to increase its market share by subjecting the price of its crude to the market, the other member countries were compelled to follow suit and offer crude at competitive prices. As the rest of OPEC members immediately followed Saudi Arabia's policy to maintain and enlarge market share, there was no longer an OPEC-fixed price. The logic of the market became the ruler of the oil business, providing an obvious blow to the Organisation's ethos. What ensued was, inevitably, a price war[19].

Saudi Arabia's policy to regain market share was implemented through the establishment of netback deals between ARAMCO and clients in key markets. The idea of sticking to a fixed price was abandoned. Within netback deals ARAMCO did not fix any specific price for the crude sold to the refineries; prices were to be calculated according to what the products fetched in the market. Under such arrangements, the refiner was encouraged to sell more products and the producer company to supply increasing volumes of crude. As a result, refineries began making profits once again, as they were called to process increasing volumes of crude. In this context of outright competition for markets, netback deals began to proliferate. Those companies which possessed refineries in key markets registered a clear advantage over those which were not vertically-integrated[20]. PDVSA's rationale for acquiring assets in the Gelsenkirchen refinery of Veba Oel obtained further significance as netback arrangements sprawled. Thus, in the 1986 context, PDVSA's policy-makers obtained political support for launching a new phase in its policy of vertical integration. ·

OPEC's production grew significantly during 1986. As a result of its policy to enlarge market share, OPEC oil production went from 16,365 million b/d in 1985 to 18,649 million b/d in 1986. However, this policy caused the price of the barrel to plummet. In this context, the budgetary situation of many OPEC governments became critical. In the atmosphere of price disarray that characterised the first half of 1986, the price of the Brent Blend that sold at \$26/b in January dropped to \$10 in April, picking up to \$15 a month later. The average price for this crude in 1986 was \$14.42, less that half the price of the previous year. Table 6.3 shows the sharp drop in spot prices for the oil barrel between 1985 and 1986.

Table 6.3   Average barrel prices for selected crudes, 1985 and 1986 (in dollars)

	Dubai (32°)	Brent (38°)	WTI (40°)
1985	26.49	27.60	27.96
1986	13.03	14.42	15.14

Source: Petroleum Economist, 1985-1986.

Most of OPEC's output increase had, in fact, found its way into stocks, a phenomenon that until then producers had not seriously considered[21]. Fearing further market disruptions, consumers began acquiring large volumes when the opportunity to obtain a lower price for the barrel arose during the first half of 1986. In the second half, however, there was no apparent need to maintain the same rate of imports, since demand had been satisfied in the short run.

The economic policy of the Lusinchi administration: from contraction to unwise relaxation

The response of the Lusinchi administration to the critical 1985 oil market situation affecting government accounts was the implementation of a policy of austerity and spending cuts, similar to that implemented at the beginning (1979-81) of the previous administration. Hopes that the conflict between Iran and Iraq would place Venezuela as the next possible candidate to make up for the loss of important amounts of crude from the world markets remained unfulfilled. The creators of the VII National Plan (1984-88) translated their expectations of high oil revenues into government guidelines that soon proved unrealistic. Government planners had estimated an important increase in the bill of oil exports. However, as Table 6.4 demonstrates both the volume of oil exports and the amounts received for them kept dwindling alarmingly after 1984.

Table 6.4 Oil production and revenues in Venezuela, 1984-1988

	Oil Production (b/d)	Revenues (million $)	Revenues (million Bs)
1984	1,799	11,000	66,050
1985	1,681	9,935	59,609
1986	1,731	7,422	44,530
1987	1,729	5,612	81,369
1988	1,825	6,316	91,581

* Between 1984 and 1986, Bs 6.00 to $1; between 1987 and 1988, Bs 14.50 to $ 1.

Source: Central Bank Data.

The acute financial crisis that inaugurated the Lusinchi administration in 1984 forced the government to adopt restrictive measures in tune with IMF recommendations. One of the administration's main targets was to reduce the fiscal deficit that had reached $2,790 million at the end of 1983. Real investment in both infrastructure and productive projects was reduced[22]. Using the devaluation of the currency mechanism to cover part of the financial deficit, the Lusinchi government implemented a new currency devaluation in February 1984: from Bs 6.00 to $1 the official rate descended to Bs 7.50 to $1[23]. A further and more drastic devaluation was applied in December 1986; the currency was devalued 93%, reaching Bs 14.50 to $1[24].

As a result of the initial contraction measures applied between 1984 and 1986, real per-capita GDP fell dramatically during those years. Inflation scored 12.5% annually. The unemployment rate went from 7.79% in 1983 to 13.06% in 1985, however improving thereafter to reach 7.32% in electoral year 1988 when the government relaxed its policies of austerity[25]. The public sector managed to consolidate huge current account surpluses of $5,300 million in 1984 and $3,000 million in 1985. These surpluses in the government's current account were used, more or less in equal proportions to foster the accumulation of foreign exchange reserves in the Central

Bank, amortise payments of outstanding foreign debt, and continue financing further capital flight[26]. From 1983 to 1985 real per-capita GDP contracted 15%, at the same time that the government's current account accumulated a surplus of $13,000 million[27].

One of the first issues the Lusinchi administration had to deal with was the service of the foreign debt, which amounted to $27,000 million in 1983, when about 52% of the public sector obligations with international creditors were due for payment[28]. The negotiations to agree on a restructuring plan began in earnest as soon as the Lusinchi administration took power in 1984. But it was only in February 1986[29] that the government signed a plan with the international creditors to pay $750 million up front and the rest in a period of twelve years and a half with interest rate payments of 1.125% over LIBOR (London Interbank Offered Rate). Severely criticised for not including a grace period for amortisation and for ruling out the possibility of acquiring new loans –contrasting with plans reached by other Latin American debtors– the first restructuring plan was soon abandoned as the collapse of oil prices rendered its observance unrealistic. Another agreement was negotiated in 1987, only adding minor modifications to the earlier plan. In the period 1984-88, the government used $9,000 million from its foreign reserves to service debt payments. The economic policy implemented by the Lusinchi administration after 1986 resulted in a dramatic depletion of the country's foreign reserves, which went from $13,750 million in 1985 to $6,671 million in 1988[30]. Venezuela was then the only Latin America country paying capital when servicing its foreign debt[31].

. After the austerity measures were slackened in 1986, a highly inappropriate moment due to the oil market situation, the government decided to boost the economy by launching the expansion of the public sector. Prices were frozen and interest rates were kept at unreasonably low levels. Also, public sector salaries were raised by decree and minimum salaries were established for both rural and urban workers. Encouraged both by high levels of government expenditures and with the measures to control prices, the inflation rate decreased from 12.94% in 1984 to 7.32% in 1988. The initial austerity measures implemented during the first two years of the Lusinchi administration had given way to a policy of high public expenditure levels, price controls, and low interest rates. The government was enjoying the benefits of the massive 1986 devaluation that increased the national currency in government accounts. And all of this in the context of collapsing oil prices.

As elections approached the government did not want to reverse to more moderate and austere economic policies. The data in Table 6.5 show the dramatic reduction in the balance of payments' current account and in the international reserves that took place during the Lusinchi administration.

Table 6.5　Selected balance of payments' account, 1984-1988 (1,000 million dollars)

	1984	1985	1986	1987	1988
Current account	5.4	3.1	-1.5	-1.1	-4.9
Trade balance	8.7	6.8	1.3	1.7	0.5
Capital account	-3.8	-1.1	-1.4	0.2	0.1
Net public borrowing	-1.8	-0.8	-1.2	-1.2	0.7
Balance of payments	1.6	2	-3	-0.9	0.5
hange in net reserves	1.9	1.8	-3.8	-0.7	-4.5
International reserves	13.7	15.5	11.7	10.7	7.8
Central Bank	12.4	13.7	9.8	9.3	6.6
FIV	1.2	1.7	1.8	1.4	0.4

Sources: M. Rodríguez. *Public sector behaviour in Venezuela, 1970-1985.* IESA, Caracas, 1988; Central Bank Data.

Government financial demands on the oil sector

The initial austerity measures implemented across the board in the public sector, especially between 1984 and 1985, meant for PDVSA a better rationalisation of its operations and expenses: cuts were implemented in wage bills and in purchases of intermediate goods and services. Oil sector investments had been sharply reduced after 1983. This allowed a high level of savings in 1984, which in turn was reduced to almost half in 1985 as government guidelines imposed a high level of transfer to the treasury. After the uproar created by the Veba Oel case, the oil industry had not undertaken any major investments. The savings and investment flows of the oil industry between 1983 and 1985 resulted in the accumulation of a significant surplus during that period. PDVSA's large surplus in 1984 was, as required by law, deposited in the Central Bank. The contributions of the oil industry were prevented from financing the additional capital needed to promote growth, as the Lusinchi administration, adhering to its initial policy of contraction, was reluctant to allow those funds to enter the economy. The data in Table 6.6 depict the behaviour of the oil sector between 1983 and 1985, which resembled that of the entire public sector subject to austerity policies.

**Table 6.6   Oil sector accounts, 1983-1985
            (% of GDP)**

	1983	1984	1985
Current revenue	22.4	27.6	23.8
Operational (sales)	21.9	27.3	23.5
Other	0.5	0.3	0.3
Current expenditures	19.2	22	21.1
Operational*	4.8	4.1	4.2
Transfer to the govt.	14.4	17.9	16.9
Savings	3.2	5.6	2.7
Investment	4	3	3.2
Surplus or deficit	-0.8	2.6	0.5

* Operational: wages, salaries, purchase of goods and services.

Sources: M. Rodríguez. *Op. cit.*; Central Bank Data.

After having declined in 1983, the government revenue situation sharply improved due to the devaluation of the bolívar in early 1984. However, it deteriorated between 1985 and 1986, only to improve again with a new massive devaluation at the end of 1986. As a result of the devaluations of 1984 and 1986, capital transfers to the central government in local currency were significant. As a consequence of a decreasing price for the barrel and of a loss of market share –exports went from 1.79 million b/d in 1984 to 1.68 million b/d in 1985– the value of the oil export bill went from $11,000 million to $9,934 million during those years. Meanwhile, oil prices kept plummeting. During 1986, the oil export bill experienced a sharp fall, largely as a result of the price war waged among OPEC members. In order to compensate for this fall, production levels increased from 1986 onwards, slightly dropping in 1985, as seen in Table 6.4. Significant changes in export revenues were not, however, noticeable until 1988, when important contributions were made to the treasury, as a result of the maxi-devaluation of 1986 that multiplied in local currency the value of the export bill in dollars. The 1986 oil sector's contribution to the treasury was of $7,422 (Bs 44,530 million; Bs 6 = $1), after having reached the level of $9,935

(Bs 59,609 million; Bs 14.5 = $1) in 1985. In 1988 it was $6,316 (Bs 91,581 million; Bs 14.5 = $1), when average annual production was higher than during the previous five-year period.

During the year 1986, as the government's financial situation deteriorated, its demands on the oil industry became more pressing. The central government increasingly demanded PDVSA to finance infrastructure projects[32]. During the year 1985 PDVSA had to close important parts of its production. Also, in order to keep a tighter grip over the industry's policies, the executive, through the Ministry of Energy, increased its control of PDVSA. Thus, the Ministry began to decide over matters which the industry considered as its sole domain, such as the appointment of presidents for the affiliated companies and the assignation of salaries to the industry's directors[33].

Conflict over price fixation formula: disagreement between the Ministry and the SOE

The way policy was formulated concerning the fixation of prices provided an interesting example of decision-making in so far as it highlighted the tension between the oil industry managers and the executive, thus reflecting the clear differentiation between 'engineers' and 'commissars' established in Chapter I. A power crisis between the two sets of oil policy-makers was set in motion. OPEC fixed crude prices. Thus, PDVSA was required to have its prices approved by the Ministry. The controversy over the oil industry's freedom to set its own prices was part of Brígido Natera's decision to resign as president of PDVSA.

At the beginning of 1986 when oil prices were at a low level, PDVSA's policy-makers, perhaps foreseeing the scenario that was to characterise that year's price collapse, were demanding for the industry the right to fix prices unilaterally, without the intervention and approval of the Ministry of Energy. Arturo Hernández Grisanti, then Energy Minister, stressed his allegiance to OPEC's precepts by refusing to allow the industry the freedom to fix export prices. This position was the source of acerbic criticism by the industry's policy-makers who thought the executive was assuming roles for which it was unprepared. Former PDVSA president, Andrés Sosa Pietri, explained as follows the Ministry's interference in what the industry considered to be one of its roles:

> Once again misinformed about the market realities, the Ministry of Energy clung to prices that kept clients at a distance. In January 1986, exports were

lower than 1 million b/d. The government was alarmed and it had good reasons for being so. Because of having been interfering in issues that did not properly understand (and does not have to understand), it reduced and controlled production, it fixed artificial prices, affecting fundamental programmes for the consolidation and the development of PDVSA[34].

In the decision-making process that leads to policy adoption the power of the industry managers is significant. One of the ways to exercise this power is by exerting control over the information handled. Since, as mentioned earlier, the Ministry requires the industry's input of information in order to establish policy guidelines, managers enjoy the best position in the decision-making process. The type of information provided to the government body often influences policy orientations. As Mancur Olsen explained:

> The covert collective action of managers can deny information to the decision-making centre. Managers can influence the decision-making in as much as they give the information they want for their own interests[35].

The dependence of the Ministry on PDVSA for information and highly specialised skills has increasingly shifted the balance of power from the executive to the industry's policy-makers within the process of oil policy-making. The Ministry's power as decision-making centre, as much as its resources, has been diminishing since nationalisation. In the following anecdotal comment, a former PDVSA manager provides an example of this shift in the balance of power in favour of the industry:

> Often, we have to pay them a taxi, so that they [Ministry officials] can come to PDVSA and discuss certain matters[36].

Natera, PDVSA's president, convinced President Lusinchi to allow PDVSA to fix prices in an autonomous way in a moment of extreme market volatility. The decision favouring the industry in the fixation of export prices was taken when the Energy Minister, Arturo Hernández Grisanti, was out of the country. PDVSA's managers explained how sales were at a minimum level and that the alarmingly low production levels registered in 1985 could not continue. In fact, the 1985 production levels of 1,681,000 b/d had been the country's lowest since 1973. When Minister Hernández, who had strongly fought this battle against PDVSA, knew of the decision taken at the highest political level during his absence, the relationship between the industry and the Ministry quickly deteriorated[37]. Quirós Corradi, former president of MARAVEN, explained this event as follows:

Once Hernández arrived, convinced that previously unquestionable powers had been taken away from him, he adopted a bitter and vengeful attitude towards the president of PDVSA, making him wait for hours for meetings, suddenly cancelling appointments, and so on. Eventually, Natera decided to resign[38].

In fact, the right to set prices by the Ministry was a hard-fought battle won against the oil MNs in 1970, a victory that the executive was not easily going to abandon. Expecting the Ministry to do otherwise would be to misunderstand the crucial role played by the Ministry and politicians in bringing about the nationalisation of the oil industry. In 1970, the Venezuelan government won the battle against the oil MNs and began fixing export values unilaterally. According to Giacopini Zárraga, long-time advisor to the presidents of PDVSA, 'this reform was attributed to AD, and in particular to Arturo Hernández Grisanti'[39]. It was then hardly surprising that in 1984, Hernández, as Energy Ministry, was not going to defend for the Ministry the battle won against the oil MNs more than a decade ago.

Policy continuation: assessment and increments on the previous implementation phase

A manager of PDVSA's subsidiary, LAGOVEN, described the process of looking for political support between the conflict-ridden time of the signing of the Veba Oel contract and the price debacle of 1986:

> From 1983 to 1985 nothing happened; no contracts materialised, even though PDVSA continued to establish contacts and kept negotiating with many companies. Contacts were made with a lot of people. In 1986 the negotiations bore fruit. The price of the oil barrel fell. It was the time when oil companies were fearful and apprehensive. The government worried and realised that the second phase of the internationalisation strategy had to be relaunched. The myth about the convenience or not of the internationalisation of the oil industry ceased. It became clear in the minds of the political élite that it was necessary. The process went on without hindrance from the political class[40].

In a Congress dominated by AD, the former opponents of internationalisation, many of them from AD, found fewer excuses to pursue their criticism of the industry's policy choice. Under President Lusinchi, PDVSA set out in 1986 'to convince the political class about the benefits of going downstream'[41]. Industry managers 'invited politicians to explain the policy to them, to convince them of the benefits of the Veba Oel contract. And they agreed'[42]. As of 1986, with the imminence of a sudden price collapse and its accompanying dramatic shortage of income for the central government, 'there was a general understanding of the fact that oil [was] a business'[43]. Between the silencing of the political opposition to PDVSA's vertical-integration strategy and the second phase of its implementation in 1986, numerous contacts were established between the industry's managers and the representatives of political parties. An industry policy-maker depicted this crucial period for the continuation of the policy as follows:

> We then called the representatives of the political parties to explain the policy. They understood that Venezuela was more and more an exporter of products, and less and less of crude. The internationalisation policy was the result of this need. There were discussions about Article 5, but they finally agreed that the internationalisation policy did not contradict the Article. This time the discussions did not go to Congress; it was only discussed with the leaders of political parties. The executive took the lead in explaining to the political forces[44].

After 'three years of fighting, talks, conferences, and contacts to convince Congress'[45], PDVSA's policy-makers were able in 1986 to gain approval for their policy-choice. President Lusinchi 'gave a blank cheque to PDVSA'[46]. In fact, he had agreed with the benefits of the vertical-integration policy before he became President, 'even since the times of President Luis Herrera'[47]. Lusinchi appeased PDVSA's policy-makers by telling them to continue with their policy choice. In their contacts with Congress and with the executive, PDVSA's policy-makers found fewer obstacles when explaining their policy choice and the benefits of increasing the vertical-integration strategy precisely in the context of loss of market share. Thus, opposition to PDVSA's policy choice gradually dwindled. Juan Chacín, PDVSA's president during most part of the Lusinchi administration depicted as follows the process that preceded the second implementation phase of the oil industry's vertical-integration policy:

> In 1985, it was decided to launch again the internationalisation process and PDVSA went to the government with those ideas. We told the government that we had to secure markets. We gathered all our efforts to try to convince the political class of the need for internationalisation. This was taken to the President [Lusinchi]; he liked the idea and gave his approval to the internationalisation programme. The President said that he would be in charge

of convincing politicians about it. There were meetings with different groups in the Presidency. We did presentations about the advantages of the strategy and about the dangers of not doing it. Then, from 1986 on, the purchase of the different systems of commercialisation of Citgo, Champlin, UNO-VEN, etc. began to be approved[48].

Despite apparent consensus, not all political factions were convinced of the benefits and needs to implement the internationalisation policy. The opposition voices were temporarily silenced, but not totally eradicated from the political arena. Since the decision to grant political legitimacy had been taken by the President, and not as a result of a Congress decision, opposition to the company's efforts to become an oil MN was not totally eradicated. As previously argued, this suggests that the policy was conferred a partial political legitimacy. Opposition to PDVSA's policy was only temporarily silenced, and was likely to reappear at a later phase of the policy implementation process. The tensions inherent in oil policy-making processes remained latent. As will be shown in Chapter VII, opposition to further internationalisation reappeared when the industry decided to acquire the remaining 50% of Citgo's share in an attempt to become the company's sole owner. Opponents to the industry's policy choice would often make themselves heard through the advocacy of more 'internalisation', referring to the need to concentrate on the upstream domestic market. As Juan Chacín put it:

> Even in 1986 not all politicians agreed with it. Pérez, for instance, during his political campaign, said no more internationalisation, but internalisation[49].

The period of calm that had followed the silencing of political opposition to the industry's policy choice was characterised by the evaluation and long-term planning of the internationalisation strategy. Consensus over the success of the implementation of the Veba Oel contract was an important factor in determining the continuation of the internationalisation policy. Despite the impasse with Congress, the implementation of the Veba Oel contract had been considered successful by PDVSA's policy-makers, as the following comments demonstrate:

> The rates of return of a business such as Veba Oel were huge, because although the prices went down, the price of products did not go down in the market that much, and Veba Oel produced mostly products[50].
> With Veba Oel PDVSA optimised volumes and logistic feasibility[51].

The association with Veba Oel had been judged a good strategic move by the industry, and there was no reason to stop implementing the policy that brought it about. In terms of financial gains, victory over Congress, and strategic development, the first policy test had given the expected results: thanks to the joint venture with Veba Oel, PDVSA had strengthened its presence in the European market. Strategic goals became more conscious policy guidelines, once the first policy test was deemed successful. A more coherent set of rationales for pursuing the internationalisation policy sprang up after 1984: the perception of policy-makers as to the undeniable success of the first phase in the implementation of the policy determined its continuation. An important policy-maker of the industry summarised this factor as follows:

> The decision would be taken in relation to the success or not of the policy. In the case of the internationalisation, the success of the first association provided the rationale for the second phase of policy implementation[52].
> There was not a think-tank permanently thinking about which strategy to adopt. Since we had registered some successes we therefore continued with policy implementation[53].

Although 'there were some strategic guidelines'[54] during the policy's formulation phase, the ensuing period was characterised by the conscious creation of policy guidelines by a team of policy-makers resembling a think-tank. PDVSA's policy-makers set out to gain strategic and technical legitimacy for the policy implemented, by seeking 'the legal, financial, and ecological advice of experts, both domestically and internationally'[55]. They sought to turn a strategic objective into a long-term policy orientation.

The reappraisal of the first phase of policy implementation was a process carried out in a rational and incremental way. It can be considered as rational in so far as policy-makers used a fair amount of information to formulate their policy orientation; and incremental as it built upon the success of the first phase of policy implementation to expand and increase the scope of subsequent implementation phases. In 1985 PDVSA's policy-makers analysed different policy options, in a clear attempt to identify and establish a hierarchy of the priorities that would best attain the goals targeted[56]. Directed by Juan Carlos Gómez, a long-time manager in the industry, a policy analysis team was designated for that purpose. Gómez pointed out the following:

> The group's role included a thorough assessment of the situation in Venezuela, regarding supply, production capacity, and needs to integrate

vertically, geographical location, types of crude, condition of the industry, types of clients, and so on. The study was confidential, and only 20 copies were made[57].

The internationalisation policy was conceived to comply with such factors. Two elements were underlined amongst the advantages presented by PDVSA: Venezuela's convenient geographic position and PDVSA's recognised efficiency in meeting commitments with its clients[58]. Paul Reimpall remarked that at that time,

All aspects of the policy and its risks were analysed... The [internationalisation] policy adopted a clearer form and was devised as a long-term strategy[59].

Gómez further depicted this period of evaluation of PDVSA's internationalisation policy as follows:

The industry's policy-makers designed how and where to go with the internationalisation, the kind of association, the kind of company, the type of partner. In September 1985, PDVSA hired the services of an external company of consultants. They had a data bank and we studied which was the best possibility... We decided to participate in everything 50-50, market decisions, decision-making, etc.[60].

The ideal partner was the one able to offer a good degree of compatibility between market position and access to the upstream sector. The proportion for the partnership adopted was the 50-50 asset ownership. This equal basis partnership was considered to be the most convenient by PDVSA's policy-makers.

It posed less problems to manage and required a constant communication with the partner; also because it provided a certain degree of security against other local companies; anyway, it was better not to be entirely foreign[61].
The 50-50 equal scheme allowed a working partnership in every sense of the term, from risk taking to an effective say in running the business[62].

The 50-50 formula finally adopted as the best form of partnership within the joint-venture associations was not, however, the first one suggested by the companies of advisors contracted out to analyse the best options. An oil industry policy-maker explained that,

National and international advisors had not advised PDVSA to go into 50-50 partnerships. They told us that it was better to accept a position of majority partner or of minority subordinate. In 50-50 associations it is difficult to establish the rules of the game. When one company has the majority there is no need to devise and plan the divorce during the honeymoon, as it would be the case when there is an equal partnership[63].

In a detailed process of selection of companies likely to be interested in associations with PDVSA, a list of more than 200 companies was drawn. Later on, fifteen of them were short-listed as possible candidates. PDVSA's policy-makers studied the background of the possible partners 'and considered if there was interest from their side'[64]. They also took into consideration the company's internal decision-making structure, 'if there existed a [close] relation between the president and the chairman, and then downwards'[65]. Possible clients were identified in Europe and in the US.

Europe was more used to processing light crude. In the US there were more refineries able to produce Venezuelan crude[66].

PDVSA's policy evaluation paper identified Citgo, Marathon, and Chevron in the US market as possible candidates. The joint-venture agreements currently implemented with Nynäs and Citgo 'were [directly] issued from the study carried out in 1985'[67]. In the US market, 'Citgo and Champlin were the favourite companies. Already, those refineries processed Venezuelan crude'[68]. As explained in Chapter III, during PDVSA's formative years refining patterns had been partially modified to satisfy the needs of the North American market: the US represented a natural target when considering purchasing refineries abroad[69]. And as a PDVSA policy-maker mentioned:

The US has refineries with very good conversion facilities. Citgo's facilities are excellent; they do not produce residuals[70].

The ideal potential refining partner had to possess an important distribution network and not be integrated upstream. Most oil MNs were integrated, and therefore were excluded from being potential partners. Furthermore, precise economic and political considerations were taken into account by the policy evaluation study.

Countries like Spain, France, and Brazil with a tradition of having regulated markets were not eligible[71].

The political system of those countries had to be stable and [present] few risks as nations[72].

PDVSA rejected several offers to establish deals that fell outside the type of downstream policy the industry had formulated. Offers from the UK, France, and Spain were considered but did not comply with PDVSA's internationalisation policy. The team of policy evaluators rejected offers from France because of its policy of *dirigisme* aimed at controlling the domestic energy market. Also, PDVSA rejected a deal from Spain's REPSOL because it did not contemplate ownership of refinery assets. In this case, PDVSA's policy-makers explained that,

> Spain wanted to keep the cake and eat it, only giving a percentage (more or less 5%) for the sales, in a sort of netback agreement. Like France and unlike Germany, Spain had a very controlled domestic market with fixed prices by the government; it also had a poor refining and manufacturing infrastructure which was used to processing crude from the North of Africa[73].
> The Spanish were ready to negotiate the association, but only as long as they kept control over the venture. They would later pay PDVSA for the supply of crude. But this did not allow us to gain access to the clients, neither did this give PDVSA a chance to participate in the decision-making process. [Spain] favoured the netback scheme[74].

PDVSA's policy-makers were seeking to purchase refinery assets abroad in order to enlarge market share and increase corporate freedom. The agreement with Veba Oel had offered this possibility. France and Spain, however, were more interested in the establishment of netback deals, which, more short-term oriented, did not allow PDVSA's managers to attain such objectives.

Rationales for policy adoption

Although most of the criteria used to implement the internationalisation policy were noticeable during the first phase of its implementation, they became clearer policy goals during the policy evaluation phase between 1984 and 1986. During this phase, PDVSA's decision-makers identified three major policy goals, loosely grouped as technical, political, and strategic[75]. With the internationalisation, PDVSA's policy-makers had sought to minimise the effects of the market's sudden upheavals, an aim that was regarded as a technical one. The political goal was the need to minimise government demands and meddling in policy orientations. Policy-makers had learnt from the experience with the political actors during the first phase of policy implementation, when the clash with the legislature had posed a real threat to policy continuation. One of the ways of minimising the possibility of Congress opposition was the *fait-accompli* approach to policy implementation, explained earlier in this chapter. In turn, becoming a MN also meant minimising the direct control of the executive on decision-making processes and, by the same token, the degree of accountability to the legislature. The third goal was a strategic one, as PDVSA sought to become a vertically-integrated oil MN, thus surpassing the stage of being merely an oil exporter[76].

Another rationale for the establishment of joint ventures was that the oil industry would pay small amounts of cash for purchasing the refineries. As will be further explained in Chapter 7, whenever there were cash payments involved in the purchase of refinery assets, PDVSA paid out relatively small amounts of money. Often, oil supplies and replacement of inventories were the main mechanisms used to obtain cash advances from different financial sources[77]. A PDVSA policy-maker recalled that,

> The money paid in cash was very little. If one considers what PDVSA actually paid for purchasing marketing channels for about 700,000 b/d it was an insignificant amount[78].

The upgrading of heavy crude as a motive for policy implementation

The large proportion of Venezuela's crude reserves, consisting mostly of heavy and extra-heavy crudes, posed particular market risks. From the outset,

> PDVSA's policy-makers had realised that the largest part of Venezuela's production, especially the heavy crude production, entailed certain risks[79].

Finding an outlet for this type of crude had been a concern of PDVSA's policy-makers since the company's creation. The internationalisation policy was a clear attempt to address this problem. The possibility of placing significant amounts of heavy crude was an important criterion when establishing association contracts. A high official from the Ministry of Energy explained the following:

> With the internationalisation the oil industry sought two objectives: to secure markets and to process and place heavy crude[80].

Although the initial supplies to Veba Oel were made up of light crude, from the start there were plans to supply and process heavy crude in the Ruhr Oel refinery. For the subsequent phase of policy implementation, the explicit intention to supply heavy crude became a more explicit policy goal.

In the US, from the beginning we talked about processing heavy crude. Both Citgo and Champlin are able to process medium and heavy crude. All of Citgo's refineries are for heavy crude. In the US the policy of securing market for heavy crude has been attained through Citgo, and to a lesser extent through UNO-VEN. By now, UNO-VEN, which is the only US refinery partially owned by Citgo (the rest are owned 100%), has been processing medium and light crude. In Europe the policy to process heavy crude has been accomplished with Nynäs and Ruhr Oel, where there are more plans to develop heavy crude processes. Swedish Nynäs is specialised in processing naphthenic lubricants, asphalt, heavy and extra-heavy crudes[81].

Increasing the sale of heavy crude was one of the original objectives to be pursued with the internationalisation strategy. However, this goal soon proved difficult to attain in the context of market realities: low processing costs and a steady demand for light crude rendered less attractive the processing of heavy crude abroad. Despite this, criticism of PDVSA's failure to channel heavy crude to its refineries abroad gradually diminished.

Minimisation of OPEC's control as a rationale for policy implementation

PDVSA's policy-makers have often considered adherence to OPEC a disadvantage, a constraint to sell crude at the price and the volumes the company deems appropriate. Between 1976 and 1986, OPEC members were restricted in their freedom to sell crude at competitive prices. PDVSA's policy-makers regarded their impossibility to fix prices as a handicap, especially in a context where competition by non-OPEC producers proved increasingly difficult to curb. As Gómez put it:

The evaluation group assessed the magnitude of the risks involved in losing markets to other non-OPEC producers[82].

Regarding the disadvantages of being part of OPEC, a PDVSA policy-maker involved in the formulation of the internationalisation policy explained the following:

The disadvantage was that we had a price fixed by OPEC. The only way to change prices was through meetings with the Organisation. The non-OPEC clients used to sell at lower prices. This sealed the decline of the Organisation. Anyway, all that ended in 1986 with the price war. The PDVSA team created to assess the first part of the internationalisation policy concluded that Venezuela had a high level of risk, because other OPEC and non-OPEC producers alike offered more advantages, in so far as their crude quality was better. The group decided that PDVSA needed to look for partners that had refineries with a market. This concept became then much clearer than during the Veba Oel contract[83].

In contrast to the view of the political leadership, most industry policy-makers mistrust OPEC and its alleged capacity to influence the market effectively. PDVSA has always had a love-hate relationship with OPEC, characterised by scepticism of the Organisation's effectiveness to regulate the market. A former PDVSA manager, Humberto Peñaloza, summarised as follows his lack of belief in the Organisation's effectiveness:

OPEC thought that the number of countries was more important than their strength, without thinking about the complexity of the decision-making process that grows according to the number of countries. If OPEC wants to play a more productive rolé it has to restructure itself by including other strong oil exporters... Now [the Organisation] works on a short-term basis. The only time a long-term committee was formed was in Algeria in 1976. Then it stopped[84].

The debate over the benefits of adhering to OPEC or not has also been at the root of the tension between the different actors responsible for oil policy-making: on one side, industry managers, on the other, government officials and political actors. Numerous are the circumstances where oil industry's policy-makers voice their discontent regarding the way government officials pay excessive observance of the Organisation's guidelines. In several opportunities, PDVSA has waged battles to modify production quota limitations. Often, like its OPEC counterparts, the industry has produced more than its assigned quotas.

Andrés Sosa Pietri's period as president of PDVSA (1990-1992) was characterised by constant clashes with Minister of Energy, Celestino Armas over observance of OPEC quotas. In relation to filling the inventories of PDVSA's refineries abroad during the summer of 1990 in preparation for a conflict in the Gulf area, Sosa Pietri wrote that '[PDVSA] had expanded its storage capacity in order to produce beyond its [OPEC] quota'[85]. Sosa Pietri's has overtly compaigned against OPEC[86]. He has repeatedly said that 'Venezuela would not lose anything by pulling out of OPEC'[87].

Government insistence to observe OPEC's policy guidelines has compelled PDVSA to devise mechanisms in order to strengthen Venezuela's bargaining position within the Organisation, in an attempt to increase production quotas. The motive behind this was the need to produce beyond production assigned quotas. Discussions about, on the one hand, the classification and crude composition of its proven reserves and, on the other, about the interpretation of quotas –i.e. whether they apply to production or to the market– are part of PDVSA's willingness to increase production levels. Part of the strategy to expand market share by seeking to increase assigned quotas is the peculiar classification of Venezuelan extra-heavy crude which allows them to be included in the country's reserves. The larger the proven reserves, the more negotiating power a country enjoys for quota allocation within OPEC. Saudi Arabia, with 261.2 billion barrels is by far the member country with the largest proven reserves. In 1995 Venezuela (64.5 billion b.) occupied the sixth position among OPEC countries having the largest crude reserves, behind Iraq (100 billion b.), Kuwait (98 billion b.), Iran (89.3 billion b.), and UAE (98.1 billion b.)[88].

Venezuela's crude classification differs from most oil producers. It is complex and partially reflects PDVSA's willingness to increase the country's proven reserves. According to PDVSA, the API (American Petroleum Industry) classification of Venezuela's crude is as follows: light, $30°$ and more; medium, $22.1°$ to $30°$; heavy, $10.0°$ to $22.2°$; extra-heavy, $0.0°$ to $10.0°$. Due to its physical characteristics and to the difficulty involved in processing it, most of the crudes in Venezuela's reserves feature in the statistics differently than other producing countries. Some observers have argued that Venezuela's extra-heavy crude from the Orinoco Belt region, similar to some tar sands or shale deposits, should not be considered as part of the country's crude reserves[89]. In Venezuela, however, a similar type of crude abundant in the Orinoco Belt, is included in the country's reserves. This type of crude, in fact, amounts to almost one third of the country's proven reserves. In 1995 Venezuela's reserves were made up of 19.8 billion b. of light and medium crude; 14.7 billion b. of heavy and extra-heavy; 29.5 billion b. of Orinoco Belt crude; and 2.3 billion b. of Orinoco bitumen. In fact, 72% of the country's reserves are made up of crude under API $22°$ [90].

The application in 1986 of a different system of accounting for the types of crude that make up the country's reserves led to the inclusion that year of 26 billion barrels of so-called 'easily recoverable' extra-heavy crude found in the Orinoco Belt area[91]. The timing for the decision was significant: the oil price collapse had generated aggressive policy responses aimed at increasing the country's market share. The shift in the criteria allowing the inclusion of extra-heavy crude in the country's proven reserves and the expansion of the second phase of the vertical integration strategy were among the most important policy responses to the oil market difficulties. If Venezuela includes its extra-heavy crude from the Orinoco Belt, it would have the largest world oil proven reserves with 333.3 billion barrels, even larger than Saudi Arabia's.

The issue regarding the interpretation of quotas is indeed more pertinent to our case study of the vertical-integration policy. If quotas refer to production, the space to manoeuvre in order to bypass them is limited. However, if they refer to exports, then there is no apparent obstacle for the purchase of crude abroad in order to maintain stocks in PDVSA's partially or totally owned refineries. During Sosa Pietri's term as PDVSA's president, conflict settled in between PDVSA, encouraging the accumulation of inventories – 'preparing for any change in the official strategy or world event that would allow it to sell beyond its quota'[92] – and the Minister of Energy, who interpreted quotas as referring to production[93].

Although some observers argue that avoiding OPEC's impact over industry policy guidelines –regarding price-fixation or quota imposition– had nothing to do with the strategy to purchase DFIs in the form of refinery assets[94], others held an opposite view and recognised the anti-OPEC element inherent in the internationalisation policy.

> The internationalisation is in collision with OPEC, and that feeds the anti-internationalisation position of Third World oriented politicians[95].
>
> The internationalisation is a way to evade OPEC's quota. There are 600,000 b/d that do not show anywhere. Where are they? The official figures do not show them. There is a suspicion that they are in inventories, being accumulated in order to ease the acquisition of new refineries abroad[96].

The vertical-integration policy, by providing PDVSA access to refineries abroad, created the possibility to accumulate significant volumes of crude inventories that can be easily released as need may arise. An oil industry manager pointed out that,

> In order to have a good bargaining position in OPEC, Venezuela needs to have a secure and large market. Other countries do not have that market and their power to negotiate in OPEC is weak. It is not so much having production capacity, but market availability[97].

Further joint ventures in the second phase of policy implementation

In 1986 the acquisition in the US and the leasing in the Caribbean of refinery assets featured the second phase of PDVSA's vertical integration policy. This took place against a background of adverse market situation and government financial crisis.

Apart from the lease of the Curaçao refinery, the first significant contract in the second phase of implementation of the internationalisation policy was the acquisition in June 1986 of 50% assets of AB Nynäs, which was owned by the Swedish conglomerate Axel Johnson and Sveriges Investeringsbank. The assets were acquired for about $23.5 million (165 million Swedish kronors).

The Nynäs's joint venture was considered a small business, one that allowed PDVSA's policy-makers to re-launch their policy without meeting the opposition of Congress. In 1986, in the middle of the price collapse,

> The Nynäs deal was accepted; it was a small business, and [at the time] politicians had other concerns[98].

The 50% acquisition of Nynäs was a step in the strategy to consolidate PDVSA's sales of heavy crude and naphthenic products in the European market. Nynäs was different from the previous deal with Veba Oel in that it 'corresponded to a strategy to defend naphthenic production in the market'[99]. The joint venture with Axel Johnson in Nynäs fitted 'perfectly well PDVSA's strategy'[100] to expand its share in the market for asphalt and lubricants. Nynäs was a long-time client of PDVSA, and by the 1980s it had become an important manufacturer of specialised naphthenic products. Nynäs possessed a significant network of distribution terminals across Europe. Thanks to the association with Nynäs, 'PDVSA has an important market for asphalt'[101]. Also, the association allowed PDVSA to gain access to three refineries specialised in heavy crude, located in Gothenburg (Sweden), Nynäshamn (Sweden), and Antwerp (Belgium). Furthermore, Nynäs owns two refineries in the UK: Dundee (Scotland) and Eastham (England), the former being totally owned by Nynäs, and the latter 50% in association with Shell. These refineries process almost exclusively Venezuelan high sulphur, extra-heavy crude. Tables 6.7 and 6.8 show key data on Nynäs.

Precisely because it is dedicated to processing heavy crude for the production of asphalt and naphthenic lubricants, Nynäs's market is limited, especially in times of oversupply of light crude. Despite the deal made by Nynäs in the acquisition of important assets of UK's Briggs Oil in 1992,

Table 6.7 PDVSA's interests in Nynäs's refinery production, 1990-1992

	1992*	%	1991	%	1990	%
Refining Capacity** Crude Oil	37		26		26	
Refinery Input Crude Oil	11		15		16	
Average API	11°		11°		11°	
Product Yield						
Asphalt	13	68.40%	10	66.70%	11	68.80%
Distillates	4	21.10%	3	20.00%	4	25.00%
Naphthenic speciality oil	2	10.50%	2	13.30%	1	6.20%
Total product yield	19		15		16	
Utilisation***		63.00%		58.00%		62.00%

* Includes the acquisition in August 1992 of the Dundee refinery with an aggregate refining capacity of 10,000 b/d and of a 50% interest in the Eastham refinery with an aggregate refining capacity of 26,000 b/d.
** Represents the average utilisation rate at the refineries in which Nynäs holds and interest, based on Nynäs's net ownership interest in the total capacity of each such refinery.

Sources: PDVSA's data; *Prospectus PDV America, Inc.*, Salomon Brothers Inc. July 22, 1993.

Table 6.8 Nynäs's refining capacity

	Nynäs's interest (%)	Total cap. (1,000 b/d)	Net. PDVSA ownerhip of ref. cap. (1,000)
Refinery			
Nynäshamn	100	25	13
Antwerp	100	14	7
Gothenburg	100	11	6
Dundee	100	10	5
Eastham	50	26	6
Total refining capacity		86	37

Sources: PDVSA's data; *Prospectus PDV America. Inc.* Salomon Brothers Inc. July 22, 1993.

the Nynäs venture is considered less successful than other refineries within PDVSA's vertically-integrated network[102]. As a result, PDVSA is not likely to increase its involvement in Nynäs. When PDVSA's Swedish partner in the venture decided to sell its shares in 1988, PDVSA declined its right of purchase and decided not to buy the rest of 50% assets: 'PDVSA was not interested'[103]. Instead, Finnish state-owned Neste Öy bought the assets[104]. The ownership transfer was considered satisfactory by PDVSA's policy-makers; 'Neste Öy is a solid company, with many distribution offices in Russia and Eastern Europe'[105].

In 1986, the agreement with Veba Oel was enlarged to cover processing a further 45,000 b/d and to acquire through Ruhr Oel an equity share participation in two refineries in Southern Germany, Neustadt (140 m/b refining capacity) and Schwedt (160 b/d). In the former, Ruhr Oel possesses 50% and in the latter, 37.5%; among the other partners are Mobil, DEA, and a French-Italian consortium[106].

Citgo: PDVSA's most important subsidiary abroad

After the diversification of markets was achieved with the ventures with Ruhr Oel and Nynäs, PDVSA's policy-makers decided to direct efforts to the US market once again, as they had done soon after nationalisation with the transformation of the refinery pattern to fulfil the needs of the US market. A high Ministry official spoke of this process as follows:

> The objective with the internationalisation was to secure and to diversify markets, because we were too concentrated on the US. We reached this goal with Veba Oel. Hence, the shift to the US: Citgo[107].

The first letter of intention leading to the final joint venture was signed between PDVSA's president Brígido Natera and Southland's president, John P. Thompson in February 1986. The initial agreement stipulated that PDVSA send 130,000 b/d to Citgo, with a capacity to process 200,000 b/d. Citgo's refinery complex was considered to be the ninth in importance in the US market[108]. Citgo Petroleum Corporation has been considered as the most successful downstream venture of PDVSA's internationalisation policy. PDVSA's policy-makers were unanimous in praising the acquisition that allowed a larger presence for Venezuelan products in the US market, as an industry manager stated: 'When PDVSA bought Citgo, it was purchasing a wonderful market network to access the client'[109].

The acquisition of Citgo by PDVSA was the result of meeting compatible needs, similar to the process that brought about the joint-venture association with Veba Oel. In 1986 PDVSA acquired Citgo with an initial amount of $290 million; $120 million were given cash and the remaining $170 million in the form of crude supplies. Although the amount paid was significantly higher than in the Veba Oel and Nynäs contracts, PDVSA's policy-makers were faithful to the policy guideline of paying limited amounts for the acquisition of joint ventures abroad, favouring other financial schemes such as inventory replacement and crude supplies. A PDVSA policy-maker who requested that his comments remain anonymous explained how the amount paid by PDVSA was significantly less than the total calculated by the two parts. According to his statements, it is not surprising that PDVSA has considered the deal as very successful from the beginning.

> When we bought Citgo, the company had capacity for 22 million barrels in inventory. We then filled the inventory, that is the 22 million barrels at $15 per barrel, which made $300 and so million. This is how the cost of the acquisition was calculated. However, the actual sale was not done at the price of $15 per barrel, but at the price it cost PDVSA to place a barrel there, a very small amount, which only covers fleet costs, etc. In fact, we paid much less than the amount calculated initially[110].

The first conversations between Southland and PDVSA to acquire Citgo began in 1984. Owned by the Thompson family of Dallas, Texas, which had interests in various businesses ranging from real estate to oil, Southland was the owner of the 7-11 'convenience stores' that combined supermarkets and petrol stations. From the beginning, the Thompson family had the intention of taking over all the 7/11 stores and the distribution networks, but not the refinery. The Thompsons wanted to avoid sharing with partners. However, as business turned difficult and outstanding loans became due for payment, Southland resorted to taking a new partner[111]. Citgo was the old City Service of Oklahoma, which later came to be owned by ARGO and then purchased by Southland, which brought the idea of associating the petrol stations and the stores[112]. Citgo possessed an important coastal pipeline and a significant network of pipelines.

PDVSA's relationship with Southland dates from the time when the latter became interested in acquiring a refinery owned by Occidental Petroleum, situated in Lake Charles, Louisiana. Hardly having any experience in marketing operations, Occidental agreed to establish a partnership with Southland for channelling products processed in the Lake Charles refinery, with a processing capacity of 320,000 b/d. Soon after, Occidental sent a representative to Caracas to negotiate with PDVSA in order to try to secure access to the upstream sector. Like most refineries that did not have secure access to crude, and in the light of general oversupply of refining facilities, Occidental was at the time experiencing losses in its Lake Charles refinery. However, Occidental, which had exploited an oil field in Venezuela between 1968 and nationalisation in 1975, had a problem pending with the government which dated from the days of nationalisation[113]. When Occidental approached PDVSA, the latter replied that no serious negotiations could be undertaken until the pending problem with the Venezuelan government was settled. Unless the issue found a viable solution, PDVSA could not sell crude to Occidental. The dispute was finally settled when the Venezuelan government decided to pay Occidental about $49 million. Consequently, Southland bought Occidental's refinery located in Louisiana, thus beginning the relationship between PDVSA and Southland[114].

The low profile that characterised the negotiations prior to the signing of the joint-venture contract with Southland at the end of 1986 awoke once again the mistrust of political actors in Congress. A PDVSA manager noted that it was difficult to know exactly how the negotiations between PDVSA and Southland took place.

> How did PDVSA go into a partnership with Southland? Nobody knows. The Thompson brothers were nice, I guess. Anyway, nobody will say how the negotiations took place. It was reported that the Thompson brothers said after the deal 'We got them', referring to PDVSA. In Venezuela that comment was very badly received. Then came to light the negative aspects of the Thompsons, that they used to bribe, and so on. A whole uproar ensued. Once again the internationalisation policy was debated and criticised...The deal turned out all right, but PDVSA had not gone into the business knowing that it was going to give good results[115].

The attacks of the old time opponents of the industry's vertical-integration policy were heard once again. In the different context of 1986, however, the opposition was insignificant compared to the one that had followed the Veba Oel contract. Despite the breathing space enjoyed by PDVSA at the beginning of 1986, allowing it to establish new contracts within its vertical-integration policy, 'the disputes with the political leaders persisted nonetheless'[116].

> There [were] new events that produced friction between PDVSA's president and the Minister of Energy. The political leaders complained about PDVSA's lack of communication, its low profile, and its attitude of secrecy[117].

PDVSA's contract with Southland had in fact become subject to a thorough investigation by Congress. After the usual hearings, questionnaires and information exchanges, Congress concluded that 'no irregularities were committed during the negotiation'[118] that led to the signing of the joint-venture deal for the purchase of Citgo's 50% assets.

The immediate success that was attributed to the venture with Southland in so far as it significantly increased PDVSA's presence in the US market calmed potential opponents and silenced further criticism. Even though PDVSA's policy-makers were convinced of the success of the policy, this was not assured until the contract began to be implemented; thereafter, it started to be recognised as a convenient policy choice by both the executive and the legislature. This degree of uncertainty inherent in the implementation of the policy made an industry manager argue the following:

> PDVSA did not embrace the internationalisation policy in a conscious manner. The deals began turning out all right...Citgo was a negotiation made by chance. Citgo was a test made by PDVSA, a spark of grandiosity... Citgo was a better deal than Veba Oel. It is an excellent investment[119].

Table 6.9 shows key data on Citgo's Lake Charles refinery located in Louisiana.

Table 6.9   Citgo's Lake Charles refinery production, 1990-1992 (Thousand b/d)

	1992	1991	1990
Refining Capacity	320	320	320
Refining Input			
Crude Oil	268	224	268
Other feedstocks	37	33	39
Total Refinery Output	305	257	307
Crude Oil Average API° Gravity	28.1°	28.1°	28.1°

Source: Prospectus, PDV America, Inc. Salomon Brothers Inc.

Champlin refinery: further expansion in the US

At the beginning of 1987, PDVSA and Union Pacific Corporation proceeded to form the Champlin Refining Company to process crude in the refining complex of Corpus Christi, located in Texas. The owner of the refinery, Union Pacific Railroad, had been in the petroleum business since the days when it was given concessions from Missouri to California[120]. The assets acquired by PDVSA included the East Plant of Corpus Christi, a petrochemical plant, and important distribution channels. The original document for the formation of the joint venture included the option for PDVSA to acquire the remaining 50% of the refinery 'within a time period of between two and six years'[121]. As contemplated from the outset, the option to buy was exercised by PDVSA in September 1988. A PDVSA manager explained:

> It was an opportunity too good to reject. Union Pacific did not want to sell, but it was in the contract and they were forced to do so[122].

With an initial investment of $30 million, PDVSA bought 50% of the assets of Champlin Refining Co., allowing it to process 80,000 b/d. After PDVSA became Champlin's sole owner in 1988, the supply of Venezuelan crude was expanded to 130,000 b/d and 10,000 b/d of naphtha. Table 6.10 shows important data on Champlin's Corpus Christi refinery[123].

Table 6.10 Corpus Christi refinery production, 1990-1992 (Thousand b/d)

	1992	1991	1990
Refining Capacity	140	140	140
Refining Input			
Crude Oil	133	125	126
Other feedstocks	49	47	58
Total Refinery Output	182	172	184
Crude Oil Average API° Gravity	24.9°	24.2°	25.5°

Source: Prospectus, PDV America, Inc. Salomon Brothers Inc.

The Caribbean refineries and storage facilities: meeting regional foreign policy objectives

In addition to the possession of DFIs in the form of refinery assets in OECD markets, PDVSA has vested interests in the Caribbean region. PDVSA's participation as lease holder of some Caribbean refineries can also be classified as part of its vertical integration strategy, since they ease the channelling of crude to key consumer markets. As former colonies, some of the Caribbean islands enjoy a special commercial treatment from the European Union. Oil products refined in the PDVSA-leased refinery in Curaçao, as part of the Netherlands, have access to the European Union without paying extra taxes[124]. Discussions for the involvement of PDVSA in the Curaçao refinery date back to nationalisation. Concrete negotiations took place between officials from the Herrera administration and the Dutch government of Prime Minister Ruud Lubbers in a 1985 visit to Caracas. Talks were then mostly based on the possibility of a joint venture between Shell and PDVSA in order to upgrade the Shell-run refinery in Curaçao, which possessed important conversion facilities and a total installed refining capacity of 335,000 b/d. Like other oil majors involved in the Caribbean, Shell was trying to withdraw its involvement due to losses experienced in its refining activities in the region[125].

With the nationalisation of the Venezuelan oil industry, Shell's and Exxon's refineries in the Dutch islands of Curaçao and Aruba were cut off from their supply of crude. These refineries were only able to survive thanks to a special netback arrangement through which PDVSA supplied crude to Shell and Exxon. Due to commercial losses, PDVSA had ceased implementing this system that favoured Exxon and Shell[126]. As a result, these companies lost access to the upstream sector allowed thanks to the arrangements with PDVSA[127].

The involvement of PDVSA in the Curaçao refinery was basically the result of a political decision, mainly aimed at avoiding an economic crisis that would jeopardise the stability of the region. At the beginning of the 1980s refinery oversupply made unprofitable many refining complexes in the Caribbean region. The sudden closure of the refinery in Curaçao by Shell was likely to have disruptive economic, political, and social consequences for the island and the whole Caribbean region. Two analysts of PDVSA's involvement in Curaçao explained this process as a result of meeting foreign policy objectives.

> In Curaçao there has been a history of social rioting, and mainly for political reasons Venezuela decided to lease the refinery[128]. We did not want a new Cuba in front of our coasts[129].

Apart from tourism and substantial aid from the Netherlands' government the refinery is the most important aspect of Curaçao's economy. 'The refinery is the island'[130]. After Shell could no longer be persuaded to maintain its presence on the island, in 1985 PDVSA decided to lease the refinery for an initial fee of $11 million per year for an initial period of five years with renewable periods of two years[131]. In addition to the refinery, PDVSA was also acquiring the right to use Curaçao Oil Terminal, with a capacity to handle tankers of up to 550,000 dwt (dead-weight-ton) at six jetties. These facilities, as well as 15 million barrels oil storage capacity, 750,000 barrels of segregated clean oil storage, a heated capacity of 1 million barrels, plus large crude blending facilities, make Curaçao's *Refinería Isla* the largest and more complete refining and trading centre in the Caribbean region[132]. *Refinería Isla* is perfectly integrated into the circuit of PDVSA's refineries operating in Venezuela. As Reimpall mentioned:

> The refinery is like the ones in Cardón or in Amuay. Curaçao sells services to the same clients as Cardón[133].

The maximisation of economic benefits was not the most important motive behind the leasing of the Curaçao refinery. In fact, PDVSA does not need it for its vertical-integration strategy or for capturing Curaçao's domestic market that is small (60,000 b/d for a population of about 150,000 inhabitants): in Amuay and in Cardón there is surplus capacity to fulfil the market of Curaçao[134]. In 1997 PDVSA supplied the refinery with 194,000 b/d (the refinery's overall capacity is of 335,000 b/d.). After the domestic market is fulfilled, the remaining volume is exported. Reimpall pointed out that,

> Nobody knows exactly if PDVSA profits or loses from its involvement in Curaçao... The island does not have a market, and the products refined are not good quality ones[135].

Despite initial hopes that most of the products from *Refinería Isla* would be directed to the European Union, Curaçao's largest markets remain the US and Latin America, with equal proportions of about 35% each; the remaining volume is destined to the Venezuelan market[136]. Even though the economic rationale for continuing leasing the refinery remains dubious, there are grounds to believe that PDVSA will continue as tenant of the Curaçao refinery in the medium term. PDVSA's involvement in Curaçao, as with other refineries in the Caribbean region, demonstrates that the industry has also followed some non-commercial goals which are characteristic of its status as SOE. In this case, PDVSA was compelled to take into consideration the government's foreign policy obligations. The Curaçao refinery issue is one that often appears on the diplomatic agenda between Venezuela and the Netherlands. A former PDVSA policy-maker referred to this issue as follows:

> In a diplomatic commission made up by Venezuela, Curaçao and Holland gathered to decide about many matters not only related to the refinery, there was one commission to deal specifically with the refinery. In case of economic and social problems, the Netherlands does not want the people of Curaçao to migrate there. The case of Suriname was an example they do not want to repeat[137].

Furthermore, PDVSA owns different storage facilities in the Caribbean that can also be considered as part of the industry's vertical-integration strategy. In the region, Venezuela has a storage capacity of 47 million barrels: 18 million barrels in Curaçao (*Refinería Isla*), 9 million b. in Bonaire (Bonaire Petroleum Corporation, BOPEC), and 20 million b. in the Bahamas (Bahamas Oil Refining Company, BORCO). A strategic drive has pushed PDVSA to establish a network of storage facilities in the area, considered by the industry and government alike to be of great geographic and economic importance. Albacete pointed out that this policy,

> Allowed [PDVSA] to keep stocks and storing facilities there. It was a strategic move, because it is not convenient to have other oil producers in the area[138].

The Caribbean facilities ease the channelling of crude to key markets. An official at the Energy Ministry explained as follows the strategic importance of having a network of storage facilities in key strategic points:

> Our ports are very shallow and that is the reason why we use the ports in the Caribbean. We fill small tankers and send them to our Caribbean facilities to fill the large tankers. The goal is to maximise net benefits in the operation...In the Caribbean there are three storage centres. In Curaçao there is one tied to the refinery. In Bonaire there is another 100% owned by Venezuela called BOPEC, which used to be owned by PAKTANK. In Bahamas there is the centre, called BORCO, previously owned by Chevron. They are used when there are surpluses of crude and production, which are in turn stored to release them when prices are better. They are also used to make mixes and later place them...In Bahamas, [PDVSA] invested $60 million

and in Bonaire $120 million. In Rotterdam, Antwerp, Hamburg and Singapore PDVSA has not invested, but it has rented facilities for storage. There is also an agreement with PETKANK, a Dutch company of distribution and storage, to supply tankers with high-sulphur fuels in those ports[139].

Although much less significant than the industry's European and US downstream network, the ability to use refineries and storage facilities in the neighbouring Caribbean region has eased PDVSA's international operations and facilitated its position as oil MN.

INTERVEN: structural adaptation to the industry's international expansion

In order to co-ordinate the management of its international ventures, in 1986 PDVSA created INTERVEN with the status of a subsidiary, to deal with the increasing significance and complexity of its international operations. The idea was to centralise the management and the expansion of PDVSA's refinery assets abroad. A PDVSA manager explained INTERVEN's origin as follows:

> PDVSA did not have a centre or a focus to manage all those companies abroad. INTERVEN was created with that intention. INTERVEN was a subsidiary of PDVSA's, whith a mandate to administer the companies abroad[140].

INTERVEN's objectives were different from the rest of PDVSA's integrated operating subsidiaries. Its objectives were mainly to identify investment opportunities in downstream facilities abroad, to administer and control the companies in which PDVSA had investments, and to evaluate results[141].

In its initial phase, INTERVEN was a short-lived organisation, a 'transitory company'[142], which ceased its operations in 1991 when the management of PDVSA's downstream ventures in the US came under the responsibility of Citgo and the European ventures under the control of PDV-Europe located in The Hague[143]. As a result of a corporate decision and of the growing significance achieved by Citgo in the US market, INTERVEN's operations were reactivated in 1996.

Conclusion

Thanks to the second phase of policy implementation PDVSA expanded its international presence and became a fully integrated oil MN. The acquisition of further DFIs in the form of refinery assets in Europe and of new ones in the US –in addition to significant storage facilities in the Caribbean– diversified the industry's international operations and enlarged its share of the market.

Despite the disappearance of the political constraints on policy implementation in 1983, it was not until 1986 that another contract for the acquisition of refinery assets abroad was signed. The impact of the controversy over the Veba Oel contract had had the immediate effect of cancelling or postponing current negotiations. In the three-year period in which no further internationalisation contract was signed the industry policy-makers evaluated the first phase of policy implementation. A combination of technical, economic, and political rationales consolidated the implementation of the internationalisation policy. Access to new refining technology, the need to minimise market uncertainty, and the intention to limit government and legislative interference in corporate policies were determinant factors in the industry's pursuit of its international expansion.

In 1986 different domestic and international contexts favoured the launching of a new and more aggressive phase of policy implementation. The price collapse of 1986 and, as a result, the government's fiscal crisis played in favour of the industry's strategy to acquire refinery assets abroad and to enlarge its market share. In 1986 there was consensus among the key policy-makers centres –PDVSA, the Energy Ministry and Congress– as to the pressing need to continue the international expansion of the oil industry. In turn, as a result of silencing the political obstacle to policy implementation, PDVSA strengthened its position as a rather powerful decision-maker within the process of oil policy-making.

The second phase of policy implementation built on the experience of the previous one. The main lesson learned from the Veba Oel experience was the way in which the industry was to deal with Congress and obtain its legitimacy for implementing future policy choices. During the first phase, the *fait-accompli* approach to policy implementation, although not used consciously, proved advantageous: Congress had not used its veto powers to reverse the policy. Subsequently, the following internationalisation contracts did not need go to Congress to gain approval.

Despite agreement between the executive and the oil SOE over the internationalisation policy during the second phase of its implementation, there was a confrontation between these policy actors regarding price fixation rights and sudden transfers of wealth to the treasury. PDVSA's success in becoming an oil MN was overshadowed by its failure to gain the right to fix export prices, a prerogative that remained with the Ministry. Neither was PDVSA capable of fending off unwelcome government financial demands. The impact of wealth transfers to the treasury jeopardised industry cash-flow availability and expansion plans. However, the very impossibility of curbing government demands provided an incentive to further the international operations of the industry. The industry's response to such government attacks was to launch a more aggressive phase in the implementation of its internationalisation strategy, purchasing further DFIs in the form of refinery assets allowing it to increase its corporate freedom. During the second phase of policy implementation PDVSA diversified its international network of refineries both in Europe and in the US. The industry's corporate response to short-term government demands was the consolidation of its long-term strategy of becoming a totally integrated oil MN.

Notes

1   Joaquín Tredenik. Director, PDVSA. *Interview*. August 13, 1993.
2   Peñaloza. *Interview*. February 2, 1993.
3   España. *Op. cit.*
4   Peñaloza. *Interview*. February 3, 1993.
5   *Idem.*
6   *Idem.*
7   Petzall. *Interview*. January 7, 1993.
8   Sosa Pietri. *Op. cit.*, p. 72.
9   *Idem.*
10 Petzall. *Interview*. February 23, 1993; John Sweeny. Oil journalist. *Interview*. August 19, 1993.
11 Sosa Pietri. *Op. cit.*, p. 73.
12 *Idem.*
13 Petzall. *Interview*. January 7, 1993.
14 Sosa Pietri. *Op. cit.*, p. 74.
15 *Idem.*
16 Robert Mabro (ed.). *The 1986 Oil Price Crisis: Economic Effects and Policy Responses*. Oxford University Press. Oxford, 1988, pp. 23-24.
17 For the deregulation policies of the Reagan administration, *cf.* John Chubb. *Interest Groups and the Bureaucracy. The Politics of Energy*. Stanford University Press. Stanford, 1983.
18 Yergin. *Op. cit.*, p. 747.
19 *Idem.*
20 Yergin. *Op. cit.*, p. 749.
21 André Giroud and Xavier Boy de la Tour.*Géopolitique du Pétrole et du Gaz*. Ed. Technip. Paris, 1987, pp. 300-302.
22 Miguel Rodríguez. 'Public sector behaviour in Venezuela, 1970-1985'. IESA. Caracas, 1988, p. 61.

23   The number of transactions that had access to the preferential rate of Bs 4.30 to a dollar was significantly reduced, including medicines and some food products. For the oil and iron industries a rate of Bs 6.00 per dollar was fixed; and a rate of Bs 7.50 per dollar was imposed on the rest of import transactions; also, a parallel and fluctuating market was maintained in order to acquire dollars for transactions considered of no priority. Toro Hardy. *Op. cit.*, p. 120.

24   For an evaluation of the somewhat arbitrary decision-making process that led to the devaluation of the currency from Bs 6 to Bs 14.50 to $1 in December 1986. *Cf.* Gerver Torres and Doramelia Salcedo 'El proceso Venezolano de toma de decisiones en política económica. Un estudio de casos'. ILDIS. Caracas, February 1988, pp. 17-31.

25   Data from Asdrúbal Baptista. *Bases Cuantitativas de la Economía Venezolana*, 1830-1989. BCV Publications. Caracas, 1989.

26   M. Rodríguez. *Op. cit.*, pp. 54-55.

27   *Ibid.*, p. 55.

28   Toro Hardy. *Op. cit.*, p. 113.

29   One of the reasons why the agreement was not reached until 1984, although the negotiations had begun two years earlier, was the recognition of the private external debt by the government. This controversial issue was settled in 1985 when the Lusinchi government recognised the validity of a private debt of $4,965 million with different international creditors.

30   Toro Hardy. *Op. cit.*, p. 136.

31   M. Rodríguez, *Op. cit.*, p. 54. For a detailed account of the terms in which the debt payment was rescheduled and on the two major agreements subscribed to service it, see William Cline, 'Estructura, orígenes y administración de la deuda pública externa de Venezuela', in *La Economía Contemporánea de Venezuela*. BCV, pp. 9-55; Pedro Palma, 'El manejo de la deuda pública externa de Venezuela: necesidad de urgentes cambios', in *La Economía Contemporánea. Op. cit.*, pp. 238-257; Ana María Alvarez de Stella, 'Crisis y manejo de la deuda externa en Venezuela', in *La Economía Contemporánea. Op. cit.*, pp. 355-402; Samuel Freije, 'The new foreign debt restructuring agreement: its terms and potential results'. *MetroEconómica.* Caracas, April 1990; 'The creditors' response to the new public foreign debt negotiation arrangement'. *MetroEconómica.* September, 1990.

32   PDVSA's CORPOVEN was requested to provide a substantial financial contribution for the construction of an important motorway in the country's eastern region. Sosa Pietri. *Op. cit.*, p. 76.

33   *Ibid.*, pp. 76-77.

34   Sosa Pietri. *Op. cit.*, p. 74.

35   Mancur Olsen. 'Presentation'. LSE. May 18, 1994.

36   PDVSA manager who requested anonymity.

37   Sosa Pietri reports having been told about this meeting by Chacín and Reimpall, among others. *Op. cit.*, p. 75.

38   *Veneconomía.* December 17, 1986. Vol 5. No. 6.

39   Giacopini. *Interview.* October 14, 1993.

40   Alfonso Albacete. LAGOVEN. *Interview.* March 4, 1993.

41   Gómez. *Interview.* August 31, 1993.

42   Albacete. *Interview.* March 4, 1993.

43   *Idem.*

44   Paul Reimpall. Former Director, PDVSA. *Interview.* August 12, 1993.

45   Pulgar. *Interview.* August 16, 1993.

46   Rodríguez Eraso. *Interview.* November 19, 1993.

47   Chacín. *Interview*. January 8, 1993.
48   *Idem.*
49   *Idem*
50   Petzall. *Interview*. September 24, 1993.
51   Gómez. *Interview*. November 17, 1993.
52   Vicente Llatas. Director, PDVSA. *Interview*. August 9, 1993.
53   *Idem.*
54   *Idem.*
55   Reimpall. *Interview*. August 12, 1992.
56   Letter by president Brígido Natera. PDVSA's *Annual Report*, 1985.
57   Gómez. Interview. August 31, 1993.
58   Peñaloza. *Interview*. February 2, 1993.
59   Reimpall. *Interview*. August 12, 1993.
60   Gómez. *Interview*. August 31, 1993.
61   Reimpall. *Interview*. August 12, 1993.
62   Chacín. *Intrerview.* January 8, 1993.
63   Llatas. *Interview*. August 9, 1993.
64   *Idem.*
65   *Idem.*
66   Reimpall. *Interview*. August 12, 1993.
67   Gómez. *Interview*. August 31, 1993.
68   Pulgar. *Interview*. August 16, 1993.
69   When the market for residuals crumbled in the US, Venezuela changed its refining pattern from residuals to fuel oil, according to the needs in the US. Reimpall. *Interview*. August 12, 1993.
70   Reimpall. *Interview*. August 12, 1993.
71   *Idem.*
72   Gómez. *Interview*. August 31, 1993.
73   *Idem.*
74   Reimpall. *Interview*. August 12, 1993.
75   *Idem.*
76   Llatas. *Interview*. August 9, 1993.
77   Reimpall. *Interview*. August 12, 1993.
78   Chacín. *Interview*. January 8, 1993.
79   *Idem.*
80   Gonzalo Castillo. Director, Ministry of Energy. *Interview*. November 17, 1993.
81   *Idem.*
82   Gómez. *Interview*. November 11, 1993.
83   Reimpall. *Interview*. August 12, 1993.
84   Peñaloza. *Interview*. February 2, 1993.
85   Sosa Pietri. *Op. cit.,* p. 171.
86   Sweeny. *Interview*. August 19, 1993. Sweeney said that Sosa had once told him that 'OPEC should be thrown in the dustbin of history'.
87   Forum in support of Oswaldo Alvarez Paz, COPEI's candidate in 1993. Tamanaco Hotel. Caracas. August 10, 1993.
88   *PDVSA. Contact.* Newsletter. No 46. Aug-Sept., 1995.
89   Boué. *Op. cit.,* p. 41.
90   *Idem.*; *Annual Report*. PDVSA, 1995.
91   Boué. *Op. cit.,* p. 43.
92   Sosa. *Op. cit.,* p. 173.

93 Sosa Pietri often referred to a conversation held on July 16, 1990 with OPEC's Secretary-General, Subruto, who told him that 'it is customary in OPEC to consider quotas as referring to market, and not to production'. Sosa. *Op. cit.*, p. 172.

94 Petzall. *Interviews*.

95 Peñaloza. *Interview*. February 2, 1993.

96 Robert Bottome. Director, Veneconomía. *Interview*. August 25, 1993.

97 Pulgar. *Interview*. August 16, 1993.

98 Rodríguez Eraso. *Interview*. November 19, 1993.

99 Gómez. *Interview*. November 11, 1993.

100 Reimpall. *Interview*. August 12, 1993.

101 Miguel Martínez. Director, PDVSA. *Interview*. October 20, 1993.

102 Llatas. *Interview*. August 9, 1993.

103 *Idem.*

104 Neste Öy is one of the largest oil refining companies operating in the Scandinavian region. It was founded after WWII to provide oil to Finland. By the time of its acquisition of Axel Johnson's assets in Nynäs, Neste used to buy up to 80% of its crude from the former USSR. 'Conocer a Neste'. Document. PDVSA.

105 Reimpall. *Interview*. August 12, 1993.

106 'La internacionalización de PDVSA'. *Op. cit.*

107 Castillo. *Interview*. November 17, 1993.

108 *El Nacional*. February 6, 1986.

109 Llatas. *Interview*. August 9, 1993.

110 Interview. PDVSA Director who requested anonymity.

111 Petzall. *Interview*. August 6, 1993.

112 Rodríguez Eraso. *Interview*. November 19, 1993.

113 Occidental Petroleum's Armand Hammer had allegedly bribed officials from the Caldera administration. Such accusations of bribery caused the Venezuelan government to refuse paying indemnities for $100 million to Occidental once nationalisation was implemented in 1975. Occidental tried to obtain the amount owed by the Venezuelan government without much success during several years. Petzall. *Interview*. August 6, 1993.

114 For this purpose, Andrés Sosa Pietri was designated negotiator for the Venezuelan government. After long legal battles, in 1991 the issue was settled and the Venezuelan government paid Occidental the pending indemnities. It was during this period that C. A. Pérez became acquainted with Sosa's work in petroleum matters and later appointed him PDVSA's president. Petzall. *Interview*. August 6, 1993. The intricacies of the dispute involving Occidental and Venezuelan government officials prior to nationalisation still remain to be clarified. *Cf.* Edward Jay Epstein. 'The World of Business. The Last Days of Armand Hammer'. *The New Yorker*. September 23, 1996, pp. 36-49.

115 Rodríguez Eraso. *Interview*. November 19, 1993.

116 Both quotes from Sosa Pietri. *Op. cit.*, p. 76.

117 *Idem.*

118 *Veneconomía*. Vol. 4, No. 42. September 10, 1986.

119 Martínez. *Interview*. October 20, 1993.

120 Petzall. *Interview*. August 6, 1993.

121 'Venezuela compró la mitad de la Champlin Refining Co.'. *El Nacional*. March 11, 1987.

122 Reimpall. *Interview*. August 12, 1993.

123 'Prospectus'. Salomon Brothers Inc., 1993, p. 40; Boué. *Op. cit.*, p. 160.

124 Petzall. *Interview*. August 6, 1993.

125 Shell, Texaco, and Exxon had been respectively involved in Curaçao, Trinidad and Aruba, but after experiencing substantial losses decided to abandon their refining activities in the area. Article by Kim Fuad, 'Pelotón de salvamento'. *El Nacional.* December 12, 1986.
126 'El subsidio petrolero debe ser condicionado'. *El Diario.* November 11, 1984.
127 Suffering from the change of policy implemented by PDVSA, a similar phenomenon was taking place in Trinidad. In 1985, the oil SOE, TRINTOC, settled the problem by acquiring two refineries operated by TEXACO. The overall capacity of the two refineries (over 300,000 b/d) far exceeded TRINTOC's limited access to crude. *Idem.*
128 Petzall. *Interview.* August 6, 1993. Successive Venezuelan governments since the end of the last dictatorship in 1958 have considered events in the Caribbean and in Central America as matters of state security. *Cf.* C.A. Pérez's comments on this issue, *Cambio 16,* June 20, 1994.
129 Quoted by K. Fuad. Article. *Op. cit.*
130 Reimpall. *Interview.* August 12, 1993.
131 Petzall. *Interview.* August 6, 1993.
132 Boué. *Op. cit.*, p. 163.
133 Reimpall. *Interview.* August 12, 1993.
134 *Idem.*
135 Reimpall. *Interview.* August 12, 1993.
136 Boué. *Op. cit.* p. 163.
137 Reimpall. *Interview.* August 12, 1993.
138 Albacete. *Interview.* March 4, 1993.
139 Castillo. *Interview.* November 17, 1993.
140 Albacete. *Interview.* March 4, 1993.
141 Peñaloza. 'Petróleos de Venezuela's Experience in Joint Venture Downstream Arrangements'. *Geopolitics of Energy-Supplement.* Conant and Associates, Ltd., 1988.
142 Albacete. *Interview.* March 4, 1993.
143 Sosa Pietri.*Op. cit.* p. 116.

Chapter 7
The third phase of policy implementation: PDVSA's consolidation as a multinational

7 The third phase of policy implementation: PDVSA's consolidation as a multinational

Introduction

PDVSA's internationalisation policy is usually regarded as a success by the policy-makers who implemented it. Thanks to it, PDVSA has been able to establish a significant network of DFIs in the form of refinery assets in OECD areas unrivalled by any other OPEC producing company. PDVSA's policy-makers regarded the acquisition of refineries abroad as the best way to strengthen the industry's position in the international oil market. One of the issues that arises when analysing PDVSA's vertical-integration strategy is whether industry policy-makers could have implemented a different policy from the acquisition of refineries abroad in order to achieve their objectives. By contrast, other oil companies chose to implement different policies in order to reach the same goals. The purchase of refinery assets was one of several options available to PDVSA in order to enlarge market share. The other and most commonly used option is the establishment of netback deals, previously discussed in Chapter IV. Usually, with a limited time lapse and periodically negotiated, netback contracts do not offer the long-term possibility to increase corporate freedom, minimise government controls and avoid unwelcome demands for transfers of wealth allowed by establishing DFIs in the form of refinery assets in key markets. It is argued here that the possibility to minimise government interference in the implementation of corporate policies was a decisive factor in PDVSA's decision to purchase refinery assets abroad. Contrary to the netback deal alternative, the option of purchasing refinery assets provided the industry with a long-term platform to diversify its operations farther away from government control and Congress scrutiny.

The purpose of this chapter is twofold. First, to assess PDVSA's preference for purchasing refinery assets as a means to enlarge market share, in the light of the experience of other oil producing companies. Second, to ascertain PDVSA's ability to minimise the adverse effects of the three variables earlier identified –i.e., political context, market situation and government financial demands– and turn them into favourable factors enabling it to continue the implementation of its policy choice in 1989. During this third phase of policy implementation PDVSA acquired further refinery assets, thus consolidating its position as an oil MN. However, as was also the case during the first and second phases of policy implementation, the findings of this study demonstrate that despite its ability to pursue the internationalisation of its operations, PDVSA proved to be less successful when trying to fend off unwelcome government financial demands.

Rationales for vertical integration

The policy aimed at enlarging market share through purchasing refinery assets abroad is often considered as 'less stabilising than direct discounts, spot sales, barters or netback deals'[1]. The findings of this research suggest that PDVSA's managers took into consideration different policy options when formulating the strategy to enlarge market share based on the purchase of refinery assets abroad. The following is but an example of a policy-maker trying to justify the industry's policy choice:

> PDVSA's vulnerability continued and we ran the risk of losing market for 700,000 b/d. We highlighted the options we had. First, to build refineries in Venezuela. Second, to establish supply agreements with the buyers. Third, to establish netback agreements like those of Saudi Arabia. Fourth, to internationalise PDVSA, in order to gain access to distribution channels and to clients. The best option was the last one[2].

Another PDVSA manager was reported saying how '[PDVSA was] looking for markets rather than assets such as refineries'[3]. In turn, an analyst of the international oil industry provided an interesting and somewhat anecdotal comment. He identified a self-indulgent motive behind the intention of PDVSA's managers to pursue the international expansion of its operations; PDVSA's policy-makers wanted to become 'international managers'[4] and one of the means of achieving it was by 'keeping assets abroad'[5]. Based on such premises, and contrary to what this study argues, the commentator went on to wonder whether the internationalisation policy as implemented by PDVSA could really be considered as an integration at all.

There is usually wide consensus regarding the benefits of achieving a good degree of vertical integration. In times of economic expansion or contraction, an integrated company fares better than a non-integrated one.

However, discrepancies arise when trying to assert the real benefits of vertical integration in times of prolonged market instability or when analysing alternatives to achieve similar goals. The following is an advice to investors from a well-known investment group:

> Integrated companies with operations in oil and gas exploration and development, refining, marketing, and chemicals, are well positioned to benefit from broad-based economic expansion. The breadth of their operations also provides some downside protection when one area of their business experiences a slow-down[6].

Among the most common benefits cited for advocating the downstream expansion of oil exporting companies are revenue stabilisation and maximisation, reduction of the effects of price competition, ability to present a consolidated balance, revenue stabilisation, and placement of heavy crude. However, all such benefits have their limitations, especially in the medium term.

The ability to increase volumes in order to maintain revenue levels is a common rationale for implementing a policy of international downstream integration. Integrating the operations of a company allows more flexibility to cope with market disruptions. According to PDVSA,

> Vertical integration guarantees that, by controlling all the segments of the industry, volumes can be maintained and revenues maximised, either from the production segment or from refining and retail sales, according to the conditions of the market[7].

The positive results of international vertical integration are better felt at the beginning of the price-cutting trend. When prices fall at the upstream level, there is still the possibility to make profits in the downstream sector. Companies with various refinery outlets and access to final consumers will be protected from outright competition only at the beginning, when it is still possible to minimise the acute imbalances inflicted by market upheavals on cash flow levels and expansion plans. Furthermore, securing direct access to a key consumer market can allow companies to minimise unwelcome and sudden government financial demands. Critics of vertical integration may argue that revenue stabilisation and maximisation occurs strictly on a short-term basis[8]. It seems more difficult to extend the benefits of vertical integration in the long term, since, most likely, other companies also seeking integration come into the picture, disputing any initial exclusivity status. In fact, OPEC members –Venezuela, Kuwait, UAE,

Saudi Arabia, Iran, and Libya– that set out to implement, at different degrees, a policy of international vertical integration at the beginning of the 1980s soon became competitors in the race for purchasing refinery assets. In the early days of the pre-nationalisation period they had also competed to attract oil MNs by offering them appealing conditions for investing in their upstream sectors.

Revenue maximisation is not, however, the direct result of vertical integration. Different forms of market strategies must accompany this policy, if the market is to be enlarged and revenue maximised. As *Petroleum Industry Indicators* commented:

> An integrated company, if it is to fully exploit the industry cycle to its best advantage, must be able and willing to alter the composition of its investment portfolio in a counter-cyclical manner[9].

Divestiture and ownership diversification are two of the schemes that could accompany vertical integration, in an attempt to palliate the counter cyclical effects of the market[10]. PDVSA's managers have taken this into consideration when implementing the internationalisation policy. The evidence shows that diversity in its refinery investments both in the US – despite a tendency to merge all deals under the control of Citgo– and in Europe has been part of PDVSA's internationalisation policy.

Another assumption used by advocates of the downstream integration strategy is that it allows oil companies a better position when competing against other producers in times of market contraction, without having to resort to significant price reductions. Such rationale is found in arguments such as the following:

> By finding a guaranteed home for a percentage of their production, [OPEC] countries can short-circuit the vicious circle of discounting price to seek more market share for their crude, which in an oversupplied market robs share from somebody else, which in turn leads him to leapfrog the first discounter[11].

Generally, this assumption applies to the first phases of the price reduction trend, when the integrated companies still enjoy unchallenged access to the final consumer. But as the price of refined products drops following the general reduction of crude prices, it is unlikely that the integrated companies continue to register advantages over their non-integrated competitors. In the context of crude oversupply and high competition, the choices are the same for an integrated company than for a non-integrated one. The main dilemma for producers remains the same: to reduce price or to reduce volume.

One of the main advantages of vertical integration lies in the possibility of preventing other companies from supplying crude to the refineries where it owns assets. This is easily attained when ownership over the refinery is 100%, or through striking a special deal with the majority partner. Again, this strategy can only bear fruit until competitors begin lowering the price for their crude in an unfavourable market context for producers. This outcome would in turn force other competitors to reduce price or close down production capacity in order to minimise losses. Price reduction can also be the result of the establishment of netback deals, as was the case prior to the 1986 oil crisis. Moreover, unlike the Seven Majors before the time of large nationalisations during the 1970s, most companies from producing countries do not have the sufficient level of control over consuming markets. They lack the necessary downstream channels to influence significantly the performance of other competitors and to force them to reduce production capacity.

Moreover, vertical integration can enable a company to present a consolidated account, and thereby be able to disguise the losses registered in its international ventures. This practice permits the concealment of possible losses incurred by refineries abroad[12], making it more difficult for goverments to assess the SOE's performance. Furthermore, the confidentiality that accompanies many of the contracts in the oil industry finds a fertile ground in the existence of assets abroad[13]. In the case of PDVSA, this difficulty in assessing the benefits and losses of its international ventures invoked Congress suspicions. The industry's internationalisation policy partly undermines accountability to the legislature. This poses clear problems for the control of the SOE, which as a result of its high degree of international vertical integration has gained more administrative freedom, and thus more independence from legislative and executive controls.

The possibility to secure access for certain types of crude difficult to market is another rationale often evoked by advocators of establishing DFIs in the form of refinery assets. PDVSA's policy-makers often used this rationale. However, the data on this issue for PDVSA's US refineries show that mainly light, more easily marketable crude is still being processed. Heavy and extra-heavy crudes are only being processed in the asphalt refineries which process feedstock lower than 15° API. The same is also true in the European refineries; the Ruhr Oel refinery largely processes medium crude[14].

This discussion suggests that the benefits of vertical integration are not often straightforward gains. However, for an oil company there are more market and strategic advantages in being fully integrated than not. The most obvious advantage is that, in times of policy shift or market upheavals, a company does not have to resort to the establishment of netback deals with refiners in an attempt to expand market share. Possessing a refinery in a given market allows to respond more rapidly to market variables and to minimise, at least in the short run, competition from other oil companies. Another incentive of vertical integration is the establishment of a long-term platform enabling the company to increase corporate decision-making freedom farther away from government meddling.

Low disbursement of cash as a rationale for refinery acquisitions

A common argument used by PDVSA's policy-makers to support their policy choice was the limited amounts of money disbursed for the acquisition of refinery assets abroad. According to Boué:

> PDVSA's preference for downstream acquisitions stems from the fact that the cost of these acquisitions can be covered by payments in kind. Thus, overseas acquisitions represent a viable way for PDVSA to add refining capacity, while getting around its grave handicap of having a very low cash ratio[15].

PDVSA's policy-makers have often stressed the fact that the refinery assets abroad were purchased with very low cash disbursements. Gustavo Roosen, PDVSA's president between 1992 and 1994 put it as follows:

> One of the characteristics of PDVSA's overseas business is its ability to be self-financing. The companies constituted abroad have needed no special monetary transfers from the holding company. Investments foreseen in medium-term planning were largely covered by the overseas companies themselves and were mainly devoted to upgrading installations in order to increase their deep conversion capacity and adapt them to be able to process Venezuelan crude, as well as to market requirements[16].

Table 7.1 shows the financial scheme through which PDVSA acquired its refineries abroad. Inventory replacement and external financing constituted the most important instruments used.

Table 7.1 PDVSA's downstream acquisitions, 1983-1991
(Million $)

Joint venture	Cash payments	External Financing	Inventory replacement	Total
Ruhr Oel	63	58	none	121
UNO-VEN	none	none	145	145
Champlin	31	89	none	120
Citgo	290	158	428	876
Nynäs	24	none	none	24
Total	408	305	573	1,286

Source: 'La internacionalización de PDVSA'. PDVSA, July 1992.

Even though disbursements were low, the purchase of refinery assets abroad required the availability of financial means. Only a few companies with excess production and means to obtain loans could envisage significant purchases of refinery assets abroad. Despite a difficult market during the 1980s, the OPEC companies that implemented vertical-integration policies enjoyed sufficient profit margins to enable them to purchase refinery assets abroad. These companies had small and easily satisfied domestic markets, allowing for the export of significant production volumes. Usually, PDVSA satisfies the Venezuelan domestic market with less than one-fifth of its production. In 1995, PDVSA produced 3.2 million b/d, of which only 657,000 b/d were aimed at the domestic market[17].

PDVSA implemented its internationalisation policy against a difficult market context. When PDVSA signed its contract with Veba Oel in 1983, the windfall effects of the Second Oil Shock were long exhausted. In 1982 the industry had suffered an important loss of its international currency reserves. In 1986, after sorting out the political obstacle restraining policy implementation, PDVSA launched a new and more aggressive strategy to purchase further refineries in Europe and in the US; this, in a context of dramatic barrel price drop and strong competition. The total purchase of Citgo in 1988, signalling the third phase of policy implementation, was carried out against a similar background of plummeting oil prices for oil products; improvements in revenues were only registered as a result of increases in the level of volumes exported.

Such evidence partly supports Boué's assumption that PDVSA's preference for purchasing refinery assets abroad was a way of coping with its chronic problem of cash flow shortages. However, such an argument does not explain why PDVSA was able to acquire refinery assets abroad in a context of financial limitations and cash flow shortages, whereas other oil companies with similar difficulties did not do the same. The fact that PDVSA had significant crude availability to replace inventories in the refineries to be purchased eased the implementation of its vertical integration policy. Other companies, such as Indonesia's PERTAMINA and Mexico's PEMEX, found it difficult to undertake a similar policy: coping with grave cash shortages and the need to fulfil their large domestic markets concentrated most of their efforts.

PDVSA's managers have almost unanimously agreed on the benefits of the industry's internationalisation policy. The following estimates by PDVSA in Table 7.2 show in an aggregated form the profits generated by each refinery abroad, by far the most profitable being Citgo[18].

Table 7.2   Profits from PDVSA's refineries abroad, 1986-1991 (Million $)

Company	1986	1987	1988	1989	1990	1991	TOTAL
Citgo	22	43	83	81	91	136*	456
Champlin **		21	22	41	18		102
UNO-VEN ***			3	22	8	33	66
Nynäs	2	3	2	3	4	5	19
TOTAL	24	67	110	147	121	174	643

*   Includes the Champlin Refinery

**   Champlin was purchased in 1987

***   UNO-VEN was purchased in 1988

Source: 'La internacionalización de PDVSA'. PDVSA. July, 1992.

Other producing countries and the internationalisation experience

Besides Venezuela, other OPEC members have made significant efforts to achieve a vertically-integrated industry as a means to expand market share. The following data in Table 7.3 show the refining capacity abroad of the OPEC companies which have undertaken significant downstream-integration strategies. Among OPEC members, PDVSA has the largest refining capacity and equity ownership of refinery assets abroad.

Table 7.3 OPEC's refining capacity abroad, 1993 (1,000 b/d)

Net Ownership in Refining Capacity

	Asia/ Far East	Western Europe	USA	Total
Iran				14.9
Kuwait		160.2		160.2
Libya		231.3		231.3
Saudi Arabia	153.4		307.5	460.9
UAE	14.9	87.6		87.6
Venezuela *		221.2	779	1,000.20
TOTAL	168.3	700.30	1,086.50	1,995.10
Refining cap.	10,488.30	15,055.70	15,145	40,689
OPEC's share	1.60%	4.70%	7.20%	4.80%

Crude Oil Refining Capacity

	Asia/ Far East	Western Europe	USA	Total
Iran	14.9			14.9
Kuwait		160.2		160.2
Libya		383		383
Saudi Arabia	328.9		550	878.9
UAE		112.8		112.8
Venezuela *		263.2	908	1,171.20
TOTAL	343.8	919.2	1458	2721
Refining cap.	10,488.30	15,055.70	15,145	40,689
OPEC's share	3.30%	6.10%	9.60%	6.70%

* Data do not include 195,000 b/d supplied to *Refinería Isla*, Curaçao.

Sources: 'La internacionalización de PDVSA'. PDVSA, 1992; *Prospectus, Salomon Brothers, Inc.* July 22, 1993.

In 1997, PDVSA had a total installed refining capacity of 3.77 million b/d, that is 1.28 million in Venezuela and 2.49 abroad (including the Curaçao *Refinería Isla*). PDVSA is one of the world's largest refiners. In 1995 PDVSA ranked third among the world's largest refiners, with a total refining capacity of 3.36 million b/d. In this category, PDVSA was only preceded by Royal Dutch/Shell (4.2 million b/d) and Exxon (3.9 million b/d)[19]. Table 7.4 shows in detail PDVSA's refinery assets in and outside Venezuela.

The purchase of refinery assets and the establishment of netback contracts: two policy options to enlarge market share

The schemes used to enlarge market share have differed from country to country. In contrast to PDVSA, most OPEC companies have preferred netback deals as a strategy to secure market share. Striking netback deals in order to increase market presence does not imply, however, achieving a long-term vertical-integration platform through the purchase of refinery assets abroad. Saudi Arabia, Kuwait, Libya, United Arab Emirates, Iraq, Nigeria, Algeria and non-OPEC Mexico have aimed at increasing their market share largely through the establishment of netback deals.

Although, as explained in Chapter IV, Saudi Arabia has often had recourse to netback deals in order to expand market share, it had also purchased significant refinery assets abroad. Whenever Saudi ARAMCO has acquired refinery assets abroad, it has favoured the establishment of 50-50 partnership schemes; in the US: Convent, Port-Arthur, and Delaware. However, in Limay, the Philippines, and in Onsan, South Korea, Saudi ARAMCO has 40% and 35% ownership respectively[20]. In the Saudi vertical-integration scheme, ARAMCO supplies all the crude to be refined. In most Saudi deals, products are sold according to the market price, following a netback pattern. In contrast to the Venezuelan experience, the petrochemical sector is often included in ARAMCO's deals as part of the integration scheme. Access to transport facilities constitutes an important part of the agreements[21], as was demonstrated by the 1988 purchase by ARAMCO of TEXACO's network in the US and which brought about the Star joint venture. Through its association with TEXACO, valued at $2,000 million, Saudi Arabia acquired 615,000 b/d of refining capacity in the US market, with refining facilities in Delaware, Louisiana, and Texas[22].

Often cited as the other pioneer country for the internationalisation of its oil industry, Kuwait began striking vertical integration contracts in 1983. Although the first Kuwaiti deals for purchasing refinery assets abroad took

Table 7.4   PDVSA's refining system (Thousand barrels per day)

	Installed Capacity	PDVSA Share (%)[1]	PDVSA crude supply[2] 1997	PDVSA crude supply[2] 1996
Venezuela				
Centro de Refinación				
Paraguaná	940	100		
Puerto la Cruz	195	100		
El Palito	123	100		
Bajo Grande	15	100		
San Roque	5	100		
Total Venezuela	1.278		1.054	1.019
Netherland Antilles				
Refinería Isla	335	3	194	186
United States				
Lake Charles, LA	320	100		
Corpus Christi, TX	150	100		
Paulsboro, NJ	84	100		
Savannah, GA	28	100		
Houston, TX	265	41.5		
Lemont, IL	160	100		
Chalmette, L	184	50		
Total United States	1191		853	632
Europe				
Gelsenkirchen, Germany	226	50		
Neustadt, Germany	144	25		
Karlsrube, Germany	275	12		
Schmedt, Germany	240	18.8		
Nynäshamn, Sweden	22	50		
Antwerp, Belgium	14	50		
Gothenburg, Sweden	11	50		
Dundee, Scotland	10	50		
Eastham, England	26	25		
Total Europe	968		272	258
Total United States-Europe	2.494		1.125	890
Total	3.772		2.373	2.095

[1] Percentage of share

[2] Includes Venezuelan crudes and crudes purchased by PDVSA

[3] Leasing agreement

Source: PDVSA, *Annual Report*, 1997.

place at almost the same time as PDVSA's deal with Veba Oel, 'Venezuela had been holding negotiations before Kuwait'[23]. With a very limited domestic market, a small population and hardly any challenge to diversify the economy, Kuwait's DFIs, in contrast to PDVSA's, have mainly been aimed at the financial sector. The 1983-created and London-based Kuwait Petroleum International (KPI) –an affiliate of Kuwait Petroleum Corporation (KPC)– has sought to invest in all the phases of upstream and downstream activities. The real momentum for the expansion of KPC was provided by the 1983 purchase of Gulf Oil's downstream businesses in the Netherlands, Belgium, Sweden and Denmark. One year later, the company further expanded its operations with the acquisition of Gulf Oil's Italian marketing and distribution outlets and later on taking over Mobil's petroleum businesses in that country. Also, in 1984, 500 petrol stations were purchased in the UK market. In 1986 KPI acquired UK's Ultramar and in 1987, thanks to the acquisition of BP's Danish assets, it became the market leader in Denmark. KPI markets its products in the European market under the Q8 label. Furthermore, KPI owns downstream interests in France, Germany, Benelux, Hungary, the Czech Republic, Spain, and Thailand[24]. In most of its vertical integration deals, Kuwait has excluded partnership agreements, preferring the exclusive ownership of assets. More recent acquisitions, however, have shown a tendency towards the adoption of 50-50 partnerships. As opposed to ARAMCO and similar to PDVSA, KPI does not demand the right to exclusively supply Kuwaiti oil to the refineries it owns in partnership[25].

For Libya, a country that has also implemented a significant vertical integration strategy, expansion overseas has a distinguishable security objective, which is that of 'winning the sympathy of the host country'[26]. Libya's presence is mostly limited to the Italian market through a partnership agreement with AGIP. In 1986, Libya's investment arm, Oil Invest, acquired the independent refiner TAMOIL, enabling it to market its products through a network of 800 petrol stations. Also in Italy, Libya has total ownership of a plant in Cremona, sold by AMOCO in 1983[27]. Besides its Italian interests, Libya's Oil Invest possesses refinery assets in Harburg, Germany (65%), and in Collombe, Switzerland (100%)[28].

In the case of Abu Dhabi, DFIs have been largely aimed at financial targets. Where the emirate has established refinery ventures abroad, it has not acquired the right to supply its crude. In turn, before its failed attempt to annex Kuwait in September 1990, Iraq had implemented a policy of competitive netback deals and attractive discounts in order to increase its presence in the US market[29]. Also Nigeria, in order to maintain a constant and acceptable level of sales, has often resorted to establishing netback arrangements[30].

Algeria's SONATRACH has also implemented a vertical-integration policy, including the petrochemical and energy-related service domains. SONATRACH, as well as Saudi ARAMCO and Nigeria, has sought to strengthen its market presence through competitive prices and netback deals[31]. In turn, Indonesia's PERTAMINA, confronted with meeting the demands of a large and ever growing domestic market, has failed to develop a policy of internationalisation. A high manager of PERTAMINA remarked that, after meeting the requirements of the domestic market, 'there is little left for export'[32]. Furthermore, PERTAMINA has a secure market share in what it considers its natural markets: China, Taiwan, South Korea, and especially Japan. Such a factor has somewhat discouraged the company from pursuing DFIs in the form of refinery assets[33].

Like PERTAMINA, Mexico's PEMEX has been long-time devoted to the domestic market, in accordance with the policy of import substitution implemented in many Latin American countries at varying degrees until the late 1960s. As a result of its concentration on the domestic market, PEMEX's efforts to regain a share of the international market have proved arduous[34]. An oil manager described PEMEX's situation as follows:

> PEMEX does not have an export vocation. It is more concentrated on the domestic market which is very large; its absence from the international market has cost PEMEX a lot; as a result, it has been more difficult to regain its market share[35].

Despite having been aiming most of its efforts to reduce costs and raise efficiency since 1982, PEMEX has never totally discarded the option of buying downstream assets abroad. Evidence of this are its associations with Shell in the Deer Park refinery in Texas and with Repsol in Spain. These are PEMEX's only associations in refineries abroad[36].

Less tangible factors influencing policy implementation

As explained, a shortage of cash flow resulting from a high taxation, a general reduction of OPEC's crude in the world markets, a low barrel price and a chronic government financial crisis have clearly influenced the formulation of PDVSA's internationalisation policy. However, other less tangible factors have also exerted an influence. Many exporting countries have underestimated the strategic importance that the countries recipient of DFIs attach to their oil sectors, often making it difficult for foreign companies to acquire refinery assets and distribution networks in their markets. Evidence of this are the difficulties experienced by Kuwait in its efforts to acquire a minority share of BP in the UK market and the judicial acrobatics orchestrated by Libya's Oil Invest to disguise its identity in its ventures in the European market[37]. The often-discriminatory treatment given to OPEC companies in OECD countries was evoked by Bonse-Geuking, Veba Oel's president:

> The largest consuming countries remain selective when granting necessary authorisation to allow companies to settle in. They may allow some asset acquisitions in the sectors with difficulty, but they are more reluctant to accept them in those areas that are profitable or deemed strategic. Thus, PEMEX, PDVSA, or Saudi ARAMCO are allowed to invest in the costly modernisation of certain refineries or in some subsidiaries in difficulty, but the acquisition of significant equities in important companies is prevented[38].

Undeniably, cultural biases play an important role in the establishment of working partnerships. Although it seems obvious to say that people who share more things in common tend to tie relationships more easily, this assumption played an important role in determining the contract between Veba Oel and PDVSA. A few years before Veba Oel signed with PDVSA, the Iranian government sought to establish a joint-venture agreement with the German company. Cultural differences and lack of trust of the potential partner made Veba Oel decline a potential partnership with Iranian Oil[39].

In order to minimise the possibility of discriminatory treatment against totally foreign-owned companies, PDVSA has had recourse to a judicial device that allows it to disguise the real ownership of its US refineries[40]. Moreover, such a device also contributes to reducing excessive tax payments. PDVSA created PROPERNYN as a legal company to represent its investments outside Venezuela. A Dutch closed limited liability corporation, PROPERNYN appears in all legal documents as the principal holding company for PDVSA's worldwide investments[41]. Keeping a low profile in the US is a way of protecting the company, even from foreign policy constraints. A PDVSA policy-maker commented the following:

> In the US there is not much knowledge of the fact that Citgo is owned by Venezuela. There was an argument, probably a political one, in the sense that if Venezuela did not pay the debt, her assets could be seized in the US. After all, PDVSA is a state company[42].

The evidence of this research showed the extent to which political and foreign policy factors could determine the successful negotiation between two companies for the establishment of joint-venture associations. The co-operation provided by the German government in 1983 in the form of tax exemptions was essential for the establishment of the joint venture between Veba Oel and PDVSA. Had it been a company from a different country than Venezuela, clashing with Germany's foreign policy objectives and with a sharply opposite set of cultural values, the outcome of the negotiations would have been different[43].

The political context to the third phase of policy implementation

The new context resulting from the change of political actors in 1988 influenced the continuation of PDVSA's internationalisation policy. The 1988 general elections gave the victory to AD's candidate, Carlos Andrés Pérez, who had already been President between 1974 and 1979. However, a different political context did not produce any significant changes to the traditional pattern of legislative policy-making based on two-party consensus. Neither was the tendency towards the exclusion of minorities transformed. In the 1988 Congress minorities were even less conspicuous than in any previous period. The 24.8% of votes obtained by minority parties only gave them 9.3% of representatives in the Senate and 18.4% in the Chamber of Deputies. AD and COPEI were once again the leading parties. AD had scored 43.26% of votes; COPEI, 31.43%. A salient point of these elections was that it was President Pérez who obtained the majority of votes, and not his party AD[44]. The fact that Pérez had reached a victory through a coalition of non-AD parties turned out to be a crucial element that subsequently widened the gap between him and his party members. President Pérez soon found out that little support could be obtained from his party for his drastic programme of economic transformation.

Prior to the December 1988 elections, PDVSA had been negotiating the purchase of the 155,000 b/d Tenneco refinery in Chalmette, Louisiana, and Coastal Corporation's refinery in Westville, New Jersey, with a capacity to process 95,000 b/d[45]. Rumours that if he won the elections Pérez would try to slow down the expansion of the internationalisation policy were making the industry act rapidly, in order to consolidate the pending negotiations for the establishment of further internationalisation contracts. During his campaign, Pérez had said that '450,000 b/d were sufficient internationalisation'[46], despite PDVSA's target of 700,000 b/d of processing refining capacity abroad. Pérez had mentioned that it was time to 'internalise'[47] the oil industry, to turn its activities inwards, 'in order to allow a larger role for private investors'[48]. Fearing a possible halt to the expansion of the policy and the failure to accomplish the goal of 700,000 b/d in refining capacity abroad, PDVSA's managers launched a third phase of policy implementation.

The possibility that Pérez would elect Celestino Armas, old foe of the internationalisation strategy, as Minister of Energy, also pushed PDVSA's policy-makers to continue implementing the industry's internationalisation policy. Armas's designation rendered PDVSA's managers apprehensive[49]. As seen, his political way of conceiving oil policy clashed with the industry's schemes and objectives. Eventually, Armas's period as Minister came to be characterised by constant differences with the industry's president, Andrés Sosa Pietri. During this period, 1989-91, the industry and the executive were in constant confrontation. The appointment of two clashing personalities as Energy Minister and PDVSA's president, with two different ways of conceiving and implementing oil policy, in turn allowed President Pérez to have the last word in key policy-making decisions.

During the first phase of policy implementation, the executive and industry managers had shared the same view regarding the benefits of the internationalisation policy. Then, Congress had criticised the behaviour of the Energy Ministry as much as PDVSA's. In the period 1989-91 it was the executive which opposed the industry's policy orientation; had the industry decided to pursue its internationalisation policy aggressively, the obstacles would have been more difficult to surmount. However, when PDVSA's policy-makers decided to slow down policy implementation, they did it not as a result of executive or Congress opposition, but of a corporate decision indicating that the main policy objectives had been successfully attained. Their decision followed a rational assessment of the policy's outcome and of the variables that rendered its continuation less attractive.

Government attempts at an economic revolution

The new set of economic policies implemented by the Pérez administration was in sharp contrast with his first mandate (1974-79), when the country enjoyed the windfall of the 1974 oil crisis. It was during Perez's former presidency that the nationalisations of the iron and of the oil industries took place. In his first administration, government policy-making was eased by the petrodollar inflow. As a result, the government subsidised the economy on a lavish scale. Populist and clientelist practices were widespread. During the 1988 elections, Perez's speeches encouraged voters' hopes about a return to the good old times associated with his first mandate. Not surprisingly, the population received the sudden implementation of a drastic neo-liberal economic programme as a shock. All too aware of the political costs of unveiling the implications of his programme, Pérez, like most Latin American presidents who ended up embracing pragmatism and departing from previous populist discourses, chose instead to tell the people what they wanted to hear in order to be re-elected. As Philip commented:

> It is notable that no recent presidential candidate in any fully democratic Spanish American country has faced the electorate with a clearly neo-liberal programme and won. Pérez in Venezuela, like Fujimori in Peru and Menem in Argentina, sounded like a populist on the campaign trail only to act like a neo-liberal once in office[50].

In January 1989 the country's economy was in sharp decline. The outgoing administration of Jaime Lusinchi had left a balance of payments' deficit amounting to 7% of GDP in 1988; operational reserves had been largely exhausted. In 1988, the current account registered a deficit of $5,800 million and the balance of payments a deficit of $4,600 million.

Within only days of taking office, Pérez implemented a drastic package of austerity measures that shocked the population and which resulted in the most serious challenge to civic order in over thirty years of democratic life. Riots in Caracas and in other urban centres were triggered by bus fare increases after petrol prices suddenly doubled, accompanied by general price increases as a result of lifting numerous subsidies. Most government attempts to rise petrol prices have been previously frustrated by the social and political costs of the measure. PDVSA, bearing alone the costs of a highly subsidised domestic market, had long advocated the liberalisation of petrol prices. In February 1989, the violent reaction to the liberalisation of petrol prices totalled over 400 dead in the capital alone.

Among the key elements of the programme were an immediate 160% currency devaluation, the liberalisation of price controls and interest rates, reduction of the fiscal deficit to 3% of GDP through cuts in public sector spending, the introduction of a sales tax, and trade policy reforms to reduce import tariffs. Incentive for debt-equity conversions and an aggressive privatisation scheme were also part of the new economic programme[51]. Seeking to open new credit lines from multilateral financial institutions, the economic adjustment programme was formulated in consultation with the International Monetary Fund (IMF).

The programme included the significant reduction of the state. Despite subsequent efforts to subsidise the private sector, in Venezuela the state has never really fulfilled its welfare functions. Successive governments have attempted to create an independent non-oil sector along with a large network of clientelist support. They failed with the former goal and succeed with the latter. In this process, the expectations of the poor remained largely unsatisfied.

Many problems and inconsistencies accompanied the implementation of the new economic measures implemented by the Pérez administration[52]. Concerned with the lack of popular support the government was experiencing, AD began to oppose the measures. Congress, where AD held a majority representation, did not approve many policies that were needed for the coherent implementation of the programme. To darken the situation, or perhaps as a result of it, in the year 1992 alone, the Pérez administration had to face two *coups d'état* attempts from military factions which used the government's lack of popular support to justify their actions. The reform programme ended up being implemented in a piecemeal manner. As with many policies, its implementation and outcome differed significantly from initial goals. For instance, the vital trade policy review was only finalised three months after the other measures were implemented. Also, following February's 1989 unrest, the government was forced to review major issues: subsidies were extended and a job creation programme implemented. The programme was adapted according to the responses its implementation was producing and in the end it bore little resemblance to the way it had been initially formulated. The programme undeniably entailed attacking the traditional manner of political practice in Venezuela and the vested interests of the key economic groups that had flourished under the state's protection. With little party and popular support, the programme seemed to be doomed from the start.

In spite of the shortcomings involved in the implementation of the economic programme, the country's macroeconomic indicators improved significantly during the first phase of its implementation. Between 1989 and 1990, GDP figures rose 6.5%; during that period the contribution of the oil sector to the GDP increased 13.9% and that of the non-oil sector 4.6%. In 1991, the GDP grew again, this time 10.4% in relation to the previous year. However, in 1991 the activity of the oil sector had reduced its contribution to the GDP, expanding 10.3% in comparison to 13.9% in 1990; in turn, the non-oil sector continued its expansion, to 8.9% in 1991[53]. Encouraged by the immediate macroeconomic results, multilateral financial institutions readily approved several disbursements. Furthermore, a significant and unexpected event came to improve government accounts during this period. A new conflict in the Gulf area erupted in September 1990 when Iraq decided to invade and annex neighbouring Kuwait. Oil prices, as a result, went soaring and the government once again welcomed with relief a new inflow of capital. PDVSA, in turn, also profited from the new windfall to implement expansion plans and increase operations.

The impact of the Gulf War

As a result of the conflict in the Gulf, in the year 1990 Venezuela received some additional $4,363 million which made its export bill rise to $17,278 million, a significant increase from the previous year's $12,915 million[54]. From $16.87b/d in 1989, the price for the Venezuelan crude basket rose to an average of $20.33b/d 1990[55]. Following the IMF's advice, the government created the Fund for Macroeconomic Stabilisation, seeking to concentrate oil revenues and prevent them from entering the economy. During the year 1990 the consolidated public sector accounts experienced a surplus of $77.8 million[56]. As a result of the expansive activity of PDVSA, triggered by the Gulf conflict, the public sector's income in 1990 rose 73% compared to the previous year. In 1990, PDVSA's operational expenditure levels rose 90% in relation to 1989. The company's contribution to the public sector during 1990 amounted to 77.6% of the government's income. In this context, PDVSA's policy-makers devised an aggressive expansion plan for the industry. Attributing the sudden growth in GDP to PDVSA's impressive investment plan, Sosa Pietri, then the company's president, pointed out that,

> The 1990-96 plan demonstrated, during its application in the period 1990-91, another reality: PDVSA is the locomotive of the Venezuelan economy. Using PDVSA's massive purchasing power in the country, we contributed, decidedly, to economic diversification, to non-traditional exports, and to lowering inflation, because the significant oil income reduced the fiscal deficit[57].
> In the 1990-1992 investment plan, PDVSA registered its highest growth period since its creation[58].

With the outbreak of the conflict in the Gulf area in September 1990, Venezuela increased production by almost 500,000 b/d. PDVSA had been preparing to raise production as soon as the conflict broke out. However, the hesitant attitude of the government, concerned not to act in opposition to OPEC's guideline, prevented the company from raising production as early as PDVSA intended. Both the Minister of Energy, Celestino Armas, and President Pérez were torn between satisfying the US call to fulfil the missing oil volumes and complying with OPEC's collective action precepts. The decision to augment production quotas came just before the conflict broke out, when OPEC members met in Geneva on August 29, 1990. All members except Iran and Iraq agreed on the production increase. PDVSA's policy-makers had achieved their goal, as Sosa Pietri commented:

> Even though I disagreed with the procedure adopted (I deemed it inconvenient, according to our policy of 'key supplier' to the US, and the fact of subordinating our decision to produce more –which had to be a sovereign one– to an international organisation), I had reached the much-desired freedom to produce[59].

As mentioned, PDVSA used the space allowed by the 1990 windfall to launch its expansion plan. During the last quarter of 1990 the company invested over $2,500 million[60]. However, after the short-lived windfall was exhausted and with the significant reduction of production later accepted by the government in the OPEC meeting of Geneva in 1992[61], PDVSA's 1990-96 expansion plan was halted and as a result the country's GDP began to plummet[62]. The annual variation in the contribution of the oil sector to the GDP descended from 10.3% between 1990 and 1991 to -1.9% between 1991 and 1992. The economy slowed its growth rate: from 1991 to 1992 GDP grew 7.3%, as opposed to the impressive 10.4% experienced between 1990 and 1991[63]. These figures highlight the impact of PDVSA's policies on the country's economy. Decisions taken by PDVSA's policy-makers have a definite impact on the overall implementation of economic policies[64].

As usual in times of sudden oil windfall, the cash that was being injected into the economy, not only as a result of PDVSA's fiscal contribution but also as a consequence of its $48,000 million investment programmes, had disruptive macroeconomic implications. The industry's expansion policy generated negative influences on the policy of restrictive monetary policy implemented by the Central Bank in accordance with the general economic programme of the Pérez administration. Sosa Pietri was a fervent advocator of the industry's expansion programme. His insistence on an aggressive expansion plan for the industry and his constant disputes with the Energy Ministry resulted in his removal as PDVSA's president in 1992. President Pérez then appointed Gustavo Roosen, former Minister of Education and asked him 'to rationalise and limit the [industry's] expansion plan'[65].

PDVSA's indebtedness and the internationalisation policy

PDVSA's problem of indebtedness had a definite impact on the development of the internationalisation policy and on the adoption of a policy aimed at allowing foreign oil companies into the country's upstream sector. Despite the 1990 windfall, PDVSA resorted to indebtedness in order to continue with the implementation of its expansion plan, which included the development of its upstream activities and the recuperation of obsolete fields. Created to contain the money inflow from the 1990 windfall, the Fund for Macroeconomic Stabilisation ended up being spent to alleviate the government's fiscal deficit. Only a small amount of the taxes paid by the oil industry had actually made it into the Fund. In 1990 PDVSA paid the treasury over $2,000 million of excess taxes, of which only a small fraction was deposited into the Fund. When the IMF asked about the Central Bank about the Fund's fate, government authorities resorted once again to PDVSA. Further loans had been conditioned on the proper management of the Fund. The company was forced by decree to provide extra sums to complete the amount requested by the IMF as a condition to continue its credit support to the government's economic programme[66].

Through loans, PDVSA obtained the difference between what was able to provide at the time, $850 million, and what the government required, $1,200 million. In turn, the government promised PDVSA that it would be allowed to make use of the Fund's money after January 1992. However, the company never succeeded in claiming those funds. In 1992 PDVSA had to rely on further loans in order to finance about 20% of its six-year plan. PDVSA's policy-makers had thus lost another battle to curb government financial demands. In the cases of the 1982 transfer of foreign assets to the Central Bank and the creation of the Fund for Macroeconomic Stabilisation in 1990, the industry had to meet the government's cash requests.

Between 1989 and 1991, 'PDVSA acquired a debt for the first time: $4,000 million in two years'[67]. In order to reschedule its debt, between 1991 and 1993 PDVSA issued bonds totalling $1,000 million in the US capital markets. Warning against what he termed the 'Pemexisation'[68] of the industry, conjuring up the deep financial crisis of the Mexican oil company due to excessive fiscal payments and massive indebtedness, one of PDVSA's former presidents summarised the company's financial situation as follows:

PDVSA's debt now (1993) amounts to $5,000 million...As a result of the fiscal system applied to the industry, its cash flow does not generate sufficient funds for the investments needed to keep up production potential, and even less to service the debt acquired with international banks. PDVSA is falling into a situation similar to that of PEMEX during the 1980s. Why did PDVSA have to acquire a $5,000 million debt? To give the money to the treasury, because the government has used PDVSA as a generator of funds. Exactly the PEMEX situation. What is more deplorable is that everyone seems to tolerate this[69].

PDVSA's financial situation has been a major source of concern for its policy-makers. Some of them have complained that politicians overlook the industry's financial problems[70]. A former member of PDVSA's Board of Directors partly blamed the industry's silence for the lack of support it encounters from external sectors. According to this policy-maker, the industry's financial problems are:

> Skeletons in the cupboard, things we do not talk about in public, only in the family. PDVSA uses this approach in relation to the public opinion. There are things that are not convenient to diffuse.
>
> The only objective of the government and its *entourage* is to become rich...No one pays attention to PDVSA [71].

PDVSA acquired most of its debt when it was registering a short windfall due to a crisis in the Gulf area. In this sense, the company was mirroring the government's situation in times of oil windfall: major indebtedness against a context of large petrodollar revenues[72]. Allegedly, PDVSA's decision to borrow from external sources relied on three conditions that the government promised to respect. First, gradual reductions of the reference tax on exports from 20% to zero. According to the reference tax mechanism, the government taxes the industry by about 13%, plus the usual 67.7% rent income tax rate. A legacy of the pre-nationalisation period, the reference tax can exceed actual earnings, with the result that PDVSA often paid taxes on amounts it does not receive[73]. Second, the increase in production in order to reach 4 million b/d by the year 2002. Third, compensation for government-imposed subsidies on petrol and fertilisers. By 1991, the government had failed to meet these commitments and in order to continue with the implementation of its expansion PDVSA was compelled to obtain cash from several sources. As a result, in 1990 PDVSA acquired a debt of $1,900 million[74]. In 1993, PDVSA launched an operation to issue senior notes in order to reschedule $1,000 million of its debt to a longer term[75]. In 1995, PDVSA's long-term debt amounted to $4,933 million[76].

PDVSA's policy-makers have had limited success in limiting government decisions regarding wealth transfers or tax reforms. In this respect, PDVSA has been treated as the rest of SOEs, forced to fulfil government short-term objectives to the detriment of its corporate policies.

Judging from the history of relationships between the industry and successive administrations over policy decisions, it seems surprising that PDVSA relied on government promises and acquired a debt that soon proved unable to service. For instance, PDVSA's decision to increase production volumes depended on the government's commitment to press for such a goal within OPEC. The industry had plans to raise production by 500,000 b/d for the year 1990 and to add between 120,000 b/d and 150,000 b/d annually until 2002 [77]. With the acquisition of important refinery assets in key markets, PDVSA has been preparing for a substantial production increase, an increase which disregards OPEC's quota restrictions. PDVSA buys crude from different sources in order to keep its refineries abroad running at a capacity enabling it to maintain and expand its significant market share. Any conflict arising in the Middle East or any sudden decision to raise production could be met immediately by PDVSA's international network of refineries and storage facilities.

As mentioned in Chapter VI, factors such as possessing sufficient proven reserves and a large market share augment a country's bargaining power within OPEC, especially when pressing for increases of production quotas. Possessing a significant network of refinery assets in key markets has contributed to strengthening PDVSA's bargaining position within the Organisation. Thanks to its international refinery network, which allows it to enlarge market share more easily by being strategically positioned within or closer to important consumer markets, Venezuela is in principle better placed to bargain for larger production quotas. As two PDVSA managers put it:

> In order to have a good bargaining position in OPEC, Venezuela needs to have a secure and large market. Other countries do not have that market and their power to negotiate in OPEC is weak. It is not so much having production capacity, but market availability[78].
> Venezuela can put pressure to change its position within OPEC. Saudi Arabia does not have as much market as Venezuela. We do not have market risks because we have the markets...The other OPEC members have risks. If they get new markets, they get them because they lower their prices or through buying refineries at high prices... No company gives away market share[79].

In this context, it is hardly surprising that PDVSA, seeking to maintain its market share, purchases between 500,000 b/d and 600,000 b/d of crude to feed its refineries abroad[80].

PDVSA's decision to become Citgo's sole owner

During the third phase of policy implementation that began in late 1989, PDVSA set out to purchase the remaining 50% of Citgo's assets. Political actors opposed the operation that made PDVSA Citgo's sole owner. This acquisition modified the policy-makers' initial commitment to having a partner in its refinery ventures abroad. PDVSA's strategy with its total ownership of Citgo was to make the company the centre of operations in the US and 'to maintain the competitive advantages acquired in the US market'[81].

Southland, PDVSA's partner in Citgo, was facing financial problems as a result of having acquired debts that proved difficult to service. Allegedly, Southland had financed many of its operations 'with the success enjoyed'[82], and not with a sound basis. Soon, Southland's financial situation became critical. When the company sought to obtain loans by indebting Citgo, PDVSA 'categorically opposed' the plan[83]. Not being able to make use of Citgo's assets to obtain further loans, Southland decided to sell its 50% shares in the company. PDVSA exercised its right as partner and became Citgo's sole owner in 1989[84]. It was a landmark operation: a DCMN (developing-country multinational) and entirely state-owned became the sole owner of a major US company. The press in Venezuela called the operation 'the most important acquisition in the US energy industry carried out by a foreign enterprise'[85].

An oil analyst narrated as follows the events that led to Southland's sale of assets and to PDVSA's transition from part to sole owner of Citgo:

> [For Southland] business turned sour. Some of its assets were sold to a Japanese company. The refinery and the 7/11 were sold to PDVSA. This way PDVSA ended up with 100%, something that was and is an adventure. The idea was to have a good partner, and the Thompsons were not. They had been involved in too many things: bread, marketing, commerce, and so on, but never in oil. They did not know the oil business. Thus, it was better not to have them as partners at all[86].

The decision to acquire the remaining 50% of Citgo's shares generated conflict with the executive and with political actors. Due to a lack of consensus regarding the advantages of the operation, the final decision to become Citgo's sole owner was preceded by a period of contradictions that highlighted the arm's-length interaction between PDVSA and the executive. PDVSA was convinced of the benefits of the venture and of the advantages of not having to share ownership of the refinery. Although it differed from the previous contracts with Veba Oel and Nynäs, this new formula of total asset ownership went in agreement with the suggestion of the policy advisors who, during the policy assessment period, warned against the disadvantages of sharing decision-making powers with a partner.

Even though PDVSA had reached the goal of strengthening its presence in the US market through owning half of Citgo, by becoming the company's sole owner, PDVSA's managers were trying to minimise the risks and inconveniences of having a partner that made decision-making a slower and more cumbersome process. An industry manager pointed out that 'when a company is owned 100%, it is easier to administer it'[87]. The experience with Southland, characterised by this company's financial problems and its lack of knowledge of the oil business, was an important factor in PDVSA's decision to acquire the remaining 50% of Citgo. The acquisition was the most important in the industry's vertical-integration policy. As a PDVSA policy-maker pointed out:

> Through Citgo, PDVSA processes whatever it wants; it serves as spearhead for the country's exports[88].

To the question of why PDVSA decided not to look for another partner instead of becoming Citgo's exclusive owner, another PDVSA policy-maker answered by pointing out the strategic convenience of not having as partner an oil company that at the same time would be a competitor. In that case,

> It would have been [more] convenient to have a financial partner. Citgo processed 50% of Venezuelan crude and 50% from other markets. Gradually, Citgo had been buying more and more Venezuelan crude. An oil partner would have wanted to place its crude, and we would have had to withdraw part of ours. That was not convenient. It would have also been complicated to have a minority shareholder like BP and Shell. We then decided to acquire the remaining 50% shares of Citgo. We got a good price from Southland and all remained in the family[89].

From PDVSA's viewpoint, it seemed advantageous to exercise the total control of a company as profitable as Citgo. However, many Congress members held an opposite view. Furthermore, the timing of the operation had been unfavourable for gaining political support. At the time, the government was in desperate need of fresh cash and it was soon preparing for a new round of debt negotiation with the international banks[90].

In a visit paid to OPEC's headquarters in Vienna in June 1989, Energy Minister, Celestino Armas, when asked about the rumours regarding PDVSA's intentions to become Citgo's sole owner replied that PDVSA will not acquire Citgo's total assets[91]. At the same venue, and perhaps in order not to contradict the Minister's words, PDVSA's officials confirmed that the industry was not negotiating with Southland Corporation[92]. Five months later, however, PDVSA bought Southland's shares in Citgo and became its sole owner. The 50% remaining of Citgo's shares were acquired by $675 million, allegedly paid with what the industry was to get from future cash flows[93].

A common argument used by politicians to oppose PDVSA's decision to become the sole owner of Citgo was the threat of a possible take-over by the

US government. Their argument was based on the fear that possessing a 100% subsidiary would make PDVSA more vulnerable to minimise eventual discriminatory treatment against totally foreign owned companies operating in the US[94]. Some politicians feared measures such as asset confiscation or outright nationalisation. In fact, Venezuelan politicians were translating to the US a way of thinking that was their own and that in many developing countries had resulted in nationalisations of the oil industry. Furthermore, there were some foreign policy concerns. PDVSA was a SOE of a country that held a significant debt with US creditors. However, PDVSA's policy-makers considered that such arguments did not stand.

> In the US the properties of foreign companies are not seized. They respect the freedom of the market. There was an argument –probably a political one– in the sense that if Venezuela did not pay the debt, its assets could be seized in the US. After all, PDVSA is a SOE... Anyway, in the US there is no much knowledge of the fact that Citgo is owned by Venezuela[95].

The following evidence depicts how PDVSA's managers went about developing a solid ground for the defence of their policy choice, highlighting that a possible take-over by the US government was unlikely:

> The political risk was not very high in having a company owned 100% by a South American MN in the US. We established some political contacts, and the Americans said that PDVSA had a respectable name in the US. The merger between PDVSA and Union Pacific in 1987 [to form Champlin Refining Company] was considered a successful one. They were content that the dependence on crude from the Gulf states would be minimised by this operation... In the US, the salesmen of Citgo's petrol stations [the Seven-Eleven stores] are the ambassadors of Venezuela[96].

After PDVSA explained to the executive and to Congress about the low amount involved in the operation and about the implausibility of seizure by the US government, opponents minimised their criticism. Thus, PDVSA proceeded with the purchasing operation. PDVSA had scored another battle in pursuing the expansion of its vertical-integration policy. Despite the criticism of many political actors, PDVSA's policy-makers were able to achieve their policy: purchasing Citgo and making it a subsidiary in the US market. The internationalisation policy had been strengthened and another confrontation with political actors was settled in a convenient way for PDVSA. Politicians accepted the operation, stressing the fact that PDVSA was to sell the shares shortly afterwards, seeking thereby to make a substantial profit.

Reducing the margin of uncertainty imposed by the implementation of import quotas and high taxation on foreign oil in the US market was also a rationale for PDVSA's acquisition of Citgo's remaining shares[97]. Since the late 1950s, when the US first imposed import quotas on Venezuelan and Middle West crude, governments have been constantly concerned with the possible implementation of a new set of discriminatory measures affecting the share of Venezuelan crude in the US market[98]. The acquisition of 50% of Citgo's shares, the subsequent total purchase of its assets, and the decision to make it the centre of PDVSA's US operations were partly a response to minimising potential US retaliatory measures against imports of foreign oil.

It would be misleading, however, to totally dismiss the political argument warning PDVSA against the possible risks involved in becoming Citgo's sole owner. The political leadership was not entirely wrong about the negative reaction the acquisition of Citgo was going to generate in the US. The timing of the acquisition of the remaining 50% shares of the company in 1989 arose the criticism of the international community of creditors. When PDVSA announced in November 1989 its intention to buy the remaining shares of Citgo for $675 million, the banks to which the government of Venezuela owed over $25,000 million were astonished: the largest Venezuelan SOE was spending in the operation an amount that the government could have used to pay part of its outstanding debt. Obviously, this did not help the Venezuelan government, that at the time of the operation was trying to obtain a substantial reduction of its debt. In 1989, Venezuela was the fourth country –after Mexico, Costa Rica, and the Philippines– that went to the negotiation table trying to obtain a substantial reduction of its debt according to the plan engineered by George Bush's Secretary of the Treasury, Nicholas Brady. During this attempt, all of the banks remarked that the amount of $675 million was slightly superior to the $600 million loan that the banks had granted the Venezuelan government the previous September[99]. The timing of the Citgo operation led bankers to believe that Venezuela, contrary to the rest of debtors, did not really need a reduction of its debt. The Venezuelan government, nevertheless, expected to receive the same treatment as Mexico, which had seen its debt reduced by 35% within the Brady Plan negotiations. Bankers insisted that the inclusion by the US government of Venezuela in the list of countries to benefit from the Brady Plan was due to a political move by the Bush administration intended to help the Pérez administration with its radical reform programme, especially after the general Riots of February 1989, and not because the country really needed preferential treatment. Bankers finally proposed alternative payment schemes, instead of allowing Venezuela important reductions of its debt[100].

Partly as a result of PDVSA's operation, the terms for rescheduling the country's foreign debt were not what the government expected. This evidence showed that what was good for PDVSA was not necessarily beneficial to the country. If the industry's investment plans may often benefit different economic sectors and help to raise GDP figures, operations such as the purchase of Citgo's remaining shares proved detrimental to the government in the particular context in which it took place. PDVSA's objective to consolidate its position as oil MN went in opposite directions to the needs of the government, grappling with its international creditors. PDVSA's corporate strategic objectives had been placed ahead of the country's short-term economic interests. The need to strike a balance between what is beneficial for PDVSA and what is convenient for the government remains a major challenge of oil policy-making in Venezuela.

Citgo's expansion and consolidation in the US market

Soon after PDVSA became Citgo's sole owner, Champlin was placed under its umbrella. 'Champlin was merged with Citgo'[101], which became 'a true subsidiary of PDVSA'[102]. The merger was however not well received by the executive. As mentioned, the executive had stressed, soon after the acquisition of Citgo's entire shares, that PDVSA was to sell them shortly afterwards. PDVSA's president Sosa Pietri reported that the Minister of Energy, Celestino Armas, often reminded him that 'the second half of Citgo was purchased with the intention of selling it after...'[103]. Therefore, any moves towards expanding the company and redefining its strategic role in the US market were not well received by the executive. PDVSA's efforts to convince the executive of the strategic importance of Citgo as an operating centre in the US market made Sosa Pietri discuss the matter directly with President Pérez. Sosa Pietri summarised his efforts as follows:

> I tried to convince him of the mistake that PDVSA would make by selling 50% of Citgo. I told him about the third dimension of the business (the market), about Citgo's strategic importance for PDVSA, about our solid growth in the US market (through Citgo), about the new mission given to Citgo, about the merging of Champlin into Citgo, the purchase of Seaview and the negotiations to acquire the Lyondell and Savannah refineries in the short term; I also told him about our global vision[104].

In order to head off the government's intention to sell 50% of Citgo's shares, PDVSA went ahead to consolidate the company as the centre of its operations in the US. By expanding Citgo and by making the rest of PDVSA's US refineries its affiliated companies, the industry's policy-makers managed to counteract the government's plans to get rid of Citgo's half assets. Policy-makers were too aware of the government's intentions when proposing the sale of half of Citgo's shares, as the following comments demonstrate:

> Those people who want to sell half of Citgo want to use the money to pay the government's bills[105].
> The executive decided that it wants to sell Citgo because the government is bankrupt...PDVSA is not interested in that. If the money were to be invested in something else, that would be fine...but to sell Citgo and give the money to the government, that no[106].

Despite the patent disagreement of the executive over the expansion of Citgo, PDVSA succeeded in carrying out as planned its consolidation in the US market. PDVSA's managers scored another victory against the executive, opposed to the company's policy choice to become Citgo's sole owner. In 1990 Citgo purchased 50% of Seaview Petroleum Company's refining interests in the Paulsboro refinery located in New Jersey, mainly specialised in processing asphalt and with a processing capacity of 84,000 b/d. The remaining 50% of Seaview's shares were purchased in February 1991. The operation allowed PDVSA to increase its presence in the US East Coast. Two years later, on April 30, 1993, Citgo purchased AMOCO's Oil Company asphalt refinery in Savannah, Georgia, with a capacity to process 28,000 b/d. AMOCO's refinery was used to processing Venezuelan Boscán crude only, and in the light of a possible closure of the refinery, Citgo decided to purchase it. Had Citgo or another purchaser not stepped in, most likely AMOCO would have closed down the refinery[107].

An important operation by Citgo was the July, 1993 acquisition of 50% shares of the Lyondell refinery in Houston. Although Reimpall pointed out that 'nobody knows [exactly] how much Citgo paid to acquire 50% of Lyondell'[108], another policy-maker asserted that 'for Lyondell, PDVSA only paid with inventories. Not one cent was given'[109]. As the time of the signing of the joint-venture contract approached, Lyondell began reducing its purchases of Mexican and Arabian crudes and increasing the shares of Venezuelan crude. Based on a formula that allowed the refinery more profits than the one provided by processing Maya crude, PDVSA had managed to offer Lyondell a better offer than PEMEX. The contract had its antecedents when, in 1992, Citgo began helping Lyondell Petrochemical Company to increase its processing capacity by 80,000 b/d. With the 1993 acquisition PDVSA sought to fulfil the entire 200,000 b/d capacity of the Lyondell complex[110]. Reimpall explained how,

Citgo sends about 130,000 b/d of heavy crude (22° API Bachaquero and others). There are plans to build a cocker to refine heavy crude at a cost of $800 million. The responsibility to build this refinery is Citgo's. By the time the construction is finished, Citgo will own 35%. By then, Lyondell will be able to process 200,000 b/d of heavier crude than the one it has been refining. Citgo will then be able to acquire 20% of the refinery, increasing its ownership significantly to 55%[111].

PDVSA's international refining capacity has significantly increased as a result of Citgo's expansion. The following data in Table 7.5 show Citgo's operations in the US market:

Table 7.5 Growth of Citgo's operations, 1986, 1992 and 1993

	1993*	1992	1986
Number of refineries	3**	3	1
Net ownership in refining capacity (Thousand b/d)	585	544	320
Branded gasoline sales (Million gallons) (***)	n.a.	5,604	2,870
Number of wholly- and jointly-owned distribution terminals	52	51	29
Number of Citgo branded retail outlets	12,173	11,953	4,175

*   As of July 1st.

**   Includes minority interest in the Lyondell-Citgo Houston refinery.

***   Total sales during the year.

Source: Prospectus, PDV America, Inc. Salomon Brothers Inc.

Further policy expansion in the US: UNO-VEN

PDVSA signed a joint-venture agreement with Union Oil Corporation of California (UNOCAL) in December 1988 to form UNO-VEN[112], based on the acquisition of 50% of a refinery located in Lemont, Illinois, with a processing capacity of up to 153,000 b/d. The deal also included partial ownership of twelve distribution terminals in five states –Illinois, Michigan, Ohio, Iowa, and Wisconsin– 131 petrol stations operating under the UNOCAL name, and 3,500 others under the brand UNOCAL-76; a terminal for aviation fuel; a plant for lubricant blending and packaging located in Cincinnati, Ohio; as well as the participation in a venture to produce and sell super-premium grade petroleum coke[113]. Currently, UNO-VEN largely processes medium and light crudes[114]. Even though the price of the operation was estimated to be about $500 million,

> PDVSA did not give a cent for UNO-VEN. Filling up the inventories was PDVSA's contribution, and this was used as a guarantee to obtain further financial funds[115].

As the only US venture that has not come under Citgo's umbrella, most likely because of its limited success, UNO-VEN is owned 50% by PDVSA and in some areas, 'it sometimes competes with Citgo'[116]. Allegedly due to the logistic problems of channelling some of the crude from the US Gulf Coast to the Chicago region through the Capline pipeline, UNO-VEN has not generated the success expected. Although Union Corporation of California has allegedly wanted to sell its part, PDVSA has not shown interest in purchasing it. 'Union is asking for too much'[117]. Through Citgo, PDVSA has sought to sell its own shares in UNO-VEN. In 1992, a possible buyer, Kuwait, backed off and declined its offer to purchase PDVSA's assets in UNO-VEN[118]. Tables 7.6 and 7.7 show significant data on UNO-VEN's refinery in Lemont.

Table 7.6 UNO-VEN's Lemont refinery production, 1990-1992 (Thousand b/d)

	1992	1991	1990
Refining capacity			
Refinery input:	153	153	153
Crude oil	138	134	138
Other feedstocks	22	19	15
Total refinery input	160	153	153
Crude Oil Average API°	29.2	29.5	30.5

Source: Prospectus PDV America. Inc., Salomon Brothers Inc.

**Table 7.7 UNO-VEN's refined product sales, 1990-1992
(Million $)**

	1992	1991	1990
Refined Products:			
Light fuels	1,255	1,432	1,579
Lubricants	49	46	2
Industrial products	124	146	165
Total revenues from sales of products	1,428	1,624	1,796

Source: Prospectus PDV America. Inc., Salomon Brothers Inc.

Nynäs expansion: Briggs Oil Ltd

Although to a much lesser extent than Citgo in the US market, Nynäs's expansion in the European market for asphalt has been significant. At the end of 1991 Nynäs acquired Neste Öy, as well as important assets of UK Briggs Oil Ltd. comprising one refinery in Scotland, with a capacity to process 10,000 b/d, and 50% of another in Eastham, England, with a capacity of 12,000 b/d [119]. Also, Nynäs purchased 50% of Shell UK's refinery located in Airtham, increasing its refining capacity by about 12,000 b/d. In Sweden Nynäs purchased 51% of the Eurobit refinery[120]. This series of acquisitions by Nynäs had allowed the company to increase its share of the European market for asphalt to an estimated 17%, rendering it the second most important regional asphalt refiner.

Policy continuation

With the third phase of implementation of the internationalisation policy identified with the 1989 acquisition of Citgo's total shares and with the company's consolidation in the US market, PDVSA exceeded its original plans of having a refining capacity abroad of 700,000 b/d. In 1997 PDVSA supplied a total of 1.31 million b/d to its refinery interests abroad, which have a total installed refining capacity of 2.49 million b/d (including the *Curaçao Refinería Isla*)[121]. Moreover, PDVSA has a storage capacity abroad of 47 million barrels. Limited by OPEC quota restrictions, through its refineries abroad PDVSA purchases an important amount of crude to feed its downstream network, thus maintaining its share of the market. An industry manager summarised this situation as follows:

OPEC's quota affects the production and therefore the supply to PDVSA's refineries. In Venezuela and abroad PDVSA buys 700,000 b/d throughout its subsidiaries. These are not exclusive purchases for refineries, but also products. LAGOVEN buys between 60,000 b/d and 100,000 b/d for Veba Oel. Citgo also buys a good amount[122].

A high official at the Ministry of Energy also commented on PDVSA's large refining capacity abroad and depicted the way in which the industry's international refineries purchase crude volumes.

Now (1993) we have a refining capacity of more or less 930,000 b/d in our refineries abroad, and this is going to grow; with Lyondell, there is around 80,000 b/d more. Actually, the nominal [refining] capacity is more, but if we reach it we would be entering the margin of inefficiency. Seaview, for instance, has more capacity, but if we were to process more, we would be flooding the market for asphalt and the prices would fall. Citgo buys some 60,000 b/d to complete its diet of low sulphur, sweet crude. It also buys Maya crude. UNO-VEN buys 15,000 to 20,000 b/d of Canadian heavy crude which is very competitive; this crude goes by pipeline from Alberta to Chicago. Ruhr Oel also buys crude from the North Sea, Russia, the Middle East, Algeria and Iran [123].

Despite the negative reaction encountered from Congress and the executive with varying intensity at different phases of the policy process, PDVSA's policy-makers had achieved their strategic and commercial objectives with the internationalisation policy. These objectives were the ability to respond better to market upheavals, the acquisition of a platform to enlarge market share, and increasing administrative freedom. The significant purchase of DFIs in the form of refinery assets in key consumer markets had turned PDVSA into a vertically-integrated oil MN.

During the Pérez (1989-93) and Caldera (1994-99) administrations, the concern of PDVSA's decision-makers shifted towards the implementation of the policy named *Apertura*, consisting of associations with foreign companies to carry out upstream activities in the country. However, attempts to continue expansion of the network of refineries abroad were not abandoned. Especially during the Caldera administration, a new *élan* was given to the policy of internationalisation. In 1993 Citgo increased its participation in the Lyondell-Citgo Refining Company from 12% to 42%; the refinery has a current capacity to process 265,000 b/d. In 1997, Citgo bought for $250 million the remaining 50% shares of UNO-VEN, becoming this refinery's sole owner. In 1997, PDVSA in association with Mobil acquired for $227 million 50% of a refinery in Chalmette, Louisiana, with a processing capacity of 180,000 b/d; Citgo has the exclusivity to purchase 50% of products processed in the refinery. In 1998 PDVSA purchased 50% of the Amarada Hess refinery in the Virgin Islands with a total capacity to refine 120,000 b/d of heavy crude; PDVSA agreed to send 200,000 b/d during a twenty-year period[124].

Conclusion

The specific form adopted by PDVSA to enlarge its share of the market –i.e. through the acquisition of refinery assets– was not only the result of corporate objectives, but also of an attempt to increase its freedom of action, away from government meddling and unexpected financial demands. In contrast to PDVSA, other oil companies favoured the establishment of netback deals in order to enlarge market share. More limited in time, netback deals do not allow, however, a long-term platform for increasing a company's freedom to implement corporate policies and to curb government meddling in the industry, notably in the form of financial demands.

After having implemented the second phase of policy implementation, PDVSA's policy-makers continued expanding the industry's refinery network abroad. Despite the persistence of political opposition to the industry's acquisition of Citgo's 50% remaining assets, PDVSA imposed its policy choice and became Citgo's sole owner in 1989. During the third phase policy implementation, PDVSA consolidated its position as an oil MN. This strategic orientation was perceived by some political actors as being detrimental to the industry's investment plans in the country, a programme considered essential for boosting important sectors of the national economy. The industry was regarded as failing to fulfil its role as direct generator of economic growth, a role commonly attributed to other SOEs. The tension inherent in PDVSA's dual nature as both the country's most important SOE and its status as oil MN became evident in this case. Such a tension was exacerbated when the government found it difficult to negotiate the terms for the payments of its foreign debt, partly due to PDVSA's recent purchase of Citgo's assets. In this case, PDVSA's intention to increase its freedom of action by pursuing the internationalisation of its operations proved detrimental to the government. What was strategically convenient for PDVSA was a hindrance for the achievement of government short-term objectives.

Despite political opposition, PDVSA exerted once again its role as main policy actor within the process of oil policy-making when it refused to sell 50% shares of its fully-owned Citgo, succeeding in keeping the company as its largest and most important subsidiary in the US market.

However, despite clear victories against Congress and the executive, PDVSA proved less successful in avoiding fiscal impositions and sudden wealth transfers to the treasury, as demonstrated in its failure to gain access to the Fund for Macroeconomic Stabilisation created as a result of the 1990 oil windfall. In turn, despite PDVSA's efforts to be able to decide over export levels, the Energy Ministry maintained this decision-making prerogative.

Also serving as an instrument to minimise non-corporate demands on its operations, PDVSA relies on its partly or fully-owned refinery complexes abroad to maintain its market share levels and, when needed, be able to circumvent OPEC quota restrictions. Thanks to its large network of refineries and storage facilities abroad, PDVSA is better placed to respond to crisis situations requiring sudden export increases and a more direct access to consumer markets.

The battles waged between the government and PDVSA over policy decisions underline the existing tensions between short-term political objectives and corporate orientations. Such tensions are inherent in the process of public policy-making and, more specifically, in the interaction between SOEs and the government. PDVSA's feature as a MN exacerbates these tensions.

Notes

1   *Petroleum Intelligence Weekly.* January 27, 1986.
2   Gómez. *Interview.* January 8, 1993.
3   *Petroleum Intelligence Weekly.* January 27, 1986.
4   Oil analyst who requested anonymity. *Interview.*
5   *Idem.*
6   'Global Investment. The Global Oil Theme'. Merrill Lynch. London. August 25, 1994.
7   CEPET, 1988, v. II, p. 175; Boué. *Op. cit.*, p. 167.
8   Boué. *Op.cit.*, p. 165.
9   *Petroleum Industry Indicators.* September 1988, p. 31.
10 Boué. *Op. cit.* p. 165.
11 *Platt's Oilgram News.* June 2, 1988, p.1.
12 Boué. *Op. cit.*, pp. 166-167.
13 This was one of the reasons why reliable information on the international operations of companies, such as Kuwait's KPC and Saudi ARAMCO, was virtually impossible to obtain for this study.
14 Boué. *Op. cit.* pp. 168 and 175.
15 *Ibid.,* p. 169.

16   Gustavo Roosen. Presentation at the 1993 Global Management Development Forum. 'Learning Across Borders'. Session 1.10. Barcelona-Sitges (Catalonia), Spain. June 14, 1993.
17   *Annual Report*. PDVSA, 1995.
18   *Cf.* Beatríz Moreno. *La Internacionalización Petrolera y su Metodología de Evaluación.* B.Sc. thesis in Economics. Universidad Católica Andrés Bello. Caracas, 1989. Moreno concluded that the internationalisation policy has been profitable. Using an incremental approach to the evaluation of the refinery acquisition policy, Moreno concluded that 'the marginal profits generated by the strategy cover the original investment' (p. 113). Moreno's study, nevertheless, is partial, in that it does not include Nynäs, a business considered less successful than the others; neither does it cover the later expansion of Citgo, nor the more recent refinery acquisitions.
19   *PDVSA. CONTACT.* Newsletter. No 46. August-September 1995. According to *Fortune*, in 1995 PDVSA ranked 11th in terms of revenues with $26,041 million and profits of $3,103 million. Exxon ranked first with $110,009 million in revenues and $6,470 million profits. Royal Dutch/Shell ranked third with $109,834 in revenues and $6,905 million in profits. *Fortune*. August 5, 1996, p. 6.
20   I. Renzetti, *Institut d'Economie et de Politique de l'Energie* (IEPE); data base of ENERDATA (MIDOIL-Refineries). In B. Bourgeois, 'Les relations entre compagnies pétrolières nationales et internationales: des accords contractuels aux relations de coopération?, p. 19. Seminar. Université Paris-Dauphine. *L'avenir des sociétés nationales des pays exportateurs d'hydrocarbures.* Paris. May 27, 1994.
21   P. Terzian, 'Downstream Investment by National Oil Companies'. *The Future of National Oil Companies in Exporting Countries.* Seminar. Université Paris-Dauphine. *Ibid.*
22   *Veneconomía.* June 29, 1988. Vol. 6, No. 32.
23   Tredenik. *Interview.* August 13, 1993.
24   *Q8.* Information document. Kuwait Petroleum Corporation (KPC). London.
25   Terzian. *Op. cit.*
26   *Idem.*
27   For the acquisition operation, the Libyan Arab Foreign Investment Bank took 70% of TAMOIL; Geneva-based company, SASEA, got 20%; and a 'First Arabian affiliate' retained 10%. TAMOIL's new president after being acquired by Libya was Giorgio Mazzanti, former president of ENI. *Petroleum Intelligence Weekly.* January 20, 1986.
28   Renzetti. *IEPE.* ENERDATA data base. In B. Bourgeois. *Op. cit.*
29   Terzian. *Op. cit.*
30   *Idem.*
31   Bouhafs. 'Stratégie de modernisation de SONATRACH'. *L'avenir des sociétés nationales des pays exportateurs d'hydrocarbures.* Seminar. Université Paris-Dauphine. Paris. May 27, 1994.
32   Sapmoko. Director, PERTAMINA, London. *Interview.* February 18, 1994.
33   *Idem.*
34   PEMEX has achieved some success by using the futures option instrument to hedge parts of its production. Boué. *Op. cit.,* p. 168.
35   Reimpall. *Interview.* August 12, 1993.
36   PEMEX possesses 5% assets of Repsol. Boué. *Interview.* February 11, 1999.
37   Bourgeois. *Op. cit.*
38   Bonse-Geuking. *Interview.* October 11, 1995.
39   *Idem.*
40   Sarkis. *Op. cit.*

41 'Prospectus'. *Salomon Brothers Inc.* July 1993.
42 Reimpall. *Interview.* August 12, 1993.
43 Bonse-Geuking. *Interview.* October 12, 1995.
44 Miriam Kornblith. 'Nuevas reglas de juego y estabilidad de la democracia en Venezuela'. UCV. July, 1993, p. 14.
45 *Veneconomía.* Vol 6. N° 37. August 10, 1988.
46 *Idem.*
47 *Veneconomía.* Volume 6. N° 28. June 1, 1988.
48 *Idem.*
49 *Veneconomía.* Vol. 7. N° 5. January 8, 1989.
50 Philip. 'Venezuelan Democracy and the February 1992 coup'. Mimeograph, p. 24.
51 Pedro Palma. *La Economía Venezolana en el Período 1974-1988: ¿Ultimos Años de una Economía Rentista?.* Caracas, October, 1989, pp. 232-242.
52 For an account of the problems faced by the programme's implementation, *Cf.* Moisés Naím. *Paper Tigers and Minotaurs: The Politics of Venezuela's Economic Reforms.* Carnegie Endowment Book. Washington, 1993.
53 José Toro Hardy. *Fundamentos de Teoría Económica. Un Análisis de la Política Económica Venezolana.* Editorial Panapo. Caracas, 1993, pp. 720-723.
54 Toro Hardy. *Venezuela. 55 Años de Política Económica.* Caracas, 1992. pp. 171-2.
55 *Ibid.,* p. 208.
56 *Ibid.,* p. 172.
57 Sosa Pietri. 'Algunas Apreciaciones sobre la Política Petrolera Venezolana'. (Second Part). Manuscript, [not dated].
58 Sosa Pietri. Talk at a forum for the candidacy of former COPEI candidate, Oswaldo Alvarez Paz. Tamanaco Hotel. Caracas. August 10, 1993.
59 Sosa Pietri. *Petróleo y Poder. Op. cit.,* pp. 177-178.
60 Sosa Pietri. 'Notas para Carlos Chávez'. Manuscript. July 19, 1993.
61 Sosa commented that PDVSA enjoyed the 'freedom to produce' until February 20, 1992 when the Minister of Mines agreed to limit the country's production in an OPEC meeting. Such a decision was one of the reasons that prompted Sosa's resignation from PDVSA's presidency in 1992. *Petróleo y Poder. Op. cit.* p. 172.
62 Sosa Pietri. Talk at the Alvarez Paz Forum. *Op. cit.*
63 Toro Hardy. *Fundamentos... Op.cit.,* p. 723.
64 The influence of PDVSA's managers is also often exerted through their direct participation in other government policy-making processes. A form of *pantouflage* –as in the French system– takes place from PDVSA to other public administration entities. Often, PDVSA's policy-makers are called to hold positions in key government agencies.
65 Naím. *Op. cit.,* p. 163.
66 Sosa Pietri. *Op. cit.,* p. 183.
67 PDVSA Director who asked to remain anonymous. *Interview.* August 25, 1993.
68 The term 'Pemexisation' has also been used in cases of political interference in the industry. *Veneconomía.* Vol. 3. N° 3. December 19, 1989.
69 Chacín. *Interview.* January 8, 1993. As of 1995, PDVSA's debt had been reduced to $4,933 million. *Annual Report.* PDVSA, 1995.
70 *Veneconomía.* Vol. 6. N° 30. June 13, 1988.
71 PDVSA Director who requested anonymity. *Interview.* August 25, 1993.
72 Gelb. *Oil Windfalls. Blessing or Curse?* The World Bank. Oxford, 1988.
73 Before 1981, there was no defined percentage by which the tax values could surpass income levels. Subsequently, the law was amended to include some limits. For the most part of 1990, the reference tax was fixed at 15% of the average realisation price

per barrel. After August 1990, the rate was fixed at 20%. As a result of the serious financial problems that affected PDVSA in 1992, the tax on export reference values was lowered to 19% in June and 18 % in October that year. The reference tax was finally written off in 1996.

74 Sosa Pietri. 'Algunas Apreciaciones Sobre la Política Petrolera Venezolana'. *Op. cit.* (Third Part), p. 2.

75 Salomon Brothers launched the operation; $25,000 million in senior notes at 7 1/4 % due in 1998; $25,000 million at 7 3/4% due in 2000; and $50,000 million at 7 7/8 due in 2003. *Prospectus. Salomon Brothers Inc.* July 22, 1993.

76 *Annual Report.* PDVSA, 1995.

77 Sosa Pietri. 'Algunas Apreciaciones... (Second Part), p. 1.

78 Pulgar. *Interview.* August 16, 1993.

79 Reimpall. *Interview.* August 12, 1993.

80 *Idem.*

81 Sosa Pietri. *Op. cit.* p. 228.

82 Reimpall. *Interview.* August 12, 1993.

83 'PDVSA no acepta que Citgo se endeude por problemas de Southland'. Article. *El Universal.* May 5, 1989; 'Petróleos de Venezuela anunció que Southland usará su participación en Citgo para obtener recursos financieros'. Document. PDVSA. May 8, 1989; 'UNOCAL y Citgo', PDVSA. Document. December 1989.

84 'PDVSA adquiere la totalidad de Citgo'. *El Nacional.* November 7, 1989.

85 *El Nacional.* November 7, 1989.

86 Analyst who requested anonymity.

87 Albacete. *Interview.* March 4, 1993.

88 *Idem.*

89 Reimpall. *Interview.* August 12, 1993.

90 *Veneconomía.* November 29, 1989. Vol. 7. No 50.

91 *Veneconomía.* June 28, 1989. Vol. 7. No 28.

92 *Idem.*

93 *Veneconomía.* November 8, 1989. Vol 7. N° 47.

94 Sosa Pietri. *Op. cit.*, p. 111.

95 Reimpall. Interview. August 12, 1993.

96 *Idem.*

97 Boué. *Op. cit.* p. 170.

98 For an account of the different import quotas imposed by the US to Venezuelan and Middle East oil since the administration of Eisenhower, *Cf.* Yergin. *Op. cit.*, especially, pp. 536-540. Even though abolished during the Nixon administration, the threat of a new imposition of quotas has not been totally eradicated.

99 Article by Jonathan Fuerbringer. *The New York Times.* 'Compra de Citgo afectará negociaciones con la banca'. This article appeared in *El Nacional.* November 11, 1989.

100 *Idem.*

101 Gómez. *Interview.* November 11, 1993.

102 Sosa Pietri. *Op. cit.*, p. 110.

103 *Ibid.*, p. 111.

104 Sosa Pietri. *Op. cit.*, p. 238.

105 Martínez. *Interview.* October 20, 1993.

106 Chacín. *Interview.* January 8, 1993.

107 Boué. *Op. cit.*, p. 175. After the acquisition by Citgo, AMOCO's president said that despite the profitability of the business, 'the capital needs faced by the refining sector in the US were forcing companies to invest in more strategically key areas'. *Platt's Oilgram News*, June 22, 1992, p. 1.

108 Reimpall. *Interview*. August 12, 1993.
109 Rodríguez Eraso. *Interview*. November 12, 1993.
110 Boué notes that the purchase did not include ownership of the petrochemical facilities. *Op. cit.*, p. 175.
111 Reimpall. *Interview*. August 12, 1993.
112 'PDVSA participa con UNO-VEN en el mercado del Medio Oeste de Estados Unidos'. PDVSA. Document. April 1992; Boué. *Op. cit.*, p. 161.
113 *Oil and Gas Journal.* December 12, 1988, p. 28; *Veneconomía*, October 25, 1989. Vol. 7 N° 25; Boué. *Op. cit.*, p. 161.
114 Castillo. *Interview*. November 17, 1993.
115 Rodríguez Eraso. *Interview*. November 19, 1993.
116 Castillo. *Interview*. November 10, 1993.
117 Petzall. *Interview*. August 6, 1993.
118 *Platt's Oilgram News*. September 1, 1992, p. 2; Boué. *Op. cit.*, pp. 162 and 175.
119 Sosa Pietri reported that the acquisition of these refineries was approved by PDVSA's Board of Directors on December 19, 1991. Act N° 91-59. *Op. cit.* p. 116.
120 Sosa. *Op. cit.*, p. 117; *Petroleum Intelligence Weekly.* January 25, 1993. Vol. XXXII, N° 4. p. 8.
121 *Annual Report*, 1995. PDVSA.
122 Ramírez. *Interview*. September 2, 1993.
123 Castillo. *Interview*. November 17, 1993.
124 PDVSA. *Annual Report*, 1997.

Chapter 8
Conclusion. The international expansion of an oil SOE: The balance between politics and corporate strategy

8 Conclusion. The international expansion of an oil SOE: The balance between politics and corporate strategy

The previous chapters explored the interaction between politics and corporate strategy in PDVSA's efforts to become an oil MN. The main tensions between the policy actors involved in the process of policy-making have been stressed throughout this book. The fact that PDVSA was the government's most important source of revenues posed a clear constraint to the industry's attempts to extend and consolidate its international operations. Furthermore, the company's international expansion threatened the government's ability to exert close control over the company's performance and policy choices. This chapter assesses the partial conclusions suggested by the findings in each chapter and links them to the main arguments proposed in the Introduction. The discussion undertaken here reflects the analytical concerns identified in the literature on MNs from developing countries and on the interaction between SOEs and governments. The discussion will revolve around three main issues: the motivations and the obstacles found in PDVSA's efforts to expand its operations abroad, the interaction between the government and the oil SOE, and the tensions inherent in the process of oil policy-making. The chapter finally proposes new areas of analysis to be covered by further research into public policy-making processes in developing country contexts.

Seeking to answer the main question at the centre of this research –how did PDVSA reconcile its efforts to become an oil MN with its role as the country's most important SOE– this concluding chapter constantly links two levels of analysis: the internationalisation efforts of a SOE and the tensions inherent in the interaction between the latter and the other actors involved in oil policy-making, notably the executive and Congress. It has been argued here that PDVSA's efforts to become an oil MN resulted in diminishing the industry's attributes as a SOE. By stressing its independence from Congress and the executive as a result of the internationalisation of its operations, the industry became less of a SOE. The reconciliation of the industry's roles as a SOE and as MN resulted in diminishing the features commonly attributed to the former: accountability to Congress, subordination to the executive, and fulfilment of non-corporate goals.

The most original aspect of this study lies in the combination of two levels of analysis: PDVSA's features as an oil MN and the constraints posed by its role as Venezuela's most important SOE. Among OPEC members, PDVSA possesses the most significant DFIs in the form of refinery assets in OECD markets. In Latin America, no other government is as dependent on one economic sector as the Venezuelan government is on the oil industry.

Motivations for the internationalisation of a SOE

At the beginning of this study it was mentioned that the motivations of a firm for pursuing the internationalisation of its operations are various. Among such motivations the most obvious are the need to expand market share, minimise market imperfections, gain access to consumer markets and technical know-how, avoid commercial restrictions, and curb government unwelcome financial demands. For many companies, the motivations for setting up a direct presence in markets abroad reflects the need to curb the restrictions posed by regulated markets, both at home and abroad. Import-substitution policies and non-tariff barriers such as quotas, preferential market agreements, and artificial quality and health controls prevent the unhindered flow of commercial exchanges, fostering the establishment of direct investments (DIs) by a foreign firm in an attempt to bypass such restrictions.

Upon its creation, and once it accomplished the corporate objectives considered essential for enhancing its operations, PDVSA sought to overcome the limitations of a small and heavily subsidised domestic market by gaining access to key consumer markets. The fear of severing the nationalised industry from international distribution channels of crude and from access to up-to-date technology prompted policy-makers to implement a process of nationalisation based on the avoidance of conflict with the oil MNs operating in the country.

Most internationalisation contracts were established with companies that were already working with the oil industry in one way or another. Knowledge of the other partner and cultural affinity were important factors for the establishment of joint ventures. Through the establishment of joint ventures as the scheme for purchasing refinery assets abroad, PDVSA gained knowledge of the local legislation and market. Another clear advantage of joint ventures was the possibility of disguising the origin of the foreign company, thus allowing products to be sold under a brand name with an already established exposure to the local market.

Initially, policy-makers advocated negotiations with totally or partially state-owned oil companies such as Veba Oel. Besides the obvious incentives offered by the German government, the non-regulated nature of the German market was a decisive factor for the establishment of subsequent joint-venture agreements, carried out almost entirely with private-owned companies.

Whenever PDVSA established joint ventures, it chose companies of countries whose markets for oil derived products were not regulated by price controls and quota restrictions. Market regulations deterred PDVSA from establishing DIs in the form of refinery assets. The existence of regulated energy markets (France and Spain), where the host government discouraged the establishment of joint ventures (Spain), or where the economic situation was uncertain (Brazil) prevented PDVSA's policy-makers from pursuing negotiations with those countries.

Non-economic factors contributed forcefully to the international expansion of PDVSA's operations. This study has argued that a crucial factor in the internationalisation of PDVSA was the goal to minimise government interference in the industry's freedom to implement corporate policies, thereby curbing the threat of sudden financial demands and its degree of accountability to the legislature. This was a determining factor in the adoption of an internationalisation policy based on the acquisition of refinery assets and not on the establishment of short-term netback deals used by many oil exporting companies as a way to enlarge market share. The industry's response to the need to strike a balance between the constraints posed by its condition as a SOE and its corporate objectives was the acquisition of an important refinery network abroad. Having a direct presence in key markets allowed the industry a long-term platform to pursue corporate goals, making it easier to respond to changes in export quotas and crude prices. Furthermore, the establishment of joint ventures abroad allowed the industry's policy-makers the international exposure and decision-making powers not offered by the rather uneventful service at home.

Interaction between an overdependent government and a powerful SOE

The attempts to reconcile both its roles as SOE and as oil MN have created a clear dilemma for the industry, a situation that has often exacerbated its interaction with the executive and Congress. The dilemma for the Ministry is how to control the industry and to profit better from its performance without hampering the implementation of its corporate policies. For the industry, the challenge is to minimise government and legislative interference in order to gain a larger degree of autonomy in the implementation of corporate objectives. Thus, by opposing government demands and Congress controls over its operations, PDVSA has sought to act more as a private company. As a result, it has minimised its status as SOE, becoming less subordinate to the executive and Congress. In turn, while pursuing corporate and long-term goals in the international oil market, the industry has strengthened its features as a private enterprise; being present in the international oil market has forced PDVSA to be highly competitive and to use state-of-the-art technology for its operations. As a result of the extent to which PDVSA pursued its international expansion, it has been increasingly more difficult for the executive and the legislature to exercise their controls over it.

The action of politics and of constantly evolving political arrangements exerted a clear influence on PDVSA's internationalisation strategy. PDVSA's efforts to consolidate its position in the international oil market faced the constraints of local politics. Congress' bargaining dynamics and government's financial demands threatened the implementation of the industry's policy to become an oil MN.

The behaviour and interests of the individuals involved in the process of oil policy-making played a significant role in the creation of agreements conducive to policy implementation. Battles were frequently waged as a result of the political aspirations of one or a group of political actors. At the time of the first phase of policy implementation, attacking the industry's policy choice was a convenient way of downplaying government performance. To a large extent, the attacks on the industry's internationalisation policy were a matter of political strategy. Later on, the settlement of the controversy over the industry's policy choice, as a result of a political arrangement at the highest level, was the work of key individuals interested in stopping persistent criticism of government performance. The reaction of elected politicians in Congress is most often predictable. As party members, they have an interest in preserving the balance of power which made their position possible; as representatives of the people, they are concerned with the SOE's commitment to the treasury and its direct involvement in economic development. Thus, political actors seek to stress the typical features of PDVSA's status as a SOE. Any attempts to diverge from such objectives are likely to bring about criticism of the industry's performance and, in some cases, the possibility of Congress exercising its veto powers.

As well as being the result of the success of previous cases of policy implementation, shifting power-distribution schemes in the interaction between the industry and the executive, and between the former and Congress, fostered clear policy responses along the policy-making continuum. The evolution of power relations among the main policy actors involved in the process of oil policy-making had a definite impact on the way the industry sought to formulate and implement its policy choice. Moreover, the successful implementation of any given policy strengthens the position of the policy actors who devised and implemented it. This was clearly noticeable in the implementation of PDVSA's internationalisation policy. Not only did the policy enable the industry to enlarge market share and better react to market changes, but it also strengthened the position of its policy-makers within the oil policy-making structure, making them in turn an important group to be reckoned with in government policy-making processes.

Gaining the President's support for policy continuation was indeed a victory for the industry over Congress. PDVSA secured political legitimacy more as a result of a non-decision from the legislature than of an agreement over the industry's policy of internationalisation. After having secured political legitimacy for its policy choice, PDVSA launched a second and more aggressive phase of policy implementation, thus purchasing further refinery assets in Europe and new ones in the US.

After having enjoyed an active role in the nationalisation of the industry, the executive lost its position as main decision-maker in the process of oil policy-making, partly as a result of the successful accomplishment of PDVSA's early corporate objectives. During the years prior to nationalisation, government officials had bargained and scored important battles against the oil MNs for tax increases and fewer concessions. During nationalisation the role of executive officials in setting the consensual basis for the process allowing the continuation of the working relationship with the MNs was both significant and successful. In turn, the oil managers had remained apprehensive throughout a process largely conducted by executive officials and politicians. During the post-nationalisation period, the role of the executive has been gradually overshadowed by the ascension of industry policy-makers as the most important actors in the process of oil policy-making. The evidence of the analysis of the industry's internationalisation policy supports this assumption. The Ministry of Energy followed a policy that was devised by the industry. In the confrontation following the implementation of the first internationalisation contract, the industry and the Ministry stood together in Congress to defend what was perceived as a government policy, as it was carried out by a SOE. Executive officials and industry policy-makers had agreed with the adoption and implementation of the industry's internationalisation policy. Signalling the growing standing of PDVSA as a decision-making centre within oil policy-making processes, the controversy over the policy choice highlighted the weak position of the Ministry and the limited capacity of Congress to influence industry policy orientations. The successful expansion of the industry's operations abroad, allowing it to be a fully integrated oil MN, further minimised the executive's role as decisive actor within oil policy-making processes.

Despite the evidence indicating PDVSA's strong position to decide over policy matters, the industry proved less successful in fending off government-imposed wealth transfers to the treasury, in seeking to fix export and local fuel prices, and in deciding over production quotas. Unexpected cash demands or the imposition of unfavourable fiscal measures by the government are a result of the government's excessive dependence on the oil sector. Regarding the right to decide export prices and quotas, the industry must take into consideration decisions emanating from the Ministry of Energy and/or OPEC. Faced with the impossibility of modifying these external variables, the industry devises policies to minimise their negative effects on the formulation and implementation of corporate policies. The internationalisation policy was partly a response to the need to counteract the adverse action of such elements on the industry's expansion plans and administrative freedom.

Congress is indeed a key actor in oil policy-making processes in Venezuela. The issue of accountability to the legislative body became a major source of conflict during the first phase of policy implementation. The legislature saw its very essence as representative of the people and its means of control over the SOE threatened by the freedom of action shown by the industry. The evidence of this study suggests that the more powerful the SOE, the more the legislature sees its supervisory functions curtailed. The spaces allowed by Congress' inability to exercise control measures over the SOE are used by the latter to display greater degrees of administrative and financial autonomy.

When the SOE is powerful as in the case of PDVSA, the legislature and the executive find it increasingly difficult to keep the firm closely under control. In Venezuela, interaction with a powerful SOE such as PDVSA makes the usual Congress-executive-SOE power equation little adapted to explain oil policy-making processes. Control and accountability, two of the main issues that characterise the interaction between governments and SOEs, are thus endowed with different meanings. PDVSA has coped with the weight of legislative control by adopting a scheme whereby accountability becomes an alternative, but not a definite means of gaining legitimacy for performance and policy implementation. Accountability to the legislature is often regarded by the industry as an uncomfortable way of gaining legitimacy for partly implemented policies. In some cases, legislative legitimacy is not considered as a strict requirement for policy implementation. As the findings of this study demonstrated, policy-makers often cope with the challenge of being responsible to Congress by adopting a *fait-accompli* approach to policy implementation.

The tensions inherent in the process of oil policy-making

The policy-making controversy that arose during the first phase of policy implementation was a major test for both oil managers and political actors in Congress, one that redefined the rules of the interaction between both sets of policy-makers. Most of the unresolved tensions between the legislature and the industry came to the fore during that initial phase. In turn, it was the first time after nationalisation that Congress so overtly opposed an industry policy choice. PDVSA's managers were not used to coping with the demands proper to the industry's status as a SOE. In turn, Congress realised that PDVSA had become a powerful SOE increasingly difficult to control. Congress' failure to understand clearly the technical details and the long-term strategic implications of the industry's policy choices prevented legislative representatives from initially granting legitimacy to the internationalisation policy. The policy's long-term components were measured against short-term political interests and the need of fulfilling the industry's role as SOE: being accountable to the legislature and meeting non-corporate criteria.

The absence of consensus between political actors and industry policy-makers over the management of oil resources has largely accounted for the persistence of tensions within the process of oil policy-making. Another source of conflict along this process is the existence of opposite views concerning the interaction between the oil industry and, on the one hand, the executive, and on the other, Congress. Usually, politicians regard oil as the government's main source for generating public goods, both material and political. In Venezuela, this interaction is even more acute due to the excessive dependence of the government on but one source of revenues. In turn, the industry's policy-makers consider oil as a commodity, subject to the uncertainties of the international market.

In 1983, removal of the political obstacle hindering policy continuation was more the result of a political arrangement at the highest level than of a consensus among policy-makers regarding oil policy. The absence of a clear decision by Congress suggests that only a partial legitimacy was conferred to the industry's policy choice. Obtaining a partial legitimacy implied that opposition to the industry's internationalisation policy remained latent and, as was later seen with the purchase of Citgo's 50% assets, likely to reappear in a subsequent stage of the policy implementation process. Furthermore, PDVSA's ability to implement its policy choices in the absence of full legislative legitimacy partly corroborates the assumption that the industry has become a significant player within government policy-making processes. The evidence demonstrated that legislative legitimacy is not always a requisite for policy implementation. The findings also suggest the limits of Congress to sanction a policy already adopted and implemented by PDVSA. As mentioned, Congress failure to reach a decision led to a settlement of the controversy at the highest political echelon. One policy actor, the President, solved the impasse. In the event of a policy impasse within the state's decision-making structure, an alternative mechanism –in this case the intervention of the country's President– was activated to settle the issue. Regardless of the high standing of the policy actor that confers legitimacy on the policy choice, it is nonetheless the action of but one actor. Such one-actor decisions can only veil the persistence of political opposition to policy choices, likely to reappear at another phase of policy implementation.

In the absence of a consensus over oil policy issues, the launching of a second, more aggressive phase of policy implementation in 1986 was the industry's response to the combination of the variables identified throughout this study: government finances, political context, and oil market situation. Key elements such as the lack of consensus over the precise role of policy actors, the industry's accountability to Congress, and the need to strike a balance between corporate policies and the government's short-term interests remain largely unresolved.

As argued above, PDVSA reconciled its role as oil MN by minimising its attributes as a SOE. Being too powerful a SOE in a developing country context where the executive and the legislature find it increasingly difficult to exert their means of control over it had the effect of minimising some of its characteristics proper to a SOE: being accountable to Congress, subordination to the Ministry, and directly contributing to economic development. In turn, as PDVSA diminishes its status as a SOE, the government finds it more difficult to diminish its dependence over it. The successful accomplishment of PDVSA's internationalisation policy has stressed this equation, highlighting the contentious interaction between an excessively dependent government and a company struggling to reconcile its roles as both a SOE and a MN.

In Venezuela, governments have proven largely inefficient at adapting to changes in the oil market and in diversifying the country's economic structure. The bipartisan scheme of party alternation and the conflict-avoidance approach to problem solving which characterised the country's political system until 1993 have been modified partly as a result of governments' inability to diminish their dependence on the oil sector. Persistent government efforts to reverse this dependence and diversify the economy will continue, regardless of their success, to inflict important changes upon the political system. Any transformation brought upon the political system will reflect the degree of success of the government's attempts to reduce its increasing dependence over the oil industry. Failure to reach this goal will result in governments continuing to rely heavily on PDVSA for the solution of many public policy-making issues, not only financially but also as a credible and efficient policy-making actor. The oil industry could become the undisputed policy actor within government policy-making processes, imbuing most policy decisions with the technical features inherent in corporate strategies. A corporate decision considered convenient for the oil industry may not be necessarily consistent with the government's economic programme and with its long-term development plans. As a result of the prominent role played by the oil industry in government policy-making processes, other decision-making centres, such as Congress and the executive, could see their roles further weakened. The exacerbation of this situation would arguably pose definite challenges to the democratic political system. In turn, by highlighting the dangers of the government's dependence on the oil sector, the existence of an ever-powerful SOE constantly seeking to pursue its corporate autonomy is likely to encourage governments to curb this very dependence. The challenge to come will be the need to strike a balance between corporate policies and government needs, allowing policy outcomes to be advantageous both to the industry and to the government. Realisation by the political leadership of its increasingly vulnerable dependence on the performance of the oil SOE could contribute to reach such a balance. Both outside and inside political circles, new actors are currently proposing, although timidly, the partial privatisation and/or divestiture of PDVSA. What is clear is that in order to reach a balance between the government and the oil industry, a new reformulation of each other's functions is at stake. Any government purporting to bring about significant economic and political transformations cannot avoid such a challenge.

Suggestions for further research

This study has opened important avenues for further research in the area of public policy-making processes in developing countries. The main arguments and the findings of this study would be enhanced by analysing other public policy cases, especially in sectors where SOEs strive to establish a balance between the need to assert greater administrative autonomy and to fulfil their role as revenue generators for the government. The study of specific public policy-making cases will shed further light on the tensions entailed in the need to meet these, at first glance, contradictory objectives. Moreover, specific policy-making studies should map the evolution of a problem into a policy decision, identifying the different phases and actors along the process. Identification of the phases described by a policy orientation contributes to understand the many-sided implications of such a process for the actors involved and for the goals to be reached. It is in this analytical attempt that are identified the often contradictory objectives of the policy actors involved. As was shown by the evidence in this study, the objectives pursued by a SOE are often in contradiction with the goals of the executive and/or Congress. Other scholarly works dedicated to the analysis of policy-making cases should further explore the question of the shifting power distribution among policy actors. Policy outcomes, that is the degree of success or failure that feature policy adoption and implementation, have a definite impact on the interaction among the policy actors involved.

In the cases where Congress and, to a large extent, the executive proved to be weak in the face of a powerful SOE, there is a need to further examine the modifications brought about by the implementation of key policies upon the political system and on the nature of public policy-making processes. There exists not only the need to assess the impact of the political system on government policy-making processes, but also the influence of policy outcomes on the former. As mentioned, in the case of PDVSA, the successful accomplishment of certain policy choices, allowing the industry to increase its freedom of action from the Ministry and Congress, boosted the position of its policy-makers in government policy-making processes. The increasing participation of industry policy-makers in such processes not directly involving the oil sector supports this assumption. There exists a clear need to further explore this aspect and to assess its impact on economic and public policy outcomes.

Policy studies should, furthermore, inquire into how a SOE policy orientation becomes part of the government's agenda. Also, such studies should shed light on the crucial issue of how SOEs seek to gain legitimacy for policy choices. Policy implementation is clearly influenced by the way SOE policy-makers go about gaining legitimacy for their policy choices.

It would be particularly insightful to focus on executive and legislative responses to the policies adopted by any given SOE seeking to internationalise its operations. The context offered by a developing country with a poorly diversified economy offers a fertile ground for testing and improving the arguments and partial conclusions stemming from the previous analysis of PDVSA's efforts to become an oil MN. Enabling it to carry an important part of its operations abroad, the internationalisation of a company renders its control difficult to exert by the executive and Congress. The context of developing countries with a democratic system where the role of the legislature is important and where public policy is the result of bargaining political processes provides an adequate context for testing and improving the findings of this study.

Bibliography

Interviews

Albacete, Alfonso. LAGOVEN.
Alcantara, Humberto. Director, Petroleum Chamber.
Alcock, Frank. Director, PDVSA.
Alfonzo Ravard, Rafael. Former President, PDVSA.
Amaro, Agustín. Strategic Planning Unit, PDVSA.
Bonse-Geuking, W. President, Veba Oel. Düsseldorf.
Bottome, Robert. *Veneconomía.* Caracas.
Boué, Juan Carlos. Commercial manager, crude oil. PEMEX
Boy de la Tour, Xavier. Institut Français du Pétrole (IFP). Paris.
Calderón Berti, Humberto. Former Minister of Mines and president of PDVSA.
Calero, Alberto. Latin American Institute of Research in the Social Sciences, Caracas.
Carabbe, Guilelmo. ENI, Caracas.
Castell, Salvador. REPSOL, Caracas.
Castillo, Gonzalo. Director, Ministry of Energy and Mines. Caracas.
Chacín Gómez, Juan. Former president, PDVSA.
Chambert-Loir, Jacques. ELF AQUITAINE, Paris.
Chirinos ,Ruben. Vice-president, CORPOVEN.
Cisneros, Alberto. Strategic Planning Unit, PDVSA.
Day, Graham. BP-Venezuela.
Espinasa, Ramón. Strategic Planning Unit, PDVSA.
Fabro-Fuad, Eda. Commercial attachée. French Embassy. London.
Fernández, Remigio. Director, PDV-UK.
Giacopini Zárraga, J. A. Former consultant to PDVSA's presidents.
Giroud, André. Institut Français du Pétrole (IFP). Paris.
Gómez, Juan Carlos. Director, PDVSA.
González, Miguel. National Federation of Petrol Workers (FENEGAS). Caracas.
Graff, Claus. Vice-president, PDVSA.
Gutiérrez, Ivan Director, PDV-UK.
Gutmann, Francis. President, Gaz de France. Paris.
Johnson, Susan. Caracas.
Keller, Jean-Bernard. Vice-President, Western Hemisphere. TOTAL. Paris.
Kelly, Janet. Institute of Superior Studies in Administration. IESA. Caracas.
Levine, Daniel. Visiting Professor. IESA.
Llatas, Vicente. Director, PDVSA.
Martínez, Aníbal. PEQUIVEN.
Martínez, Miguel. Director, PDVSA.
Marty, Pierre. Technical Coordinator for Venezuela, TOTAL. Paris.
Mommer, Bernard. Strategic Planning Unit, PDVSA; St Antony's College. Oxford.

Odell, Peter. Professor Emeritus. London School of Economics.
Olorunfemi, Mr. Nigerian Delegate, OPEP. The Hague
Parra, Alirio. Former Minister of Energy and Mines; Centre for Energy Studies. London.
Peñaloza, Humberto. Consultant and former PDVSA Director.
Petzall, Wolf. Former vice-president, PDVSA.
Plaza, Gonzalo. Venezuelan Delegate, OPEP. Vienna.
Pulgar, Juan. Strategic Planning Unit. PDVSA.
Rainault, Elionora. LAGOVEN.
Ramírez, Daniel. LAGOVEN.
Reimpall, Paul. Former Director, PDVSA.
Ren, Mignot. Coordinator for Latin America, TOTAL. Paris.
Rheinheimer, Hans. Veba Oel. Caracas.
Rodríguez, Mario. Director, PDVSA.
Rodríguez Eraso, Guillermo. Former President, LAGOVEN.
Salvadore, Andrea. Former director, LAGOVEN.
Sapmoko, Mr. Director, PERTAMINA. London.
Simoneau, Noel. ELF AQUITAINE. Paris.
Sosa Pietri, Andrés. Former president of PDVSA.
Sweeney, John. Oil journalist. Caracas.
Tredenik, Joaquín. Director, PDVSA.
Viergutz, Alan. Former president, Venezuelan Petroleum Chamber.
Zemella, Jorge. Director, BITOR.

Selected Books, Articles, and Dissertations

Agarwal, Jamuna Prasad. *Third World Multinationals.* A case study of India. Kiel University. Tübingen, 1989.
Agmon, Tamir and Charles Kindleberger (eds). *Multinationals from Small Countries.* The MIT Press. Cambridge, Massachusetts, 1977.
Aharoni, Yair. *The Evaluation and Management of State Owned Enterprises.* Ballinger Publications. Cambridge, Massachussets, 1986.
Aharoni, Yair (ed.). *Coalitions and Competition. The Globalization of Professional Business services.* Routledge. London, 1993.
Al-Chalabi, Fadhil. 'El desarrollo del mercado durante 1982 y 1983. Las condiciones que influyeron en la reducción de precios de la OPEP'. Boletín Mensual, N. 17. MEM, 1984.
Alfonzo Ravard, Rafael. *Siete años de una Gestión.* PDVSA. Caracas, 1982.
Allison, Graham. 'Conceptual Models and the Cuban Missile Crisis'. *The American Political Science Review.* September, 1969. Vol. LXIII, No. 3.
Allison, Graham. *Essence of Decision. Explaining the Cuban Missile Crisis.* Little Brown. Boston, 1971.
Alvarez de Stella, Ana María. 'Crisis económica y manejo de la deuda externa en Venezuela'. *La economía contemporánea de Venezuela.* BCV. Caracas, 1988.
Anderson, James. *Public Policy Making.* Praeger Publisher. New York, 1977.
Aranda, Sergio. *La Economía Venezolana.* Siglo XXI Editores. Bogotá, 1977.

Arreaza A., Julio César.*1976-1985 Diez años de la industria petrolera nacional. Aspectos históricos y jurídicos.* CEPET. Caracas, 1986.

Arroyo Talavera, Eduardo. *Elections and negotiation: the limits of democracy in Venezuela (1958-1981).* PhD thesis. LSE. London, 1983.

Ashford, Douglas E. 'In Search of French Planning: Ideas and History at Work'. *West European Politics.* Vol. 11. No 3. July, 1988.

Atencio Bello, Heraclio. 'Venezuela: Development Experiences and Options for the 1990s'. International Seminar. Stockholm. September, 17-18, 1990.

Ayoub, Antoine. 'Le Modele OPEP: Ajoustements ou Nouvelle Logique?'*L'avenir des sociétés nationales des pays exportateurs d'hydrocarbures.* Seminar. Université Paris-Dauphine. Paris. May 26-27, 1994.

Baena, César E. *Le processus d'apprentissage politique dans la transition vers la démocratie au Venezuela.* M. Sc. thesis. Université de Montréal. Département d'histoire, 1989.

Baptista, Asdrúbal. *Bases cuantitativas de la economía venezolana, 1830-1989.* Ediciones María Di Mase. Caracas, 1991.

Baptista, Asdrúbal and Bernard Mommer. *El petróleo en el pensamiento económico venezolano. Un ensayo.* IESA. Caracas, 1990.

Barrios T., Thaís. *La diversificación de los mercados internacionales: El caso de Venezuela.* UCAB. B. Sc. thesis. Caracas, 1989.

Betancourt, Rómulo. *Venezuela. Política y Petróleo.* Editorial Senderos. Bogotá, 1969.

Bina, Cirus. *The economics of the oil crisis.* Martin Press. New York, 1985.

Blair, John M. *The control of oil.* Pantheon Books. New York, 1976.

Boy de la Tour, Xavier and André Giroud. *Géopolitique du Pétrole et du Gaz.* Editions Technip. Paris, 1987.

Bond, Robert. *FEDECAMARAS in the Venezuelan Economic Arena.* PhD thesis. Vanderbilt University, 1975.

Boué, Juan Carlos. *Venezuela. The Political Economy of Oil.* Oxford University Press. UK, 1993.

Boué, Juan Carlos. *The political control of state oil companies. A case study of the international vertical integration programme of Petróleos de Venezuela (1982-95).* PhD thesis. Oxford University, 1997.

Bouhafs, Abdelhalk. 'Stratégie de Modernisation de SONATRACH'. *L'avenir des sociétés nationales des pays exportateurs d'hydrocarbures.* Seminar. Université Paris-Dauphine. Paris. May 26-27, 1994.

Bourdeau, François. *Histoire de l'administration française. Du XVII au XX siècles.* Montchrestien. Paris, 1989.

Bourgeois, Bernard. 'Les relations entre compagnies pétrolières nationales et internationales: des accords contractuels aux relations de coopération?'. *L'avenir des sociétés nationales des pays exportateurs d'hydrocarbures.* Seminar. Université Paris-Dauphine. Paris. May 26-27, 1994.

Bourguignon, François. 'Le choc pétrolier au Venezuela: 1973-1982'. In *Problemes d'Amérique latine.* N° 75. Paris, 1985.

Boussena, Sadek. 'L'adaptation des compagnies nationales au nouveau contexte pétrolier'. *L'avenir des sociétés nationales des pays exportateurs d'hydrocarbures.* Seminar. Université Paris-Dauphine. Paris. May 26-27, 1994.

Brewer-Carías, Allan. *Instituciones Políticas y Constitucionales.* Vol 2. Universidad Católica del Táchira. Caracas-San Cristóbal, 1985.

Brogan, Christopher J. *The oil crisis in Ecuador: The search for an external solution, with special reference to the period 1979-1983.* PhD thesis. LSE. London, 1990.

Buchanan, James and Gordon Tullock. *The Calculus of Consent.* University of Michigan Press. Ann Arbor, Mich., 1962.

Bulmer-Thomas, Victor. *The Economic History of Latin America since Independence.* Cambridge University Press. Cambridge, UK, 1994.

Calderón Berti, Humberto. 'Intervención en la Camara de Diputados'. Caracas. May, 1983.*Capacidad institucional del estado para formular opciones de política y adoptar decisiones en materia económica. Aspectos administrativos, de recursos humanos, legales y técnicos.* Edited by ILDIS. Caracas, Venezuela, 1988.

Calderón Berti, Humberto. *Oposición y Petróleo en Venezuela. Cronología de una gestión errática.* Ediciones Centauro. Caracas, 1988.

Chacín, Juan. *Perspectives of an oil exporter: Repositioning for flexibility.* Cambridge Energy Forum. Cambridge, Massachusetts,1986.

Chubb, John. *Interest Groups and the Bureaucracy. The Politics of Energy.* Stanford University Press. Stanford, 1983.

Clark, Robert. *The LAFTA Debate in Venezuela: A Test Case in Building Consensus.* PhD thesis. The John Hopkins University. Baltimore, 1968.

Cline, Wiliam. 'Estructura, orígenes y administración de la deuda pública externa de Venezuela'. *La economía contemporánea de Venezuela.* BCV Publications. Caracas, 1987.

'Conocer a Neste'. PDVSA Publications, [not dated].

Coronel, Gustavo. *The Nationalization of the Venezuelan Oil Industry. From Technocratic Success to Political Failure.* Lexington Books. Lexington, 1983.

De la Vega Navarro, A. 'Dynamiques des économies des pays expotateurs et réorganisation de leurs indrustries pétrolières'. *L'avenir des sociétés nationales des pays exportateurs d'hydrocarbures.* Seminar. Université Paris-Dauphine. Paris. May 26-27, 1994.

Diario de Debates. Congress of Venezuela. Caracas, 1974.

Díaz-Alejandro, Carlos F. 'Foreign Direct Investment by Latin Americans'. In Agmon, Tamir and Charles Kindleberger (eds). *Multinationals from Small Countries.* The MIT Press. Cambridge, Massachusetts, 1977.

Dorian, James P. and Fereidun Fesharaki, (eds). International Issues in Energy Policy, *Development and Economics.* Westview Press, Inc. USA, 1992.

'Downstream joint-ventures'. Publication. PDVSA, [not dated].

Dror, Yehezkel. *Public Policy-making Re-examined.* Chandler. San Francisco, 1968.

Dror, Yehezkel. *Design for Policy Science.* Elsevier. New York, 1971.

Dror, Yehezkel. *Policy-making under Adversity.* Transaction Publications. New Brunswick, 1986.

Duby, Georges. *Atlas Historique.* Larousse. Paris, 1989.

Dunleavy, Patrick. *Democracy, Bureaucracy and Public Choice.* Harvester/ Wheatsheaf. UK, 1991.

Dye, Thomas. *Understanding Public Policy.* Prentice-Hall, Inc. New Jersey, 1992.

Easton, David. *The Analysis of Political Structure.* Rutledge. New York, London, 1990.

Easton, David; John Gunnel and Luigi Graziano (eds). *The Development of Political Science. A Comparative Survey.* Routledge. London, New York, 1991.

Eklof, Dennis. 'The downstream adapts: markets and strategies'. *Cambridge Energy Forum.* Cambridge, Massachusetts, 1986.

El Mallakh, Ragaei, Oystein Noreng and Barry W. *Poulson. Petroleum and economic development. The cases of Mexico and Norway.* Lexington Books. D.C Heath and Company Lexington, Massachusetts, 1986.

Enright, Michael, Antonio Francés, Edith Scott Saavedra. *Venezuela: el reto de la competitividad.* Ediciones IESA. Caracas, 1994.

España, Luis Pedro. 'El futuro político de las minorías partidistas'. *SIC.* Centro Gumilla. January-February, 1989.

Espinasa Vendrell, Ramón Juan. *The long term dynamics of international petroleum production and price formation.* PhD thesis. Cambridge University. December, 1984.

Espinasa, Ramón and Bernard Mommer.*Venezuelan Oil Policy in the Long Run.* East-West Center, Hawaï, 1992.

Espinosa, Javier. 'OPEC's second wind: restraint market share'. *Cambridge Energy Forum.* 1986.

Estrada, Javier. 'Relationship between the Norwegian state and Statoil: challenges to come'. *L'avenir des sociétés nationales des pays exportateurs d'hydrocarbures.* Seminar. Université Paris-Dauphine. Paris. May 26-27, 1994.

Etzioni, Amitai. *Public Policy in a New Key.* Transaction Publishers. New Brunswick and London, 1993.

Faundez, Julio and Sol Picciotto. *The Nationalisation of Multinationals in Peripheral Economies.* MacMillan Press. London, 1978.

Feigenbaum, Harvey. *The Politics of Public Enterprise. Oil and the French State.* Princeton University Press. New Jersey, 1985.

Fitzgibbon, Russell and Julio Fernández. *Latin America: Political Culture and Development.* Prentice-Hall, Inc. New Jersey, 1981.

Freije Rodríguez, Samuel. 'The new foreign debt restructuring agreement: its terms and potential results'. *MetroEconómica.* Caracas. Abril, 1990.

Galal, Ahmed. 'Public Enterprise Reform. Lessons from the Past and Issues for the Future'. *World Bank Discussion Papers,* 119. Washington, D.C., 1991.

García, Gustavo, Rafael Rodríguez, Silvia Salvato de Figueroa. 'Dinámica de la tributación en Venezuela 1980-1994: Un período de turbulencia y contracción. *DEBATES IESA.* Vol. 3. N 3. January-March 1998.

Garip-Bertuol, Patricia. 'Cristóbal Colón and two heavy crude associations get the green light. *Veneconomía.* Draft paper, [not dated].

Geddes, Barbara. 'A Game Theoretic Model of Reform in Latin American Democracies'. *American Political Science Review.* Vol. 85. No. 2. June 1991.

Gelb, Alan. *Oil Windfalls. Blessing or Curse?.* The World Bank. Oxford, 1988.

Guevara, Rafael M. *Petróleo y Ruina.* Ediciones Instante. Caracas, 1983.

Gil Yépez, José Antonio. *El reto de las élites.* Editorial Tecnos. Madrid, 1978.

Giordani, Jorge. 'La planificación en Venezuela, de la experiencia nacional al plan corporativo petrolero'. In *Vigencia y Perspectivas de la Planificación en Venezuela.* Colección Jorge Ahumada, No 5. CENDES. Caracas, 1995.

Godoy, Ana María. 'Racionalización de operaciones interfiliales en el mercado interno'. *Boletín Mensual.* MEM. Caracas. January-June 1984.

Gómez, Emeterio. *Dilemas de una Economía Petrolera.* Editorial Panapo. Caracas, 1991.

Gómez, Juan Carlos. 'Se nacionaliza, luego se internacionaliza...?' *Gerente.* October, 1992.

Greene, William. *Strategies of the Major Oil Companies.* Umi Research Press. Ann Arbor, Michigan, 1985.

Grindle, Merilee and John Thomas. *Public Choices and Policy Change. The Political Economy of Reform in Developing Countries.* The John Hopkins University Press. Baltimore and London, 1992.

Ham, Christopher and Michael Hill. *The policy process in the modern capitalist state.* Harvester/Wheatsheaf. UK, 1993.

Hausmann, Ricardo. *Shocks Externos y Ajustes Macroeconómicos.* Publicaciones IESA. Caracas, 1992.

Heald, David. 'Performance Measurement of Public Enterprises: Resolving Conceptual Issues'. *Public Finance and Performance of Enterprises.* Proceedings of the 43rd Congress of the International Institute of Public Finance. Paris, 1987. Wayne State University Press. Detroit, 1989.

Heald, David. 'The Economic and Financial Control of UK Nationalised Industries'. *The Economic Journal,* 90. June, 1980, pp. 243-265.

Heclo, H. *Modern Social Politics in Britain and Sweden.* Yale University Press. New Haven, 1974.

Heclo, H. 'Review Article: Policy Analysis', *British Journal of Political Science,* 2. UK, 1979.

Hein, Wolfgang. 'Value aspects of dependence from exporting oil'. *International commodity trade Latin America-EEC.* CEDLA. Incidentele Publicaties 20. Amsterdam, 1980.

Hernández Acosta, Valentín. *Apuntes sobre la Nacionalización de la Industria Petrolera.* PDVSA Publications. Caracas, [not dated].

Hernández Grisanti, Arturo. *Significación histórica de la nacionalización petrolera.* MEM. Caracas, 1985.

Hernández Grisanti, Arturo. 'Discurso pronunciado por el Ministro de Energía y Minas, Dr. Arturo Hernández Grisanti, en la inauguración de la IV Exposición Latinoamericana del petróleo'. *Boletín Mensual.* MEM. Caracas. June, 1984.

Hogwood, B.W. and L.A. Gunn. *Policy Analysis for the Real World.* Oxford University Press. Oxford, 1984.

Hughes, Steven and Kenneth Mijeski. *Politics and Public Policy in Latin America.* Westview Press, 1984.

'Internacionalización. Con la Ruhr Oel, en Alemania Petróleos de Venezuela fortalece su participación en territorio europeo'. *Petróleos Informa.* August, 1992.

'Interven, la empresa de la internacionalización'. *PDVSA Publications.* June, 1986.

'Intervención del Ministro Humberto Calderón Berti en la Cámara de Diputados'. *Boletín Mensual.* MEM. Caracas, May, 1983.

'Intervención del Ministro de Energía y Minas, Dr. Arturo Hernandez Grisanti, en el bautizo de la biblioteca Juan Pablo Pérez Alfonso'. UCV. June 26, 1984. *Boletín Mensual.* MEM. July-December 1984.

'Intervención del Ministro de Energía y Minas, Dr. Arturo Hernandez Grisanti, en la Comisión de Energía y Minas del Senado. April, 25, 1984'. *Boletín Mensual.* MEM. January-June 1984.

Jenkins, W. I. *Policy Analysis.* Martin Robertson. London, 1978.

Jenkins, Gilbert. *Oil Economists' Handbook.* Penguin Books. London, 1989.

Jones, Charles. *An Introduction to the Study of Public Policy.* Duxbury. Boston, 1978.

Jones, Leroy P. (ed.). *Public enterprise in less-developed countries.* Cambridge University Press. Cambridge, 1982.

Johnson de Vogeler, Susan. *Organizational adaptation in the Venezuelan petroleum industry after nationalization.* PhD thesis. MIT. Massachusetts, 1987.

Kay, John and David Thompson. 'Privatisation in the United Kingdom. Regulatory Failure in the Public Sector'. *Public Finance and Performance of Enterprises.* Proceedings of the 43rd Congress of the International Institute of Public Finance. Paris, 1987. Wayne State University Press. Detroit, 1989.

Kaplan, Marcos (ed.). *Petróleo y Desarrollo en México y Venezuela.* Editorial Nueva Imagen. Mexico, 1981.

Karl, Terry Lynn. 'Petroleum and political pacts: the transition to democracy in Venezuela'. *Latin American Research Review.* Vol. XXII, No.1 1987, pp. 63-94.

Kastner, George and Daniel Yergin. 'Venezuelan Oil: Curse or Blessing'. Prepared for the Nomos Project at the Center for International Affairs. Harvard University. September, 1983.

Katz, Jorge and Bernardo Kosacoff. 'Multinationals from Argentina'. In *Sanjaya Lall. The New Multinationals. The Spread of Third World Enterprises.* John Wiley and Sons. New York, 1983.

Keliher, Leo. *Policy-making on Information Technology: the Alvey Report.* PhD thesis, LSE. December, 1987.

Kelly, Janet (ed.). *Empresas del Estado en América Latina.* IESA. Caracas, 1985.

Kelly, Janet. 'Comparing state enterprises across international bounderies: the Corporación Venezolana de Guayana and the Companhía Vale do Rio Doce'. In Leroy Jones (ed.). *Public enterprise in less developed countries.* Cambridge University Press. Cambridge, 1982.

Kelly, Janet. 'Venezuela: Letting in the Market'. IESA, [not dated].

Khan, Khushi (ed.). *Multinationals of the South: New Actors in the International Economy.* Frances Pinter Publishers. London, 1987.

Kimenyi, Mwangi S. and John M. Mbaku. 'Rent-seeking and institutional stability in developing countries'. *Public Choice 77.* The Netherlands, 1993.

Kornblith, Miriam. *Nuevas reglas de juego y estabilidad de la democracia en Venezuela* Mimeograph. IESA. Caracas. July, 1993.

Kornblith, Miriam. *Venezuela en los 90. Las Crisis de la Democracia.* Ediciones IESA. Caracas, 1998.

Kornblith, Miriam and Daniel H. Levine. *The life and times of the party system.* Kellogg Institute. University of Notre Dame. Indiana, USA. June, 1993.

Krapels, E. N. *Oil Crisis Management: Strategic Stockpiling for International Security.* John Hopkins University Press. Baltimore, 1980.

Kumar, Krishna and Maxwell G. McLeod. *Multinationals from Developing Countries.* Lexington Books. Lexington, Massachusetts, 1981.

'La compañía UNO-VEN. Refinación y mercadeo de petróleo. La atención al Medio Oeste'. PDVSA Publications. Caracas, 1989.

'La internacionalización. Nuevo elemento en la estrategia de comercialización'. PDVSA Publications. Caracas, 1986.

La Industria venezolana de los hidrocarburos. 'Síntesis de actividades relevantes'. CEPET. Caracas, November, 1989.

Lall, Sanjaya. *The New Multinationals. The Spread of Third World Enterprises.* John Wiley and Sons. New York, 1983.

Lall, Sanjaya. *Multinationals, Technology and Exports.* Selected Papers. Macmillan Press. London, 1989.

Lane, Jan-Erik. *The public sector. Concepts, models and approaches.* SAGE Publications Inc. London, 1993.

Larraín, Felipe and Marcelo Selowsky (eds). *The Public Sector and the Latin American Crisis.* ICS Press. San Francisco, 1991.

Laswell, H. 'The Policy Orientation'. In D. Lerner and H. Lasswell (eds). *The Policy Sciences.* Stanford University Press. Standford, 1951.

Leca, Jean and Madelaine Grawitz. *Traité de Science Politique.* Presse Universitaire de France. Paris, 1986.

'Ley Orgánica que reserva al Estado, la industria y el comercio de los hidrocarburos y sus reglamentos parciales No 1,2,3 y 4'. Eduven, C.A. Caracas, 1992.

Lieuwen, Edwin. *Petróleo en Venezuela, una Historia.* Cruz del Sur Ediciones. Caracas, 1964.

Lijphart, Arendt. *Democracies.* Yale University Press. New Haven, 1984.

Lindblom, Charles. *The Policy-Making Process.* Prentice Hall. New Jersey, 1968.

Livingstone, J.M. *The Internationalization of Business.* The Macmillan Press Ltda. London, 1989.

Lorenzo, María del Carmen. *PDVSA y el proceso de internacionalización de la industria petrolera: una visión a través de la prensa.* B.Sc. thesis. UCV. Caracas, 1992.

Mabro, Robert (ed.). *The 1986 oil price crisis: economic effects and policy responses.* Oxford University Press. Oxford, 1988.

McGrew, Anthony and M.J. Wilson (eds). *Decision-making. Approaches and Analysis.* Manchester University Press. 1988.

McLean, Iain. *Public Choice. An Introduction.* Blackwell. Oxford, 1993.

Mangone, Gerard J. (ed.). *Energy Policies of the World.* American Elsevier. New York, 1976.

March, J. G. and H. Simon. *Organizations.* Wiley. New York, 1958.

Martínez, Aníbal R. *Cronología del Petróleo Venezolano.* Ediciones Foninves. Caracas, 1976.

Martínez, Aníbal R. 'Reserves Nomenclature World-Wide: A Utopia?'. II LAPEC. Caracas, March 11, 1992.

Martz, John and David Myers (eds). *Venezuela and the democratic experience.* Praeger. New York, 1986.

Mazzolini, Renato. *Government Controlled Enterprises. International Strategic and Policy Decisions.* John Wiley Publishers. Columbia University. New York, 1979.

Marx, F. M. *The Administrative State.* University of Chicago Press. Chicago, 1957.

Megateli, Abderrahmane. *Petroleum Policies and National Oil Companies.* Austin University Press. Austin, Texas, 1978.

Megateli, Abderrahmane. *Petroleum Policies and National Oil Companies: A Comparative Study of Investment Policies with Emphasis on Exploration of Sonatrach (Algeria), NIOC (Iran), and Pemex (Mexico), 1970-1975.* PhD thesis. University of Texas at Austin, 1978.

Mendoza Pottellá, Carlos. *El Poder y la Economía Petrolera Venezolana.* UCV. Caracas, 1995.

Mikdashi, Zuhayr. *The Community of Oil Exporting Countries. A Study of Governmental Co-operation.* George Allen and Unwin Ltd. London, 1972.

Mikdashi, Zuhayr. *Transnational Oil. Issues, Policies and Perspectives.* Frances Pinter Publishers. London, 1986.

Milloz, Pierre. *Le mal administratif. La fonction publique est-elle ingouvernable?* Bordas. Paris, 1987.

Mommer, Bernard. 'Oil Rent and Rent Capitalism. The Example of Venezuela'. Review. Fernand Braudel Center. Vol. XIII, No 4. New York, 1990.

Mommer, Bernard. 'The Political Role of National Companies in the Large Exporting Countries: the Venezuelan case'. *L'avenir des sociétés nationales des pays exportateurs d'hydrocarbures.* Seminar. Université Paris-Dauphine. Paris. May 26-27, 1994.

Mommer, Dorothea. *El Estado Venezolano y la Industria Petrolera.* Santiago, Chile, 1981.

Mora, Jesús. 'Associations stratégiques de PDVSA: forces et faiblesses'. *L'avenir des sociétés nationales des pays exportateurs d'hydrocarbures.* Seminar. Université Paris-Dauphine. Paris. May 26-27, 1994.

Nagel, Stuart. *Policy Studies. Integration and Evaluation.* Greenwood Press. New York, London, 1988.

Nagel, Stuart (ed.). *Policy Theory and Policy Evaluation.* Greenwood Press. New York, London, 1990.

Naím, Moisés. *Paper Tigers and Minotaurs.* A Carnegie Endowment Book. Washington, 1993.

Naím, Moisés. 'The Politics of Public Policy Implementation'. IESA. Caracas, 1983.

Nationalisation Law. August, 1975.

Noreng, Oysten. *The Oil and Government Strategy in the North Sea.* Croom Helm. London. 1980.

Odell, Peter R. *Oil and World Power.* Penguin Books. London, 1986.

Odell, Peter R. and Kenneth Rosing. *The Future of Oil*. Kogan Page, London, 1980.

Official Gazette. Government of Venezuela. No. 1784. December 18, 1975.

O'Neill, Bard E. 'The Analytical Framework'. *Energy crisis and US foreign policy*. Prage Publishes. N.Y., 1975.

Olson, Mancur. 'The Devolution of Encompassing Organizations: The Rise and Decline of Nations since 1982'. Paper presented at the LSE. Michaelmas term, 1994.

Pachauri, Rajendra K. *The Political Economy of Global Energy*. The John Hopkins University Press. Baltimore, 1985.

Palma, Pedro A. *La economía venezolana en el período 1947-1988: ¿Ultimos años de una economía rentista?* Caracas. October, 1989.

Palma, Pedro A. 'El manejo de la deuda pública externa de Venezuela: Necesidad de urgentes cambios'. In *La economía contemporánea de Venezuela*. BCV. Caracas, 1988.

Palma, Pedro A. 'Contracción de los precios de exportación, deuda y crecimiento en economías en desarrollo: el caso de Venezuela'. IESA. Caracas, 1988.

'PDVSA adquiere el 50 por ciento de la nueva empresa Champlin Refinig Company'. *Petróleos Informa*. Caracas, March 13, 1987 .

PDVSA. 'La internacionalización de PDVSA'. PDVSA Publications. July 6, 1992.

'PDVSA participa con un 50 por ciento. Nynäs consolida posiciones en el mercado europeo de asfaltos'. *Petróleos Informa*. Caracas. December, 1992.

'PDVSA afianza su presencia en el mercado estadounidense'. PDVSA Publications. Aug., 1992.

Peñaloza, Humberto. 'Las relaciones entre el estamento político y la industria petrolera nacional: un juego de aproximaciones recelosas'. *Cuarto Congreso Venezolano de Petróleo*. Caracas, Venezuela. July16-21, 1990.

Peñaloza, Humberto. 'Petróleos de Venezuela's experience in joint-venture downstream arrangements'. *Geopolitics of Energy-Supplement*. Conat and Associates, Ltd. and Petroleum Analysis, Ltd. New York. September 29-30, 1988.

Peñaloza, Humberto. 'Los grandes números financieros del petróleo (1976-1989) y las exigencias del futuro'.*Petroplus. Boletín de opiniones y comentarios sobre petróleo y temas afines*. Published by Petro-Ger S.A. Caracas, July 10, 1990.

Petras, James F.; Moris Morley and Steven Smith. *The Nationalization of Venezuelan Oil*. New York, London. 1977.

'Petróleos de Venezuela anunció que Southland usará su participación en Citgo para obtener recursos financieros'. PDVSA Publications. Caracas, May 8, 1989.

'Petróleo y gas. Proyección hasta el consumidor final. PDVSA participa con Uno-Ven en el mercado del medio oeste de Estados Unidos'. *Petróleos Informa*. April, 1992.

'Petroleum. Hard luck, soft prices'. *The Economist*. April 16, 1983.

Petroguía. PDVSA Publications. Caracas, 1987.

Pérez Alfonzo, Juan P. *El Pentágono Petrolero*. Revista Política. Caracas, 1967.

Philip, George. 'Venezuelan Democracy and the February 1992 coup attempt'. Mimeograph, 1992.

Philip, George. *Oil and politics in Latin America. Nationalist movements and state companies.* Cambridge University Press. Cambridge, 1982.

Pinto, Helder Junior. 'Les structures de financement des compagnies pétrolières internacionales constituent-elles une norme por les compagnies nationales des pays exportateurs?'. *L'avenir des sociétés nationales des pays exportateurs d'hydrocarbures.* Seminar. Paris, May 26-27, 1994.

'Plan de negocios de la industria petrolera venezolana y su impacto macroeconómico'. Strategic Planning Unit. PDVSA, 1993.

Pozen, Robert. *Legal Choices for State Enterprises in the Third World.* New York, 1976.

Pressman, J. and Aaron Wildavsky. *Implementation.* University of California Press. Berkeley, 1973.

'Prospectus Emission of Senior Notes. PDV America, Inc.' Salomon Brothers, Inc. July 22, 1993.

Przeworski, Adam. *Democracy and the Market.* Cambridge University Press. Cambridge, 1992.

Randall, Laura. *The Political Economy of Venezuelan Oil.* Praeger Publishers. New York, 1987.

Randall, Laura. *The Political Economy of Brazilian Oil.* Praeger Publishers. New York, 1993.

Ramamurti, Ravi. *State-owned entrerprises in high technology industries. Studies in India and Brazil.* Praeger. New York, 1986.

Ramanadham, V.V. *Studies in Public Enterprise. From Evaluation to Privatisation.* Frank Cass. London, 1987.

Ramanadham, V.V. (ed.). *Public enterprise. Studies in Organisational Structure.* Frank Cass. London, 1986.

Ramanadham, V.V. *The Nature of Public Enterprise.* Croom Helm. London, 1984.

Ramanadham, V.V. (ed.). *Public Enterprise and the Developing World.* Croom Helm, London, 1984.

'Refinación. PDVSA participa con un 50 por ciento. Nynäs consolida posiciones en el mercado europeo de asfaltos'. *Petróleos Informa.* December, 1992.

Riemens, Patrice. *On the Foreign Operations of Third World Firms. A study about the background and consequences of 'Third World Multinationals'.* Nederlandse Geografische Studies 100. Amsterdam, 1989.

Rodríguez, Miguel. 'Public sector behaviour in Venezuela, 1970-1985'. IESA. Caracas, 1987.

Rodríguez, Mario. 'The View from Venezuela'. *L'avenir des sociétés nationales des pays exportateurs d'hydrocarbures.* Seminar. Université Paris-Dauphine. Paris, May 26-27, 1994.

Rodríguez Padilla, V. 'Les Sociétés Nationales et la modernisation du régime fiscal dans les pays exportateurs'. *L'avenir des sociétés nationales des pays exportateurs d'hydrocarbures.* Seminar. Paris, May 26-27, 1994.

Reed, Robert (ed.). *The Oil Market in the 1990s.* Challenges for the New Era. London, 1989.

Roosen, Gustavo. *Learning across borders.* The 1993 Global Management Development Forum. Barcelona, June 14, 1993.

Russell H. Fitzgibbon and Julio A. Fernández. *Latin American: Political Culture and Development*. Prentice Hall Inc. New Jersey, 1981.

Sabatier, P. 'Top-Down and Bottom-Up Approaches to Implementation Research: A Critical Analysis and Suggested Synthesis'. *Journal of Public Policy*, 6 (1), 1986.

Sabatier, P. and D. Mazmanian. 'The Conditions of Effective Implementation: A Guide to Accomplishing Policy Objectives'. *Policy Analysis*, 1979.

Salcedo, Doramelia and Enrique Rodríguez. 'Un primer acercamiento a la comprensión del funcionamiento del despacho de la Presidencia de la República en Venezuela'. ILDIS.   Caracas, 1988.

Salcedo, Doramelia (ed.). 'Capacidad institucional del Estado para formular opciones de política y adoptar decisiones en materia económica. Aspectos administrativos, de recursos humanos, legales y técnicos'. ILDIS. Caracas, 1988.

Sarkis, Nicolas. 'La réintegration de l'industrie pétrolière: mythes et réalités'. *L'avenir des sociétés nationales des pays exportateurs d'hydrocarbures*. Seminar. Université Paris-Dauphine. Paris, May 26-27, 1994.

Self, P. *Political Theories of Modern Government*. Allen and Unwin. London, 1985.

Selznick, P. *Leadership in Administration*. Harper and Row. New York, 1957.

Sigmund, Paul E. *Multinationals in Latin America. The Politics of Nationalization*. The University of Wisconsin Press. Wisconsin, 1980.

Singh, Chaitram. *Multinational, the State and the Management of Economic Nationalism. The Case of Trinidad*. Praeger Publishers. New York, 1979.

Sosa Pietri, Andrés. *Petróleo y Poder*. Editorial Planeta. Caracas, 1993.

Stallings, Barbara and Robert Kaufman (eds). *Debt and Democracy in Latin America*. Westview Press. London, San Francisco, Boulder, 1989.

Stauffer, Thomas R. 'Accounting for 'Wasting assets': Measurements of Income and Dependency in Oil-Rentier States'. *The Journal of Energy and Development*, Vol 11, N.1, 1986.

Stevens, Paul (ed.). *Oil and Gas Dictionary*. London, 1988.

Stepan, Alfred. *The State and Society. Peru in Comparative Perspective*. Princeton University Press. Princeton. New Jersey, 1978.

Stiles, Kendall. 'IMF Conditionality: Coercion or Compromises? *World Development*. UK. Vol. 18, No. 7, 1990, pp. 959-974.

Szyliowicz, Joseph and Bard O'Neill (ed.). *The Energy Crisis and US Foreign Policy*. Praeger Publishers. New York, 1975.

Tanner, James. 'Estados Unidos empieza a tomar en cuenta a Venezuela ahora que ha reajustado sus estimados de reservas petroleras comprobadas'. *The Wall Street Journal*. May 1, 1987.

Tanner, James. 'Change of Heart. Venezuela now woos oil firms it booted in '70s nationalization'. *The Wall Street Journal*. October 2, 1992.

Teichova, Alice; Maurice Lévy-Leboyer and Helga Nussbaum. *Multinational enterprises in historical perspective*. Cambridge University Press. Cambridge, 1985.

Terzian, Pierre. 'Downstream Investment by National Oil Companies'. *L'avenir des sociétés nationales des pays exportateurs d'hydrocarbures*. Seminar. Université Paris-Dauphine. Paris, May 27, 1994.

Tétrault, Mary Ann. *The Organization of Arab Petroleum Exporting Countries.* Greenwood Press. Connecticut and London, 1981.

'The creditors' response to the new public foreign debt renegotiation arrangement'. *MetroEconómica.* Caracas. September, 1990.

'The changing world oil supply'. *Shell Briefing Service.* June, 1980.

'The Energy Transition in Developing Countries'. *The World Bank.* Washington D.C., 1983.

Toro Hardy, José. *Venezuela 55 Años de Política Económica.* Caracas, 1992.

Torres, Gerver and Doramelia Salcedo. *El Proceso venezolano de toma de decisiones en política económica. Un estudio de casos.* ILDIS. Caracas, 1988.

Tsebelis, George. 'Decision-making in Political Systems: Comparison of Presidentialism, Parliamentarism, Multicameralism, and Multipartism'. Draft paper. April, 1993.

Tugwell, Franklin. *The Politics of Oil in Venezuela.* Standford University Press, 1975.

Tullock, G. *The politics of Bureaucracy.* Public Affairs Press. New York, 1967.

Turner, Louis. *Oil Companies in the International System.* Allen and Unwin. London, 1983.

'Unocal y Citgo PDVSA'. PDVSA Publications. December, 1989.

Vallenilla, Luis. *Oil: the Making of a New Economic Order. Venezuelan Oil and OPEC.* McGrawHill. USA, 1975.

Vernon, R. *The Hungry Giants: The United Nations and Japan in the Quest for oil and ores.* Cambridge, Massachusetts, 1983.

Viergutz, Alan J. '1993: Año de Parálisis?' *Gerente.* December, 1992.

Viloria Vera, Enrique. *Planificación de Organizaciones. La experiencia de PDVSA.* Editorial Anri. Caracas, [not dated].

Villela, Annibal. 'Multinationals from Brazil'. In Sanjaya Lall. *The New Multinationals. The Spread of Third World Enterprises.* John Wiley and Sons. New York, 1983.

Weber, Max. *The Theory of Social and Economic Organizations.* Free Press. Glencoe, Ill., 1947.

Wells, Louis T. *Third World Multinationals. The Rise of Foreign Investment from Developing Countries.* The MIT Press. Cambridge, Massachusetts, 1983.

White, Eduardo. 'The International Projection of Firms from Latin American Countries'. In Kumar, Krishna and Maxwell G. McLeod. *Multinationals from Developing Countries.* Lexington Books. Lexington, Massachusetts, 1981.

Whitehead, Laurence. 'Political Explanations of Macroeconomic Management: A Survey'. *World Development.* Great Britain. Vol. 18, No. 8, 1990, pp. 1133-1146.

Wildavsky, Aaron. *Speaking Truth to Power: The Art and Craft of Policy Analysis.* Little Brown, Boston, 1979.

Wildavsky, Aaron. *The Politics of the Budgetary Process.* Little, Brown. Boston, 1984.

Williams Howard R., and Charles J. Meyers. *Manual of Oil and Gas Terms.* Matthew Bender. New York, 1976.

Williamson, O. 'A rational theory of the federal budgetary process'. In G. Tullock
(ed.). *Papers on Non-Market Decision Making.* Thomas Jefferson Centre
for Political Economy. Charlottesburg, Virginia, 1966.

Wirth, John (ed.). *Latin American Oil Companies and the Politics of Energy.*
Lincoln. London, 1985.

Worldwide Refining Business Digest. Hydrocarbon Publishing Co. Southeastern,
PA. March, 1992.

Yergin, Daniel. *The Prize. The Epic Quest for Oil, Money and Power.* Simon and
Schuster. New York, 1992.

Specialised journals and publications

Barriles, 1991-1993.
Boletín Mensual. Ministry of Energy and Mines (MEM), 1984-1993.
Fortune. Selected issues.
Gerente, 1991-1993.
MetroEconómica. Selected issues.
Middle East Economic Survey. Selected years.
PDVSA Annual Reports, 1976-1995.
PDVSA. CONTACT, 1991-1995.
Petroleum Economist, 1983-1995.
Petroleum Intelligence Weekly, 1983-1995.
Pétrostrategies, 1992.
Petróleos Informa. PDVSA, 1986-1991.
Platts Oilgram News. Selected issues.
The Economist. Selected issues.
The Oil and Gas Journal. Selected years.
Veneconomía, 1983-1995.
SIC. Centro Gumilla. Selected years.

Newspapers

Economía Hoy, 1990-1993.
El Diario, 1990-1993.
El Nacional, 1983-1993.
El Universal, 1983-1993.
The Daily Journal, 1983-1993.
The Financial Times. Selected issues.
Ultimas Noticias, 1983-1993.

Index